Edmund J. Luck, Anonymous

Short Meditations for Every Day in the Year, Inteded Chiefly for the Use of Religion

Vol. II

Edmund J. Luck, Anonymous

Short Meditations for Every Day in the Year, Inteded Chiefly for the Use of Religion
Vol. II

ISBN/EAN: 9783337279073

Printed in Europe, USA, Canada, Australia, Japan

Cover: Foto ©Lupo / pixelio.de

More available books at **www.hansebooks.com**

SHORT MEDITATIONS

FOR EVERY DAY IN THE YEAR, INTENDED CHIEFLY FOR
THE USE OF RELIGIOUS, BY AN ANONYMOUS
ITALIAN AUTHOR.

Translated by
DOM EDMUND J. LUCK, O.S.B.,
PRIEST OF THE CASSINESE CONGREGATION OF THE
PRIMITIVE OBSERVANCE.

Prefaced by a Recommendation from
HIS EMINENCE CARDINAL MANNING.

VOL. II.

LONDON:
R. WASHBOURNE, 18 PATERNOSTER ROW.
1879.

SHORT MEDITATIONS

FOR

EVERY DAY IN THE YEAR.

TRINITY SUNDAY.

Tres sunt, qui testimonium dant in cœlo, Pater, Verbum et Spiritus Sanctus, et hi tres unum sunt.—1 Joan. v. 7.
There are three who give testimony in heaven, the Father, the Word, and the Holy Ghost ; and these three are one.

I. CONSIDER that amongst the distinctive marks of Christianity, faith in the adorable mystery of the most holy Trinity is peculiar to itself—that faith by which we believe in one only God and one only Divine Essence in three Divine Persons;—one only God Who contains in Himself every kind of infinite perfection ; our first beginning and our last end ; our Lawgiver and supreme King. *Videte, quod ego sum solus, et non est alius Deus præter me*—Deut. xxxii. 39 —*See ye that I am alone, and there is no other God besides Me.* It is on this belief that the obligation, under which thou liest, rests, of obeying and serving God only, of acknowledging Him to be the only source of all the good thou canst hope for, of looking to Him alone for real happiness, of keeping thy heart turned towards Him, and of loving Him above all things as thy supreme good. But how often hast thou not made the will of God secondary to thy own capricious whims! How scanty are the thanks thou hast given Him for all the goodness He has shown thee! How very little hast thou placed thy trust in Him! and alas! how much more love hast thou thrown away on poor miserable creatures than thou hast given to thy God and only good! Be ashamed of thyself, and in the grief of thy heart exclaim with S. Augustine: *Sero te amavi—too late have I loved thee!*

II. Consider how, though God Almighty is but one in His essence, He is three in person, forasmuch as by contemplating and fully comprehending Himself, He generates a substantial image of Himself, whole and perfect in every way, which is the Word. On beholding this beauteous image of Himself, Who is *Splendor gloriæ, et figura substantiæ ejus*—Heb. i. 3—*The brightness of His glory and the figure of His substance,*—the Eternal Father loves Him with an infinite love; the Divine Word on His side reciprocates this love in an infinite degree in regard of His eternal Father; and this reciprocal love produces the third Person—the Holy Ghost, there being in all three the greatest perfection, complete equality, and perfect unity of will. Christ's prayer in the supper-room was to this effect, that the concord and union of will which reigns among the Divine Persons might reign also amongst His followers: *Ut sint unum sicut et nos unum sumus*—Joan. xvii. 11—*That they may be one, as We are one.* It must therefore be thy earnest endeavour to establish and maintain a like concord and harmony of will in thy relations with God, with thy superiors and with thy neighbour generally, in order to recopy as faithfully as may be that most perfect union which exists between the Divine Persons.

III. Consider that thou hast been made after the likeness of God and of the most august Trinity inasmuch as thy Creator has given thee a soul with three powers substantially united to it, yet distinct amongst themselves. Now since thou art an image of God, thy perfection consists entirely in bringing out the resemblance to thy divine original by imitating, not indeed His power, as Lucifer tried to do with such sorry success, nor His knowledge, as Adam unfortunately strove to do, but His holiness, as in so many words we are bid to do by God Himself: *Sancti eritis, quia ego sanctus sum*—Lev. xix. 2—*Be ye holy, because I am holy;* and on which account—viz., by reason of His holiness—He receives the especial homage and praise of the angelic spirits who sing *Sanctus, Sanctus, Sanctus, Dominus Deus*—Apoc. iv. 8—*Holy, Holy, Holy, Lord God Almighty.* Make therefore the most earnest endeavours to model thy life on the perfect holiness of God.

MONDAY AFTER TRINITY SUNDAY.

Ipse vobis demonstrabit cœnaculum grande stratum: et illic parate nobis.—Marc. xiv. 15.

He will show you a large dining-room furnished; and there prepare ye for us.

I. CONSIDER, with a view to preparing thyself during these days that precede the solemnity of the most adorable Sacrament, in what the preparations consisted which Christ Himself made. In the first place He sends two of His disciples to get ready a large and well-furnished room — *Cœnaculum grande stratum* — and why, pray? If Jesus was ever so enamoured of poverty that He was content with a manger at His birth, with a scanty cell during His lifetime, and at His death had not even a draught of water wherewith to quench His thirst—why go in search of a stately and richly-adorned room in order to spread

the Eucharistic table before a few poor fishermen? The reason is to give thee to understand what thy preparation ought to be on drawing near to this sacred table, and on receiving thy God into the lodging of thy heart. In what has thy preparation hitherto consisted on approaching the altar to receive Communion or to say Mass? Hast thou drawn near well prepared, or perhaps from mere custom, as thou wouldst to any other ordinary repast?

II. Consider that Our Lord caused to be got ready a large room or hall—*cœnaculum grande;*—such also must thy heart be to receive therein a divine and adorable guest; thy heart must be large and spacious, because thy Lord will pour His heavenly treasures into it in proportion to the room He finds there: *Dilata os tuum et implebo illud*—Ps. lxxx. 11—*Open thy mouth wide and I will fill it.* But in order that thy heart may be made fit thou must strive to empty it of all disorderly and earthly affections; that it may become large and roomy thou must widen out thy desires and thy aspirations. Thou hast hitherto derived so little fruit from the many Communions thou hast made, because thou hast gone to receive thy Lord with a heart encumbered with a thousand disorderly whims and attachments which have cloyed thy longing and taken away thy hunger after this heavenly bread. When the stomach is laden with crude humours, it feels no hunger: and so also it is with thy heart. In order to derive nourishment from this heavenly table, empty thy heart of everything earthly, and so wilt thou feel a hunger for it and derive benefit from it: *Famelici saturati sunt*—1 Reg. ii. 5—*The hungry are filled.*

III. Consider that the hall was moreover richly furnished and adorned with precious vessels, thus showing that thou hast to enrich and adorn thy heart with virtue when thou approachest Holy Communion.

These acts of virtue ought to consist before Communion in acts of real humility and true contrition on beholding, on the one hand, thy own worthlessness and guilt, and on the other, the excellency and dignity of that good Lord so wantonly offended by thee, and Who is now about to come from heaven to take up His abode in thy breast in the excess of His wonderful condescension and tender love. After Communion thou hast to adore Him with acts of profound worship, to thank Him for so great goodness, and to beg Him to come to thy relief in all thy various needs, for He cannot refuse thee what thou askest for, when it is to thy spiritual advantage, since He comes to bestow on thee His whole Self with all His treasures for thy sanctification.

TUESDAY AFTER TRINITY SUNDAY.

Immolabit agnum universa multitudo filiorum Israel.—Exod. xii. 6.

The whole multitude of the children of Israel shall sacrifice it.

I. CONSIDER the motives Our Lord had in initiating the Eucharistic supper by the eating of the Paschal lamb. The first was in order to convey to our minds the fact, that just in the same way as amongst the Jews the supper of the Paschal lamb was the highest festival and greatest mystery of the Mosaic law, so also the Eucharistic supper is the highest festival and greatest mystery of the Evangelical law, of which the former was but a mere shadow and figure. Now, if the Jews by express command of God solemnised their mysterious supper with so much preparation, so many rites, and such great pomp, with how much more preparation and devotion ought not Christians to celebrate the great mystery of the Eucharistic supper! Hitherto thou hast made but too little account of this mystery. Begin at least now, during these days of preparation, to ponder on its greatness, and so conceive a more tender devotion towards this most adorable Sacrament.

II. Consider the second motive Our Lord had in first of all commemorating the supper of the Paschal lamb. It was this, that as the lamb was wont to be eaten by the Jewish people with great solemnity, in memory of their having been freed from the slavery of Pharaoh, so also the Eucharistic supper serves us as a memory of our having been freed by the pure blood of Jesus from the slavery of sin, of the devil and of hell. Now, just as the boon of our having been set at liberty from the slavery of guilt and of the everlasting death of the soul, through the divine blood of Jesus, is immeasurably greater than the benefit the Jews derived in being freed from the bondage of Pharaoh and the temporal death of the body, through sprinkling their door-posts with the blood of the lamb, so also is it fit and proper that we should partake of this Eucharistic supper with a proportionably greater devotion and preparation.

III. Consider that this law-established supper was held by the Jews once a year, on account of their having been on one only occasion set at liberty from the bondage of Egypt. But we, who by virtue of the blood of our Redeemer are day after day cleansed from our faults, daily celebrate this sacramental supper, which is at once a remembrance of the boon conferred upon us by Our Lord in ransoming us, and a renewal or repayment of our purchase-money. Hence this festival of the Blessed Sacrament is the greatest of the solemnities of the year; because all the other principal feasts of the Nativity, Resurrection, and Ascension are nothing more than a simple commemoration, a mere calling to mind of these mysteries, whereas the feast of the Blessed Sacrament is a real repetition of the great mystery celebrated by Our Lord in the supper-room. If thou givest serious attention to these truths, thou wilt adore thy God with greater devotion and piety in His churches and when thou assistest at the holy Sacrifice of the Mass, and thou wilt draw nigh to receive Him in Holy Communion with more earnest preparation.

WEDNESDAY AFTER TRINITY SUNDAY.

Cœpit lavare pedes discipulorum, et ex'ergere linteo quo erat præcinctus.—Joan. xiii. 5.

He began to wash the feet of the disciples, and to wipe them with the towel wherewith He was girded.

I. CONSIDER how our Redeemer, just before the sacramental supper, took off His upper garments, girded Himself with a coarse towel, and, after filling a laver with water, began to wash the feet of His disciples on His knees like a humble menial, to show forth in a lively manner to what a degree He lowers Himself in the Blessed Sacrament, where He strips Himself of all outward majesty, covers Himself with the lowly accidents of bread and wine, and comes down from the bosom of the Eternal Father, to enter into the heart of man, to cleanse him with His own precious blood, and feed him on His own divine flesh: *Declinavi ad eum ut vesceretur*—Osea xi. 4—*I put his meat to him that he might eat.* But if the Apostle S. Peter was so wonder-stricken and touched on beholding his divine Master thus humbly kneeling at his feet, that in his utter astonishment he exclaimed: *Non lavabis mihi pedes in æternum—Thou shalt never wash my feet*, how much greater sentiments of awe and reverence ought to awake in thy heart on beholding with the eye of faith Jesus reduced to so lowly a condition under the appearance of bread and wine, in order to wash thee with His blood, and feed thee with His flesh!

II. Consider that Jesus washed the dirt from the feet of His Apostles before giving them Holy Communion, to signify the cleanness of heart that is required by way of preparation for Holy Communion, inasmuch as this cleanness of heart ought to consist in freedom, not only from mortal sin, but also from venial faults, and from all inordinate and wrong motions of love and hatred which are, as it were, the feet of the soul. In order to acquire this cleanness of heart, thou must needs wash thy soul by sacramental confession, and also immediately before Communion make acts of contrition in imitation of holy Job, who said: *Antequam comedam suspiro*—Job iii. 24 —*Before I eat I sigh*. It is well that these acts of sorrow should be general, including all thy sins, known or unknown, confessed or not confessed, because if by any chance thou shouldst receive Communion in a state of mortal sin, in good faith, through some inculpable ignorance, thou wouldst be enabled by means of this general sorrow, although itself imperfect, to rise from the death of sin to the life of grace in virtue of the Blessed Sacrament.

III. Consider that by means of this typical washing of the feet Our Lord teaches thee what are the acts of virtue thou oughtest to practise with regard to thy neighbour, by way of preparation for Holy Communion. They consist in acts of humility and charity, in imitation of the example Jesus has set thee: *Exemplum dedi vobis, ut quemadmodum ego feci vobis, ita et vos faciatis*—Joan. xiii. 15—*I have given you an example, that as I have done, so do you also.* Thou must also elicit acts of these two virtues of humility and charity in honour of thy Saviour, Who lowers Himself to such a degree to manifest the extreme refinement of His love for thee in this sacrament. Would to God that on His entrance into thy breast, Jesus be not forced to reproach thee as He did the Pharisee of the Gospel: *Intravi in domum tuam ; aquam pedibus meis non dedisti*—Luc. vii. 44—*I entered into thy house ; thou gavest Me no water for My feet*—the water, namely, of wholesome compunction of heart, with which to wash at one and the same time My feet and thy own soul : *oleo caput meum non unxisti*—*My head with oil thou didst not anoint*, by pouring forth from thy heart the sweet-smelling oil of devout affections : *osculum mihi non dedisti*—*thou gavest Me no kiss*, as a sign of love and peace never more to be violated.

THE FEAST OF CORPUS CHRISTI.

Cum dilexisset suos qui erant in mundo, in finem dilexit eos.—Joan. xiii. 1.
Having loved His own who were in the world, He loved them unto the end.

I. CONSIDER the excessive tenderness of the love of Jesus in the institution of the Holy Eucharist, firstly by reason of the gift itself, in which under the sacramental species He bestows on thee His flesh, His blood, His soul, and His Divinity, with all its untold treasures : and in such a manner, too, that in giving thee this morsel, He gives thee all that He has that is precious in the treasures of His divinity. And wilt thou not even take the trouble of thanking Him for so great a gift, and feel thyself constrained to love Him in return for such boundless love? Any trifling token of love thou receivest from a fellow-creature smites thy heart, and forces thee to love him in return; and can it be that a God Who gives thee His whole Self in the excess of His love, cannot succeed in winning over thy heart, and oblige thee to love Him in return? Dost thou not blush at thy chariness in the scanty return thou hast hitherto made for the prodigal liberality of thy God?

II. Consider the wondrous tenderness of Jesus' love in the manner in which He gives thee Himself, coming down from the bosom of His Eternal Father to clothe Himself with the sacramental species, in order thus to enter thy breast, and become one with thee after the fashion of food, thus linking, as it were, together His own most holy body with thy sinful flesh, His own divine Spirit with thy soul, His divinity with thy humanity. There is no one thing that is more closely united with us than our food, which, once assimilated to the system, cannot possibly be disparted. How far dost thou on thy side further this so close a union, invented by the love Jesus bears thee? how far dost thou endeavour to keep lovingly united to Him in thought and affection? It is, alas! to be feared that even during the short space of time that He actually tarries in thy breast, thou art perhaps far away from Him in both thought and affection!

III. Consider what was the end and intent Jesus proposed to Himself in the sacramental union. It was no other than that He might sanctify our bodies with His most pure flesh, sanctify our souls with His soul and divinity, to such a degree that we should be animated with His Spirit and live a life more divine than human, according to the saying of the Apostle: *Vivo ego, jam non ego; vivit vero in me Christus*—Gal. ii.

20—*I live, now not I; but Christ liveth in me.* The alchemists of old pretended to be able to give any base metal the beauty and valuable qualities of gold, by means of a certain extract obtained from gold by dint of fire and labour. So also Jesus unites Himself with us under the sacramental species containing the quintessence of all that is divine, in order to change us into divine beings. But what effect can these inventions of divine love work in thee, if whilst Jesus is intimately present to thee, thou knowest not how to keep thyself present to Him by means of the powers of thy soul? If thou wouldst reap abundant fruit from this blessed union, thou must, when thou receivest Jesus into thy breast, keep thy heart aloof from all created things, and withdraw thy soul into its own solitude to entertain there thy God alone: thus will be verified in thee those words of Isaias, xlv. 14: *Tantum in te est Deus—Only in Thee is God;* only Jesus in thy memory; only Jesus in thy understanding; Jesus alone in thy will.

FRIDAY WITHIN THE OCTAVE OF CORPUS CHRISTI.

Sciens Jesus quia venit hora ejus, ut transeat ex hoc mundo ad Patrem . . . . in finem dilexit eos.—Joan, xiii. 1.

Jesus knowing that His hour was come, that He should pass out of this world to the Father . . . . He loved them unto the end.

I. CONSIDER what great lustre the mystery of the Holy Eucharist receives from the circumstances of the particular time when it was instituted by our divine

Redeemer. Knowing that the hour had arrived for Him to leave His disciples, He determined on making good the privation of His natural and visible presence by His sacramental presence, and thus to give the finishing stroke to the work of our salvation. As he had come down on earth to put on our mortal flesh without leaving His Father, so now He wished to return to His Father without leaving His disciples. He thus gave proof of how strongly He was bound by the ties of love to His disciples, since He could not make up His mind to part from them even in death. *Deliciæ meæ esse cum filiis hominum*—Prov. viii. 31—*My delight is to be with the children of men.* But if Jesus cannot for an instant be at a distance from His ungrateful creatures, how canst thou be so little anxious to betake thyself to His loving presence in the Blessed Sacrament, where He awaits thy coming and offers Himself to thee, to be thy guide, thy physician, thy consolation and thy strength! *Venite ad me omnes qui laboratis et onerati estis, et ego reficiam vos*—Matth. xi. 28 —*Come to me, all ye that labour and are burdened, and I will refresh you.*

II. Consider a further and still greater refinement of love in the circumstance of the particular time of the institution, on which the Apostle dwells: *In qua nocte tradebatur*—1 Cor. xi. 23—*the same night on which He was betrayed;* thus contrasting an excess of treachery with an excess of love, and causing the light of His goodness to shine forth all the more brilliantly 'mid the darkness of human malice : *Lux in tenebris lucet*— Joan. i. 5—*The light shineth in darkness.* Is it not enough to make one shudder to see men plotting against the life of Jesus in order to drive Him far from them, whilst He, on that memorable night, is contriving by such wondrous means to remain with them on earth ? to see Him spreading a banquet of heavenly delights for His disciples on that very night when He was about to be betrayed by one, denied by another, and abandoned by all of them into the hands of His enemies? Wilt thou not learn from these instances of such surpassing love, to return good for evil and to love him who hates thee?

III. Consider that when Jesus instituted this most Holy Sacrament He foresaw that the only return He would receive for this excess of love in our regard would be an excess in the opposite direction of the most disgraceful treatment at the hands of men. He foresaw how His sacred Body would be trampled under foot by unbelievers, and insulted in the most shameful way; and, what is still worse, how amongst the faithful themselves, who profess to believe in His real presence in the consecrated Host, He would be left in utter abandonment on the altar, wearied and grieved by a thousand irreverences, and would even be received sacrilegiously into many a heart stained by most hideous crimes. And yet in the midst of all this darkness, our good Jesus did not withdraw the bright light of this His excessive love and undaunted patience: *Hospitabitur, et pascet, et potabit ingratos; et ad hæc amara audiet*—Eccl. xxix. 31—*He shall entertain and feed and give drink to the unthankful; and moreover he shall hear bitter words.* Now if Jesus has chosen to submit in the Blessed Sacrament to so many and so great injuries and insults, and all for thy sake, why shouldst not thou also for His greater glory put up willingly and cheerfully with what is distasteful to thee? Why not endeavour, as far as it lies in thy power, to make Him some little compensation for the coarse ingratitude He meets with at the hands of the greater part of mankind, by oft-repeated visits and acts of adoration, which will cost thee only a few steps; humbling thy soul in His presence and bending thy knees to honour Him and offer Him thy tribute of adoration by thy interior and exterior acts of worship?

SATURDAY WITHIN THE OCTAVE OF CORPUS CHRISTI.

Ecce ego vobiscum sum omnibus diebus usque ad consummationem sæculi.—Matth. xxviii. 20.

Behold I am with you all days, even to the consummation of the world.

I. CONSIDER that the object Jesus has in view in abiding with us in the Blessed Sacrament is to perpetuate in our behalf all the advantages which His visible presence on earth brought with it; to instruct and enlighten our minds, to heal our ailings, to encourage and strengthen us in the attainment of virtue. His first object then is to instruct and enlighten us from the tabernacle, as from His professor's chair. *Non faciet avolare a te ultra præceptorem tuum*—Isa. xxv. 20—*He will not cause thy teacher to flee away from thee any more.* And, pray, what wholesome truth is there that thou needest which Jesus does not teach thee as He darts forth from the sacred Host bright rays of light to enlighten thy mind and silently speaks to thy heart?—*loquar ad cor ejus*—Osea ii. 14.—S. Thomas Aquinas learnt more by devoutly remaining in the presence of the Blessed Sacrament than by reading the most learned books. *Qui appropinquant pedibus ejus, accipient de doctrina illius*—Deut. xxxiii. 3—*They that approach to His feet shall receive of His doctrine.* Oh how fortunate thou art to be able at all hours to hearken to the teaching of so great a master! But to what extent dost thou frequent this school? How far art thou anxious to learn His heavenly doctrine? Remember, too, that if thou wouldst be taught by thy Lord, thy mere bodily presence is not enough unless thou draw nigh in spirit also, placing thyself, like Magdalene, at His feet, to listen to His words and His teaching. *Accedite ad eum et illuminamini*—Ps. xxxiii. 6—*Come ye to Him and be enlightened.*

II. Consider that Christ remains on our altars to heal thee as of old Moses raised the brazen serpent in mid-air to heal the Israelites of the venomous bites of the serpents: *Qui percussus aspexerit, vivet*—Num. xxi. 8—*Whosoever being struck shall look on it, shall live.* During the interval that our divine Redeemer held visible intercourse with men on earth, He continually worked miraculous cures on behalf of the bodily health of those who appealed to Him. Even more wondrous and oft-repeated favours does Jesus still confer, veiled under the sacramental species, on those souls who make devout recourse to Him. How many there are who when they run for help to Jesus in the Blessed Sacrament, are healed of their poisoned wounds! and if thou canst not succeed in recovering from thy own spiritual ailings, it is because thou art careless in betaking thyself to Jesus Who alone is able to make thee sound.

III. Consider that Jesus remains on our altars to encourage and urge thee on to acquire the virtues thou needest, by the examples He brings to thy mind of the virtues He Himself practised during His mortal life, as also by the examples of the virtues He actually gives thee under the sacramental species. The Blessed Sacrament, therefore, is a remembrance of all Jesus has done and undergone for thee, and it is on this account called by St. Augustine: *Sacramentum memoriæ—a sacrament of memories.* Moreover, because this mysterious love-token is full of life and animation, it imparts courage and vigour to follow in Jesus' footsteps. Still more does it strengthen and encourage thee by reason of the example it puts before thy eyes of the virtues which Jesus actually shows thee therein: as for instance of obedience in coming down from heaven under the species at the bidding of the priest; of humility and patience by remaining so close a prisoner under the accidents and by putting up with so many irreverences and affronts for thy sake. Place thyself in the presence of Jesus and turn over diligently in thy mind the various virtues of which this sacrament is a memorial, and the virtues which He actually displayed therein. Imagine thou hearest the Eternal Father speaking to thee, and saying as He did to Moses from the tabernacle, *Inspice et fac secundum exemplar*—Ex. xxv. 40, and so thou wilt take fresh courage in the pursuit of virtue.

SUNDAY WITHIN THE OCTAVE OF CORPUS CHRISTI.

Hoc facite in meam commemorationem—Luc. xxii. 19.
Do this for a commemoration of Me.

I. CONSIDER that Jesus comes under the sacramental species not only to dwell amongst us, but also in order to offer Himself up as an unbloody victim in the sacrifice of the Mass, in which He daily renews the sacrifice of Calvary, thus giving us to understand how much He has at heart that we should bear in mind the bitter death He underwent for our sakes on the cross. The Holy Sacrifice of the Mass represents His death and sacrifice on the cross to us in several ways. It represents it mystically by the separate consecration of the precious Blood under the appearance of wine, and of His adorable Body under the appearance of bread. It represents it virtually by the Body of Christ remaining under the accidents as it were in a state of death. It represents it really by Our Lord's losing, when the species are consumed, that sacramental existence which by means of the consecration He again acquires. How then canst thou assist at this representation of the death of the Son of God with less attention and interest than thou wouldst bestow on the representation of some fictitious tragedy on a stage?

II. Consider that in the sacrifice of the Mass there is not merely a representation—but a renewal of the great sacrifice offered on Calvary to the Eternal Father, to whom it is just as acceptable as the bloody sacrifice on the cross. The reason is because in the Mass, the same victim is offered up as was offered up on Calvary; it is also the same High-Priest that offers it up, since Jesus is the primary minister in the Mass, and He offers it up to His Eternal Father for the same end and with the same intensity of love with which He offered up His bloody sacrifice. It is just as though he were again to shed the last drop of His blood on the cross. Moreover the worth and value of the Mass is not lessened one tittle by reason of the unworthiness of the priest who celebrates. This renewal of the sacrifice of the cross which is daily offered up on our altars was invented by Jesus in order that we might daily satisfy the debts and obligations we have contracted with Almighty God. Our first and chief obligation is that of honouring Him, and the Mass meets this requirement inasmuch as it is a holocaust: we have to appease Him for our sins, and it does this inasmuch as it is a propitiatory sacrifice: we owe Him thanks for benefits received, and we can fulfil this obligation in virtue of its being a Eucharistic Sacrifice, or Sacrifice of thanksgiving: and, finally, we have to beg from Him further blessings we stand in need of, and it effects this inasmuch as it is a pacific sacrifice or peace-offering. Oh, what a wonderful mystery is this! When thou celebratest, or assistest at the Holy Sacrifice, endeavour to offer it up and direct it to each and all of the ends just mentioned, namely, to honour the infinite majesty of Almighty God, to appease Him, to thank Him, and to beg graces from Him. If, moreover, thou unitest these thy intentions with those of Jesus, the primary minister in the Mass, they will be all the more acceptable to God and profitable to thyself.

III. Consider that this unbloody sacrifice of the cross is not less profitable to us than the bloody sacrifice of the cross. This latter was the general cause which wrought and completed the treasury of Christ's merits, for the benefit of all men in general. The former applies these merits and distributes them for the benefit of each individual, by bestowing on us the actual possession of these merits in proportion to the dispositions and co-operation it finds in each one. Since therefore thou art aware that Jesus on the altar places at thy disposition during the time of Mass such an inexhaustible fund, in order to enrich thee with His heavenly treasures, how canst thou remain listless and thoughtless during that time without heeding the greatness of the mystery and without eliciting those acts of worship and devotion which are absolutely required to render the Holy Sacrifice profitable in thy regard?

MONDAY WITHIN THE OCTAVE OF CORPUS CHRISTI.

Qui manducat meam carnem et bibit meum sanguinem, in me manet et ego in eo.—Joan. vi. 57.
He that eateth My flesh and drinketh My blood, abideth in Me, and I in him.

I. CONSIDER that in the same way that our most loving Redeemer has deigned to institute in the Mass a renewal of the sacrifice of the cross, so also He has had the wondrous goodness to institute in the Holy Eucharist a prolongation and extension, as it were, of the mystery of His divine Incarnation. On the worthy communicant He bestows, by means of the sacramental union, a share of those exhaustless treasures which were the result of the hypostatic union of His most Sacred Humanity with the Eternal Word. See what an honour and dignity it was for Jesus to be assumed, as man, to the intimate communion of the Godhead; and yet He is loth to keep the benefit of this privilege to Himself alone, but would wish us also to be in a certain manner partakers of the same by means of Holy Communion. *Claritatem quam dedisti mihi, dedi eis.*—Joan. xvii. 22— *The glory which Thou hast given Me, I have given to them,* said He in His prayer to His heavenly Father—in the supper-room after He had given Holy Communion to the Apostles. He meant by these words that He had made His disciples partakers of that glory which He had received through the union of His human nature with the Word, by giving them His own Body and Blood in the Blessed Sacrament. Oh wondrous bounty of Jesus! Let it never be true that thou shouldst be slow to thank Him for so wonderful a mystery, or fail to conceive a great esteem for it.

II. Consider that although this sacramental union is lower in dignity than the hypostatic union of Christ's manhood to the Eternal Word, it is nevertheless the closest and most intimate union we can hope for in this life, because at one and the same time it unites us with Christ bodily, spiritually and mystically. Firstly, it unites us bodily by the physical contact of His most pure flesh which sanctifies our bodies: it unites us spiritually with the Divinity which is hypostatically united with His sacred Body: it unites us mystically by making us mystical members of Jesus, animated by His divine Spirit and raised to a divine life: *Qui adhæret Domino, unus spiritus est*—1 Cor. vi. 17—*He who is joined to the Lord is one spirit.* This divine life which sacramental union with Our Lord confers on us, is alluded to in these words: *Ego vivo propter Patrem: et qui manducat me, vivet propter me*—Joan. vi. 58—*As I live by the Father; so he that eateth Me the same also shall live by Me.* As I live a divine life which is communicated to Me by means of the divine union of Persons, so also he that eats My flesh and drinks My blood lives a divine life by means of the sacramental union. How can we hear these truths and believe that Jesus is so intimately united with us, and yet live far from Him in thought and affection?

III. Consider that the sacramental union with Christ is called Communion, because by means of it He communicates to us all the treasures of His merits and satisfaction which He has gained for us: *Pasceris in divitiis ejus*—Ps. xxxvi. 3—*Thou shalt be fed with His riches*, without any other limitation than that of our own dispositions and capacity: *In omnibus divites facti estis in illo.*—1 Cor. i. 5—*In all things you are made rich in Him*, being put in possession of all the riches Jesus possesses as Man-God. In giving Christ to us the Father has given us all things, according to those words of S. Paul: *Quomodo non etiam cum illo omnia nobis donavit*—Rom. viii. 32—*How hath He not also, with Him, given us all things.* So also Christ bestows on us all He has in giving us Himself in Holy Communion. But after so many Communions what fruit hast thou reaped ? One Communion alone ought to suffice to make a saint of thee; and yet so many Communions have not been enough even to make thee live like a real religious.

TUESDAY WITHIN THE OCTAVE OF CORPUS CHRISTI.

Parasti in conspectu meo mensam adversus eos, qui tribulant me.—Ps. xxii. 5.

Thou hast prepared a table before me, against them that afflict me.

I. CONSIDER that Holy Communion serves us in a threefold capacity—as medicine, as armour, and as food. It serves as a medicine to cure the diseases of our ill-regulated passions. All our passions, whether of soul or body, are caused by the connection we have contracted with the sinful flesh of Adam; it is to cure these spiritual infirmities that Jesus comes in Holy Communion to unite His own deified flesh most intimately with our own, under the appearance of food, in order that if we have inherited our spiritual sickliness through our connection with the sinful flesh of Adam, so also by our union with the flesh of Christ our Redeemer we may obtain a remedy and a cure. Thus Holy Communion is our best and most efficacious remedy against the sting of our rebellious flesh and the best means of checking the vicious whims of the old man. In proportion therefore as thou findest thy passions more boisterous and thy flesh more rebellious, approach Holy Communion with greater devotion and frequency, since it is a universal remedy that will heal all the diseases of thy soul.

II. Consider that Holy Communion is the best armour we can use against the assaults of the devil, as it possesses an especial virtue to put the infernal spirits to flight and conquer them—a power which was shadowed forth in the unleavened loaves of Gideon, who routed the army of the Madianites. A soul that is well fortified with the Eucharistic Bread will never be overcome by the united efforts of all the legions of devils; they have an exceeding fear of the soul with whom Jesus is present, and who even after the sacramental species have ceased to exist, is defended in an especial manner by His loving Providence. If the sign of the cross is enough to put the evil spirits to flight, how much more Jesus Himself in Person ? *Si Deus pro nobis, quis contra nos?*—Rom. viii. 31—*If God be for us, who is against us ?* Endeavour therefore to keep closely united with Jesus, and thou wilt be victorious over all thy spiritual foes.

III. Consider that Holy Communion gives nerve and strength to work and toil for God much more effectually than the ember cakes which enabled Elias to walk for forty days and ascend the heights of Horeb. In this pilgrimage of life thou lackest the necessary strength to mount the cragged steeps of virtue and to overcome the hindrances that corrupt nature puts in thy path: and lo! Jesus sets before thee this banquet of His own most Holy Body and Blood, to strengthen thy weakness, to give thee courage to overcome the difficulties of the undertaking, and enkindle in thy heart a generous resolution to run in the pursuit of virtue. It was formerly a common belief that pearls and gold administered in a potable form had the power of dilating and strengthening the human heart. And this is what in reality this divine banquet effects. Take heed, therefore, that thou avail thyself of it, to cure thy ailings, to defend thyself against thy foes, and to strengthen thy weakness.

WEDNESDAY WITHIN THE OCTAVE OF CORPUS CHRISTI.

Caro mea vere est cibus, et sanguis meus vere est potus.
—Joan. vi. 56.
My flesh is meat indeed, and My blood is drink indeed.

I. CONSIDER that of all the sacraments only this one of the Holy Eucharist is given us by way of food; because the other sacraments are as it were so many channels to convey a certain amount of sanctifying grace to our souls, whereas this sacrament of the altar puts us in possession of the source itself of all grace. We could not obtain this actual possession in any better form than by way of food and drink, as there is nothing over which we obtain more complete dominion than over our food, inasmuch as there is no distinction between the dominion we have over ourselves and that which we have over our food. When thou beholdest Jesus thy God, thy Creator, thy Redeemer, come into thy breast to bestow on thee the possession and mastery of His entire self, wilt thou refuse to allow Him to take full possession of thee, once for all placing thyself without reserve in His hands, that He may dispose of thee absolutely according to His own good pleasure?

II. Consider that Jesus is given to us by way of food, to signify that He works in our souls those same effects which material food works in our bodies. The sacraments are at one and the same time both signs and causes which produce what they shadow forth. Hence, as it is the office of material food to maintain and increase the life of the body, so also it is the office of this spiritual food to maintain and increase the life of the soul: with this difference, however, that whereas material food can increase the life of the body only to a certain extent, and so check the progress of death for a short time, the Eucharistic food on the contrary improves the life of the soul to any degree, by causing it to grow without let or hindrance and making it immortal. It is called *Panis vitæ*—Joan. vi. 35—*the bread of life*, because it imparts all the advantages of true and real life—bestowing on us the life of grace, the life of glory, and, after the days of our pilgrimage are over, undying life to our very bodies. Are not all these benefits enough to excite in thy heart an insatiable hunger after this divine food? Remark, however, that as the food thou givest thy body is of little avail in maintaining and increasing life unless it be well masticated and unless the stomach be in a healthy condition, so also does the same hold good with regard to the Eucharistic food and the disposition of thy soul. How many Communions hast thou made with little or no fruit, because thou hast partaken of this heavenly bread without the mastication of devout reflections and with thy soul tainted with vice!

III. Consider that this Eucharistic table is spread by Jesus under the appearances of bread and wine, to signify that He gives thee a full meal wherewith to satisfy the hunger of thy soul, just as bread and wine constitute a complete meal to satisfy the hunger of thy body. And pray, what soul can ever suffer hunger whose nourishment is God Himself, the source of every good? Solomon says, *Anima saturata calcabit favum*—Prov. xxvii. 7—*A soul that is full shall tread upon the honeycomb;* and can the heart that has fed on its God hesitate to despise all the miserable pleasures which the goods of this world can bring with them? All other gifts we receive at the hands of the divine bounty are not God Himself, nor do we in them enjoy the possession of God Himself. It is only at the Eucharistic table that we enjoy the possession of God Himself, where He becomes our real food and our real drink under the sacramental species. Oh, surely this divine food ought to extinguish in thee the hunger and thirst of of all that is earthly! *Quid enim bonum ejus, et quid pulchrum ejus, nisi frumentum electorum, et vinum germinans virgines?*—Zach. ix. 17—*For what is the good thing of Him, and what is His beautiful thing, but the corn of the elect, and wine springing forth virgins?*

OCTAVE OF CORPUS CHRISTI.

Qui manducat meam carnem et bibit meum sanguinem habet vitam æternam.—Joan. vi. 55.
He that eateth My flesh and drinketh My blood hath everlasting life.

I. CONSIDER that in these words it is not said that he who partakes of the Body of Jesus in the Blessed Sacrament *shall* have life eternal, but that he *has* life eternal—*habet vitam æternam*. The reason of this is, that in giving Himself to be our food, our divine

Lord gives us a pledge of future glory which certainly differs but little from its actual possession, in so far as the pledge we are put in possession of as a warranty is in nowise inferior in worth to the object we hope for. Who would think of distrusting the promises of a man that gave himself as a surety? And wouldst thou doubt the promises of a God-man Who gives Himself to thee in the Blessed Sacrament as a pledge of future glory? Each time, therefore, that thou receivest Holy Communion, say from thy heart, *Deus spei meæ*—*Thou art the God of my hope;* Thou art, oh my God, the assurance of all my hopes; Thou comest from heaven to earth to abide thus meekly and humbly in my heart, and thus Thou givest me a sure hope that Thou wilt one day receive me into Thyself in glory: *Speret in Domino et innitatur super Deum suum*—Isa. l. 10—*Let him hope in the name of the Lord, and lean upon his God.* What remains to be seen is whether a hope, which is immovably firm as far as Jesus in the Blessed Sacrament is concerned, may not waver on thy own account, and even fail thee altogether through thy own fault.

II. Consider that Jesus in the Blessed Sacrament is a pledge of the glory that awaits thee—*Pignus futuræ gloriæ*—but a pledge which at one and the same time aids thee to strive after it and renders it easy of attainment, by giving thee strength to overcome concupiscence, to resist temptation, and do all that is needed on thy side to merit eternal glory. Indeed, the chief end and object of this sacrament is precisely to serve thee as a viaticum, or provision on the journey to eternity, and to bring thee happily to a never-ending rest. Whenever, therefore, thou goest to Communion, get thyself ready to receive thy Jesus as a viaticum, as though it were for the last time, and as though thou wert just about to go into the next world. This practice will prove of great benefit to thee, if thou also addest the intention of fulfilling the precept of receiving Communion at the end of thy life, especially in the event of thy being overtaken by a sudden death.

III. Consider how, by means of Holy Communion, those words of Our Lord are verified : *Ecce regnum Dei intra vos est*—Luc. xvii. 21—*The kingdom of God is within you :* for we receive Him into our breasts in His entirety Who constitutes the whole happiness of the denizens of heaven ; He gives us at the Eucharistic table that same food which satisfies the cravings of even an angel's love : *Panem angelorum manducavit homo*—Ps. lxxvii. 25—*Man ate the bread of angels.* The only difference is that the blessed in heaven feed on their God in the light of glory, whilst we pilgrims on earth do the same in the light of faith. The blessed are seated at this table of delight to their own enjoyment and bliss, and we to the increase of our own grace and merit. How, then, comes it that thou feelest not a continual and eager hunger for this divine banquet, which forms the delight of the whole court of heaven ? The blessed in heaven can brook no separation from their supreme good, which they possess and enjoy in the light of glory ; so also thou oughtest not to remain at a distance from thy supreme good, though thou canst enjoy it only by the light of faith, but live united by love with Jesus, by means of frequent visits to Him in the Blessed Sacrament, by a loving remembrance of Him, and by thy Communions both sacramental and spiritual. Then wilt thou truly say with S. Peter : *Bonum est nos hic esse*—Matth. xvii. 4 —*It is good for us to be here.*

FRIDAY AFTER THE OCTAVE OF CORPUS CHRISTI.—THE FEAST OF THE SACRED HEART.*

Haurietis aquas in gaudio de fontibus Salvatoris.—Isa. xii. 3.
You shall draw waters with joy out of the Saviour's fountains.

I. CONSIDER how great must have been the joy of the Israelites when, after journeying for a long time in the desert, and in the greatest distress for want of water, they at length reached the fountain of Elim, whence each one could draw as much water as he wished. But there is no comparison between this fountain of Elim and that of Calvary, where that Sacred Heart was pierced whence Jesus pours forth streams of living grace on thy behalf. This is the fountain from which thou must draw as large a supply as thou art able, to refresh thee during thy journey in the dreary desert of this world. Divine grace is called in Holy Writ by the name of water, to express its qualities, and hence just as water possesses the properties of cleansing, fertilising, and quenching thirst, so also does grace produce corresponding effects in the soul. If thou endeavourest to grasp the meaning of these important qualities of grace, thou wilt be all the more eager to draw the waters of grace from the never-failing well-spring of the Sacred Heart of Jesus.

* As the Meditation assigned by the author to this day had no especial bearing on the Feast of the Sacred Heart, I have taken the liberty of transposing it to the Friday in the Seventeenth week after Pentecost, and have inserted here the Meditation assigned to that day, with a slight adaptation to to-day's feast.—THE TRANSLATOR.

II. Consider that the first property of this water of divine grace is, that it washes away the defilement, not indeed of the body, but of the soul, imparting at the same time fresh energy, and bestowing on it a degree of beauty capable of making Almighty God Himself in love with it. In the next place, it fertilises the soul by beautifying it with the flowers of good works, like a well-watered garden, and enabling it to produce fruit well pleasing to Almighty God. The third property of this water that flows from the Heart of Jesus, is that it destroys the evil thirst arising from the fever of ill-regulated passions, and at the same time encourages a wholesome thirst that is the effect of a healthy disposition of soul. It destroys the evil thirst by killing useless desires and bad inclinations, or at least by checking them and hindering them from grievously vexing and harassing thee; according to those words: *Qui biberit ex aquâ hâc quam ego dabo ei non sitiet in æternum*—Joan. iv. 13—*He that shall drink of the water that I shall give him, shalt not thirst for ever*. It also encourages a wholesome thirst, by fostering the wish of loving and serving Almighty God, of enjoying Him, and being united with Him for ever. This is the water that flows down from the Heart of Jesus as its source, and in finding its level bears the soul up with it again to the Heart of Jesus, as its resting-place: *Fons aqua salientis in vitam æternam*—Joan. iv. 14—*A fountain of water springing up into life everlasting*. Why, then, shouldst thou doubt that it is thy privilege also to draw these waters with joy, out of the Saviour's fountains, to thy heart's content?

III. Consider that, if thou dost not enjoy an abundant supply of this life-giving water, thou hast no one to blame but thyself, because the Heart of Jesus is a fountain that is open to all: *Fons patens domui David* —Zach. xiii. 1—*A fountain open to the house of David*. All that is required in order to obtain it, is to ask for it earnestly; thou needst never fear that it will be denied thee, provided only thou art ready to ask for it, because Jesus is more desirous of bestowing His grace on thee than thou art of receiving it. Resolve, therefore, to take up thy abode close by this wellspring of grace. Let the Sacred Heart of thy crucified Jesus always be before thy eyes; call upon it, adore it, because from it thou hast to draw all thy good. Thy real good consists in laying aside vice and acquiring virtue, and in wishing for nothing else in this world but thy God alone. These dispositions will draw an abundance of that water of divine grace which springs from the Sacred Heart of thy Saviour, if only thou wilt have recourse to it with confidence, and take up thy abode therein. *Haurietis aquas in gaudio de fontibus Salvatoris—You shall draw waters with joy out of the Saviour's fountains.*

SATURDAY AFTER THE OCTAVE OF CORPUS CHRISTI.

Si quis sermonem meum servaverit mortem non videbit in æternum.—Joan. viii. 51.

If any one shall keep My word, he shall not see death for ever.

I. CONSIDER that the sayings of Christ are not unlike those simple substances and herbs endowed in themselves with wonderful properties, but which are overlooked and unheeded by the inexperienced shepherd that treads them under foot, though the skilled simplicist most diligently searches after them, and gathers them in order to carefully lay them by and make use of them for his own advantage. The same thing precisely occurs with respect to the words and sayings of the Gospel. One that is not acquainted with their wonderful virtue and power, gives no heed to them; another, who does know their worth, will consider them attentively and store them up. Supposing there were a certain herb that possessed the virtue of keeping death away from thee for several centuries, with what diligence wouldst thou not go in search of it, and, when found, with what care wouldst thou not store it up? And yet with still greater care and diligence oughtest thou to store up the sayings of Christ, since they have the power of keeping death away from thee for ever.

II. Consider how it comes to pass that the words of Our Lord possess so great a power? We are liable to a twofold death—death of the body, and death of the soul. As regards the death of the body—he that keeps the words of Our Lord *mortem non videbit in æternum—shall not see death for ever;* not that he has never to die, but because after death he shall one day recover life in a more excellent form, and in which he will never see death again—a benefit which is not shared by the damned, who will live for ever, only to undergo the torments of dying for ever. Then as regards the death of the soul, which is sin—he that keeps Our Lord's words *mortem non videbit—shall not see death—*by ever incurring the guilt of grievous sin, because whosoever lives up to the teaching of Our Lord will never lose the life of grace. *Serva mandata et vives*—Prov. vii. 2—*Keep My commandments and thou shalt live.* The life of grace is usually lost, either owing to the ill-ordered state of the passions, or on account of the dangers and occasions of sin to which one is exposed, or through the assaults of diabolical temptations; or, finally, from a combination of all these three causes. Now the words of Our Lord have a very special power to regulate our passions, to preserve us from the danger of falling into the occasion of sin, and to ward off the assaults of the devil. See, then, how great is their worth, and how much thou oughtest to esteem them. *Fili mi ad eloquia mea inclina aurem tuam, vita enim sunt invenientibus ea*—Prov. iv. 20—*My son, hearken to my words, and incline thy ear to my sayings, for they are life to them that find them.*

III. Consider in what manner thou hast to keep these words and sayings of Our Lord if thou wouldst turn them to good account. Thou must keep them *corde, ore et opere*—in thy heart by meditating on them in due season, by loving them with the affections of thy will, and by frequently recalling them with thy memory, especially when thou art in danger of sinning. *Ore*—*In thy mouth*, by showing that thou settest a high value on them, and this by willingly making them the subject of conversation and not being ashamed to make open profession of them before the world. *Opere*—*in deed*, by putting them faithfully into execution : so that thou also mayest be able to say with truth : *Levavi manus meas ad mandata tua quæ dilexi*—Ps. cxviii. 48—*I lifted up my hands to Thy commandments which I loved.* Wouldst thou perchance say that this will cost thee too much trouble ? but reflect how great is the fruit, because it is a fruit of life—*verba vitæ;* and not of any life, but of life eternal.

THIRD SUNDAY AFTER PENTECOST.

Vadit ad ovem, quæ perierat, donec inveniat eam, et cum invenerit eam, imponit humeris gaudens. — Luc. xv. 4.

He goeth after the sheep that was lost until he find it, and when he hath found it, he lays it upon his shoulders rejoicing.

I. CONSIDER that thou art that strayed sheep of the Gospel which the divine Shepherd has endeavoured with such toil and hardship to bring back to His fold and place in safety, because whilst thou didst live in the world thou didst wander but too far from thy Shepherd, and didst tread a path fraught with numberless dangers of losing thyself altogether. Whilst thy Lord has left so many others in the midst of the perils of the world, He has sought thee out and after a deal of pains has succeeded in leading thee into the religious state in order to secure thy salvation. Recognise the great obligation thou art under to Almighty God for thy vocation, and thank Him with all thy heart: for although thou hast served Him ill in religion, thou wouldst have served Him still worse in the world.

II. Consider what it has cost Our Lord to draw thee out of the world and lead thee into religion. How many inspirations and interior voices did He not make thee feel in thy heart and which thou didst leave unheeded! how many lights and impulses did He not employ to which thou didst only offer a long resistance! and yet all the while our good God never ceased from renewing the invitations and multiplying His graces. Then again in order to merit these inspirations and graces in thy behalf, what toil, what labours, what torments, did He not undergo in life and in death! Whatever

He did or suffered for the salvation of all, He did and suffered for thy salvation alone, just as though there had been no one else in the world to save: *Dilexit te et tradidit semetipsum pro te*—Gal. ii. 20—*He loved thee and delivered Himself for thee.* If such then be the case, it may well be said that He has carried thee on His own shoulders and taken all the burden on Himself. Neither could Jesus have been led to show thee such a marked love for any need He had of thee, but solely because thou stoodst in so great need of His especial love, foreseeing as He did that thou wouldst have been lost for a certainty if He had not drawn thee from the dangers of the world. What correspondence hast thou shown so far to such signal mercy and love?

III. Consider that it is mentioned in the Gospel narrative that the good shepherd was congratulated on having reclaimed the strayed sheep and brought it back to the fold, because the angels rejoice and congratulate Our Lord when they behold a soul raised up after falling into sin, and so put out of danger of being lost. In like manner there was rejoicing in heaven when thou didst abandon the world and didst enrol thyself in the service of God in holy religion; but beware lest these rejoicings should be changed into wailings: *Versa est in luctum cithara mea*—Job xxx. 31—*My harp is turned to mourning*, if perchance thou art more taken up in serving the world than God. If thou wouldst that the rejoicing in heaven should continue, make up thy mind to attend in good earnest to the acquisition of the virtues proper to thy state, to the correction of thy faults and imperfections—and thus thou wilt complete the joy and gladness of Jesus Christ and of all the heavenly court.

MONDAY IN THE THIRD WEEK AFTER PENTECOST.

Attendite ne justitiam vestram faciatis coram hominibus, ut videamini ab eis.—Matth. vi. 1.

Take heed that you do not your justice before men, to be seen by them.

I. CONSIDER that the word justice here signifies all good works: these are reducible to three sorts—fasting, under which are comprised all penitential works which justify us with regard to ourselves; almsdeeds, which comprise all works of charity which regulate our conduct towards our neighbour; and prayer, which comprises all acts of religious worship which regulate our lives with regard to Almighty God. Now it is well that all these virtuous and meritorious works be seen by others in order to give good example; but it is not Our Lord's intention that thou shouldst do them with a view to gain the approbation and praise of men. Reflect and consider with what intention thou performest these good works.

II. Consider that there are two kinds of good works: some are proper to thy state of life and are performed by all the community, others are singular and extraordinary. It is safer and better that thou shouldst perform in private such works as are singular, in order to avoid giving any occasion for wonder or admiration; but as regards all common acts, thou art bound to perform them with that amount of publicity which is customary in thy own community; and thou oughtest on no account to withdraw thyself from their observance, so as not to give scandal. But alas! how easily thou neglectest these good works, time after time, not in order indeed to shun vainglory but to pander to thy own sloth and ease.

III. Consider how important it is thou shouldst have this upright intention in thy works. Every act of vanity which moves thee to perform thy good actions, takes away thy merit; so that thy whole reward will consist merely in the esteem thou wilt have won here on earth in the eyes of men—that esteem which thou hast preferred to the good pleasure of Almighty God; and so thou wilt obtain nothing from Almighty God for eternity. Observe however, that not always does any act of vanity deprive thee of all merit before God. It is only that which precedes thy action and proposes, as its end, the good pleasure of man; this is that hidden worm that spoils the good work in its entirety. Any little act of vanity that accompanies or follows upon a good work does not spoil it entirely,—although it is wrong and blameworthy,—because the good work does not depend on it as its end and object. Reflect then, how important it is that thou shouldst direct thy intention from the very beginning of thy actions, and that thou shouldst make it thy study to perform them, not to please men, but to please Almighty God alone.

TUESDAY IN THE THIRD WEEK AFTER PENTECOST.

Dedit ei locum pœnitentiæ, et ille abutitur eo in superbiam.—Job xxiv. 23.
God hath given him place for penance, and he abuseth it unto pride.

I. CONSIDER what a matter for astonishment it is that God Almighty, the Lord of infinite majesty, after having been most outrageously insulted by man—by a vile worm of the earth—should of His own mere goodness, and from no sort of obligation, give him every means of repentance and of returning to His favour and grace, *dedit ei locum pœnitentiæ*—by giving him time and grace, impulses and helps—and that man should abuse all this mercy and employ it only to go on sinning all the more wantonly. Yet how far more wonderful still it is that, in thy own case, after having offended thy God so often, He on His side should in His mercy have called thee to the religious state in order thus to give thee more time and greater convenience for doing penance and amending thy life; and that thou on thy side shouldst make such ill use of all this mercy by increasing thy sins and thy ingratitude! Admire the great goodness of Almighty God in thy regard, and bewail thy own ingratitude.

II. Consider that the reason why the sinner makes such ill use of the time granted him, is because he argues falsely. He comes to the conclusion that as Almighty God did not punish him on the instant, but still allows him the enjoyment of life and prosperity, that he was not after all guilty of any great harm. If Almighty God had punished his sins the instant they were committed, oh how profoundly would he humble himself! *Quia non profertur cito contra malos sententia, absque timore filii hominum perpetrant mala*— Eccl. viii. 11—*Because sentence is not speedily pronounced against the evil, the children of men commit evils without any fear.* And wouldst thou be of the number of those who abuse the kindness and patience of God in bearing up against them? If instead of calling thee to religion to do penance for thy sins, Almighty God had cast thee into hell which thou hast so often deserved, then indeed in the midst of those devouring flames wouldst thou know and recognise the heinousness of thy sins and detest thy own folly, but to no purpose. Why then dost thou correspond so ill with divine grace, and make such bad use of so great mercy? What penance hast thou hitherto performed, in anywise proportioned to the grievousness of thy sins? Even the mere observance of thy rule appears to thee too burdensome and difficult!

III. Consider that the sinner grows presumptuous because, as he sees that Almighty God bears up with him so long, he rashly reckons on having time and opportunity in the future for saving his soul, and for putting his conscience in order at the end of his life. But how deceitful is this lying hope of the sinner! and how many in consequence make a bad end, and are therefore damned! Remember, too, that the same thing happens to not a few religious, who by their ungrateful abuse of divine mercy are at last abandoned by it. Reflect, therefore, for what purpose Our Lord has granted thee this period of religious life: it is for no other than that thou shouldst have time to do penance. Humble thyself, therefore, and be ashamed of thyself: beware of abusing so great mercy on the part of God, for by so doing thou art guilty of a grievous injury against Him, and inflictest the most serious loss on thyself.

WEDNESDAY IN THE THIRD WEEK AFTER PENTECOST.

In omnibus operibus tuis memorare novissima tua, et in æternum non peccabis.—Eccl. vii. 40.

In all thy works remember thy last end, and thou shalt never sin.

I. CONSIDER what a worthy object of our desires it is to avoid mortal sin. It was in order to obtain this boon that the Saints importuned heaven with their prayers, and this same privilege is within thy reach also, if only thou makest up thy mind to remember thy last end in all thy works. But it is not enough to bear in mind the thought of death only, which is the beginning of thy last end; for in many instances the thought of death has been only the occasion of sinners allowing themselves still greater liberty: *Transibit vita nostra . . . venite, ergo, fruamur bonis*—Sap. ii. 3, 6—*Our life shall pass away . . . come, therefore, and let us enjoy the good things that are present.* That the thought of death may be of profit to thee, thou must also remember that after death will come a severe judgment, and with this judgment will go hand-in-hand a sentence of either eternal punishment or of eternal reward—either hell or heaven. Here it is that the efficacy and power of the remembrance of thy last end is to be found.

II. Consider whence proceeds the wonderful power of this remembrance. It is because by bearing in mind these four last things, thou acquirest the habits of the four cardinal virtues, by which all thy faculties are ordered to their right end. Prudence regulates thy reason so that it may not swerve. Justice directs the will that it may be upright. Temperance puts a bridle on thy concupiscence, so that it may not run after the enticements of vice. Fortitude keeps under thy anger, so that thou mayest patiently overcome the difficulties of the practice of virtue. Now the remembrance of the four last things causes these virtues to gain the ascendancy in thy heart more efficaciously than anything else, because the remembrance of death disperses from thy mind all those fumes of ambition and haughtiness which obscure thy intellect, and endows thee with prudence. The remembrance of judgment causes thee to appear in spirit before that rigorous Judge Who will one day examine the account of thy stewardship, and so puts thee in possession of justice. The remembrance of hell bridles thy craving after those unlawful pleasures which will be turned into such grievous pains, and imparts temperance to thee. The remembrance of heaven lessens the dread of those evils which will be changed into never-ending joy, and gives thee fortitude. Thus how will it be possible for thee to commit grievous sin? *Memorare novissima tua, et in æternam non peccabis—Remember thy last end, and thou shalt never sin.*

III. Consider that this promise of Ecclesiasticus is in many cases not verified, because so many reflect on the four last things in the abstract only, although they discourse about them, discuss them, and even represent them on paper or in marble; but they do not bring them home to themselves as truths that immediately concern them individually. For this reason it is said, *memorare novissima tua—remember thy last end.* It is needful that thou shouldst realise that it is thou thyself that wilt ere long be stretched on thy deathbed, laid out on the bier, and consigned to the grave: that thou thyself art the one who is concerned in that dreadful judgment, that for thee are destined those eternal torments if thou yieldest to temptation, and that for thee likewise are prepared those heavenly rewards if thou standest fast. It must be a practical remembrance: *in omnibus operibus tuis—in all thy works.* It will avail thee little to keep beautiful pictures of the four last things in thy cell, or to write or preach beautiful descriptions of them—all these are but dead pictures. Thou must keep them alive before thy eyes in all thy actions. This lively remembrance, which, perchance, appears distasteful to thee now, will afterwards become most pleasant to thee, because it will maintain in thee the peace of a good conscience, which is the greatest of all joys, according to that of Ecclesiasticus: *Non delectamentum super cordis gaudium—*

xxx. 16—*There is no pleasure above the joy of the heart.*

THURSDAY IN THE THIRD WEEK AFTER PENTECOST.

Similiter odio sunt Deo impius et impietas ejus.—Sap. xiv. 9.

To God the wicked and his wickedness are hateful alike.

I. CONSIDER that the hatred Almighty God bears sin is equal to the love He bears Himself, which is immense, infinite, essential. This is the reason why He has always pursued sin with such terrible punishments, such as deluges of water, rains of fire, plagues, earthquakes, and numberless other evils. But all this is as nothing. That Almighty God can vent His hatred for sin, there must needs be a hell ; and not even this is enough, for even after millions of ages, it will not be true that He has received a fitting satisfaction from the sinner, overwhelmed though he be by those awful torments. In order to show His great hatred of sin, and receive adequate satisfaction for it, He has gone so far as to punish sin in the person of His own Divine Son—though He had not in Himself aught of sin but its appearance and likeness—by handing Him over to the death of the cross, *ad ostensionem justitiæ suæ*—to *show His justice.* Is not this sufficient to give thee some idea of the great hatred God has for sin ?

II. Consider that so intensely does Almighty God hate sin, that all the boundless love He has for all the good and meritorious works that have ever been performed by the purest of His creatures—by the Patriarchs, Prophets, and Martyrs—if placed in the balance of His Justice, does not outweigh the hatred He bears to a single one of thy sins: so that were He capable of pain and grief, He would be more distressed at one sin of thine than He would be gladdened by the accumulation of all the good works of all the Saints together, although so noble and worthy from another point of view. Hence, were it possible that the performance of all these good works should depend on the commission of even the slightest sin, He could never wish—though He might permit—its commission; nor could it be His Will that thou shouldst wish it. Thus if, for instance, by telling a lie, thou couldst bring about the conversion of the whole world to the true faith, thou couldst not in conscience tell it. Oh, what an intense hatred for sin must not this be!

III. Consider that in the same degree that Almighty God hates sin, does He also hate thee if thou art a sinner: *similiter odio sunt Deo impius et impietas ejus—to God the wicked and his wickedness are hateful alike.* Hence, in that case, it would be a lesser evil for thee to be a reptile or a wild beast than to be wicked—seeing that God hates none of His creatures, but sin only. What a great misfortune thou wouldst deem it, didst thou come to incur the hatred of all thy acquaintance or of all thy fellow-townsmen? Yet is it not far worse for thee to be the object of the hatred of God Almighty and of all the citizens of heaven? There is, however, this difference between the hatred that God bears to the sinner and to his sin, that sin cannot but be hated by God at all times and in all places; whereas the sinner can, if he chooses, come to be the object of God's love, by ceasing to be a sinner, by becoming the object of his own hatred, and by bewailing from his heart the evil he has committed. If, then, thou wouldst but begin to be indignant with thy own rebellious flesh and wayward appetites by mortifying them, thou wilt cease to be guilty in the sight of God, and He will begin to love thee. But if thou hast already by God's merciful grace abandoned this state of sin and guilt, never cease to thank thy Lord for it, and to be strenuous in thy endeavours to make Him some satisfaction for thy past sins. Remember that in the religious life thou art not safer against a fall than Adam was in a state of innocence, or than Lucifer was on the threshold of heaven.

FRIDAY IN THE THIRD WEEK AFTER PENTECOST.

Qui sunt Christi carnem suam crucifixerunt, cum vitiis et concupiscentiis.—Gal. v. 24.

They that are Christ's have crucified their flesh, with the vices and concupiscences.

I. CONSIDER that the sign of being especially beloved by Christ is not the being a worker of miracles, or a great preacher, or a learned man, but the being interiorly and greatly mortified; which is a thing that all can arrive at by the help of God, provided only they wish it. This interior mortification is called a crucifixion because it has to be practised from a devoted love for our crucified God, and with a desire of being made like unto Him; and, again, because the practice of this mortification ought to be painful and persevering, like the crucifixion that Jesus underwent, Who remained immovably nailed to the cross in the greatest agony, until He expired. Reflect whether thy spirit of mortification bears any resemblance to this, or rather if it be not inconstant; and whether perchance thou shunnest to the utmost of thy power every occasion for practising it. The less thou lovest mortification, the less wilt thou be beloved by Jesus.

II. Consider that thou oughtest to mortify thy flesh in the first place, in order thus to put the axe to the root. The flesh is the root of all the evils that affect the soul, and if thou wouldst set about the cure of the soul it behoves thee to get the upper hand of the flesh. Now, before God, what corporal penances dost thou perform? Art thou intent on bringing thy flesh under subjection, or art thou perchance intent on pampering it? Remember, too, that the mere exterior mortification of the flesh is not enough. Of what use is it to take away the cause of the fever if the fever itself is not at the same time destroyed? Hence to exterior mortification thou must join interior mortification; indeed the former has to be employed only as a means for the attainment of the latter, which is the all-important mortification.

III. Consider what it is that has to be pulled down and destroyed by this interior mortification. It is *thy vices*, or in other words, thy sins, and *thy concupiscences;* that is to say, thy passions. Thou must first of all set to work at thy sins, by cleansing thy soul of them, and then turn thy attention to thy passions, by bringing them into subjection. Which are the passions that hold greater sway over thee? Endeavour to find them out with a view to mortify them, so that if they must live they may at least live fastened to the cross. By vices are to be understood, not, properly speaking, actual sins, but habitual sins. It is difficult to arrive at such a degree of mortification as not to commit any actual sin at all, but it is quite possible to arrive at that degree which excludes all habitual sin. Hence it is to the mortification of thy vices, whether little or great, that thou must give thy particular attention, and not content thyself with allowing them to live although fastened to the cross, but persecute them till they die on the cross. By the help of God's grace thou wilt be enabled to attain even this triumph over thy vices, if only thou art determined to mortify them in real earnest.

SATURDAY IN THE THIRD WEEK AFTER PENTECOST.

Sagittæ tuæ transeunt : vox tonitrui tui in rota.—Ps. lxxvi. 18, 19.
Thy arrows pass : the voice of thy thunder in a wheel.

I. CONSIDER that all the various evils, such as sickness, trials and misfortunes, which come to thee in this world from the hand of Almighty God, are so many arrows which He darts at thee from His throne in heaven, either to punish thee or to try thee. These are arrows that smart—it cannot be denied—sharp arrows that pierce through and through and make us bleed; but, after all, they are arrows that pass swiftly by. *Sagittæ tuæ transeunt—Thy arrows pass.* In what, then, can that dread calamity consist which is never to pass away? It will be that dreadful sentence which Christ Our Lord will thunder forth on the last day in the ears of sinners, and which will drive them away from Him when He shall say : *Discedite a me maledicti in ignem æternum*—Matth. xxv. 41—*Depart from Me, ye cursed, into everlasting fire.* This dread sentence will resound for ever in the ears of the damned as the great wheel of eternity revolves in its never-ending circle; for ever will it strike dismay and despair into their aching hearts. How comes it, then, that thou, who art so fearful of, and art so much upset by, the temporal misfortunes which befall thee, and which pass swiftly by like arrows—how comes it that thou remainest unmoved and undismayed at the danger of those eternal woes that threaten thee?

II. Consider that that voice with which Christ will pronounce sentence on the damned is called *a voice of thunder—vox tonitrui;* because just as the thunder is produced by the coalition of the electric fluids that have been pent up in, and have overladen, the clouds, and at length bursts forth in awful grandeur to give vent to its power and fury, striking awe in all who witness the storm, so also on that dreadful day the voice of Christ will be a voice of thunder; it will give expression to the just indignation and wrath that He has for so long a while withheld and smothered in His heart, and which will burst forth with so much the more fury on these wretched outlaws in proportion as He will have delayed and put off the manifestation of His anger. It will overwhelm them with such fear and dread that they will call upon the mountains to bury them and swallow them up in the depths of the earth. *Tacui semper et silui, patiens fui, ut parturiens loquar, destruam et absorbebo simul*—Isa. xlii. 14—*I have always kept my peace, I have kept silence, I have been patient, I will speak now as a woman in labour: I will destroy, and swallow up at once.* This is what He tells thee by His Prophet Isaias, and wouldst thou now be so rash as to have no fear of provoking Him to anger? Set thyself to ponder earnestly on this voice of thunder, *Discedite a me maledicti in ignem æternum—Depart from Me, ye cursed, into everlasting fire,* and thou wilt willingly bear with patience the trials that Our Lord sends thee in this life, to escape hearing this voice of thunder burst over thy own head on His judgment day.

III. Consider that it is said that the sound of this thunder will be *in rota—in a wheel,* because it will fill the whole circuit of eternity, which will never come to

an end; so that when millions and millions of ages
shall have passed away, there will always be a still
longer period remaining in the future. The wheel of
eternity, whether it be a happy or an unhappy eternity,
is stationary. Whosoever once finds himself at the
top of this wheel will for ever remain there, and whosoever has the misfortune to find himself at the
bottom of it, will remain in the depths for ever. Oh,
what would become of thee if it were thy lot to find
thyself at the bottom of this wheel? *Perditus in æternum eris*—Jer. li. 26—*Thou shalt be destroyed for ever.*
Time will whirl round, but not so the fate of him that
has no longer time to do good. Do thy best, therefore, to put thyself in safety by doing good now that
thou hast the time.

FOURTH SUNDAY AFTER PENTECOST.

Per totum noctem laborantes nihil cæpimus—Luc. v. 5.
We have laboured all the night, and have taken nothing.

I. CONSIDER who are they that labour a great deal in
the night of this world, but without any fruit. They
are, in a particular way, those religious that busy
themselves in worldly matters and undertakings which
are unbecoming their state of life; they are those that
are occupied in the otherwise religious duties of studying, preaching, and fulfilling their daily occupations,
only doing all this, not with the end of serving God,
but from other human motives, either to gain esteem
and applause, or to obtain some higher position or
greater ease and comfort. Finally, they are those that
perform their actions, either good or indifferent, as it
were in the dark, without setting before themselves any

virtuous and praiseworthy motive. All such as these
will, when the night of their lifetime is over, behold
all their toil and work lost, like the arrow that misses
the target, and, indeed, what is worse, fit only for fuel
to feed the flames. *Labores populorum ad nihilum, et
gentium ad ignem*—Jer. li. 58—*The labours of the people
shall come to nothing, and of the nations shall go to the
fire.* Enter seriously into thyself and reflect on the
manner in which thou performest thy actions, in order
not to incur so grievous a disappointment.

II. Consider what Our Lord said to S. Peter with
a view to enable him to take a large draught of
fish after having toiled all the night and laboured in
vain: *Duc in altum—Launch out into the deep.* He tells
him to draw away from the shore and betake himself
to the deep sea. The same thing must thou also do if
thou wouldst labour with fruit; thou must detach
thyself from all affection to the fleeting goods of earth,
and raise thy mind to the deep consideration of
heavenly and eternal truths. So long as thou remainest tied fast in thy affections to the present and
turnest not thy mind's eye to the future, thou wilt
never succeed in raising thy thoughts to God or to the
acquisition of the only real treasures of heaven, but
thou wilt always in thy undertakings keep thy eyes
fixed on earthly ends such as honour, comfort and
worldly advantages; all *labores ad nihilum—labours that
come to nothing.* Therefore *duc in altum—launch forth
into the deep*, raise up thy thoughts, thy intentions,
thy affections, to God and to heaven.

III. Consider that Peter took so abundant a draught
because he cast his net in the name of Our Lord and
at the bidding of Our Lord. See here the real way of
enriching thyself and of laying out thy labour to advantage. Let all thy actions be regulated by obedience
and by the routine laid down for thee in thy rules, by
directing all thy actions—even the most indifferent—

in the name of, and to the glory of, Almighty God. *Omne quodcumque facitis in verbo aut in opere, omnia in nomine Jesu Christi facite*—Colos. iii. 17—*All whatsoever you do in word or in work, all things do ye in the name of the Lord Jesus Christ.* In this manner all thy toils will gain for thee a plentiful draught for eternity.

MONDAY IN THE FOURTH WEEK AFTER PENTECOST.

Bonum facientes non deficiamus; tempore enim suo metemus non deficientes.—Gal. vi. 9.

In doing good let us not fail; for in due time we shall reap, not failing.

I. CONSIDER that whosoever is engaged in sowing seed—in a spiritual sense—is entitled to so great gain that he must not lose any time nor grow weary of his work. Thou perchance didst begin thy religious career in thy early youth: go on with thy work, by all means, although thou be now far advanced in virtue and years. *Mane semina semen tuum, et vespere non cesset manus tua*—Eccl. xi. 6—*In the morning sow thy seed, and in the evening let not thy hand cease.* Beware therefore of allowing thyself to be overcome by weariness and disgust, because *Qui parce seminat parce et metet*—2 Cor. ix. 6—*He who soweth sparingly shall also reap sparingly.* As regards, therefore, these good works of mortification and penance, of charity and devotion, which once upon a time thou didst take upon thyself, thou canst not be too anxious to keep up the practice of them with eagerness and cheerfulness; *Bonum facientes non deficiamus*—*In doing good let us not fail;* because if thou leavest off sowing thy seed, it is very easy to lose all.

II. Consider that there is nothing better calculated to relieve the toil of the poor husbandman than the thought of the future harvest. Yet with how much greater reason mayest not thou encourage thyself to bear up perseveringly against the toil of good works by the thought of the future recompense that awaits thee? The reward thou wilt reap in eternity from thy good works will be a harvest of glory and happiness that will know no end. If, therefore, the yield will last for ever, it is not at all the proper thing that so long as the few days of life granted thee by Almighty God last, thou shouldst withdraw thy hand from the work through weariness or tediousness. The labourer toils a great deal when sowing his seed, and when he gathers in he rejoices—yet not without having to toil then also. Thou, on the other hand, hast to toil but for a very short time on sowing thy seed, and wilt gather in to thy heart's content without ever growing weary. *Qui seminant in lacrymis, in exultatione metent*—Ps. cxxv. 6.—*They that sow in tears shall reap in joy.*

III. Consider that in order to succeed in obtaining this blissful harvest in the next world, which though not certain is, when obtained, most abundant, it is needful not only to scatter the seed of good works perseveringly, but it is moreover necessary to protect it from destructive birds, as is the wont of the careful sower who protects his seed by afterwards well covering it over. Such also is the practice of the humble. They are careful to conceal their good actions as fast as they perform them: whereas the vainglorious make no difficulty in allowing their good works to be seen, and in consequence, if they do not lose all their merit they lose a great part of it: *Seminasti multum, et intulisti parum*—Agg. i. 6—*You have sowed much, and brought in little.* If thou wouldst gain a great deal from the good thou dost, hide it when it is thy duty to hide it, and beware at all times of thoughts of vainglory, which are the birds that prey on it: *Volucres cœli comederunt illud*—Luc. viii. 5—*The fowls of the air devoured it.*

TUESDAY IN THE FOURTH WEEK AFTER PENTECOST.

Quid faciam cum surrexerit ad judicandum Deus? et cum quæsierit, quid respondebo illi?—Job. xxxi. 14.
What shall I do when God shall rise to judge? and when He shall examine, what shall I answer Him?

I. CONSIDER that that very same Jesus Who when He came on earth for thy salvation shed the last drop of His blood for thee, and whilst He is seated at the right hand of His Father, performs in thy regard the office of advocate in thy behalf, will the very moment thou breathest thy last, rise up and come to meet thee, no longer indeed as thy advocate but as thy supreme Judge. Oh, what will become of thee in that dread hour, when thou wilt have lost such a patron? Whatever good thou now enjoyest, all that forbearance that is shown in thy regard on the part of divine justice—all comes to thee through Jesus' pleading for thee. But at that last hour, at thy death, Jesus will lay aside this office of mercy, and thou wilt behold Him before thee not as thy Advocate, but changed into thy supreme Judge; —a Judge thoroughly well informed of thy every thought, thy every word, thy every action—because He has witnessed all, heard all, and has been most intimately present to all. Oh, what wilt thou do at this sudden and changed appearance of thy Jesus, foreboding such painful revelations?

II. Consider what kind of policy thou wilt be able to adopt under these woeful circumstances. Wilt thou seek to appease Him, or to excuse thyself? Thou certainly wilt not appease Him, because it will be no longer the time for putting forward petitions, but for undergoing punishment. He is a Judge who will prove Himself to be so much the more inexorable after death in proportion as He has been forbearing and merciful all thy life long: it will be useless therefore to hope to obtain pardon or to succeed in prevailing on Him to lay aside that anger which is called the anger of the Lamb, precisely to show that it will be implacable: *Abscondite nos ab ira Agni*—Apoc. vi. 16 —*Hide us from the wrath of the Lamb*. Set thyself therefore to think over again *quid facies—what wilt thou do?* Wilt thou perchance fall to thy prayers and beg that the mountains may crush thee and bury thee in the depths of the earth, and so hide thee from His wrath? Oh, vain hope! thou must perforce listen to a most minutely detailed account of thy whole life, in order that thou mayest receive the final sentence that depends on it from His own divine lips.

III. Consider that neither wilt thou be able at that dreadful hour to defend thyself or excuse thyself: certainly not to defend thyself, because thy guilt will be clear and certain: nor to excuse thyself, because these excuses are reducible to two heads—either to ignorance, or to frailty. But how wilt thou be able to plead ignorance, who hast been brought up in the Church of Christ, who hast lived in the religious state, with such abundance of clear light, virtuous example, and sound teaching? Hast thou closed thy eyes in order not to see the light? Thy ignorance will only prove thy severer condemnation. Wilt thou perhaps betake thyself to the excuse of frailty? But how canst thou do that, when this very frailty was thy own choice, seeing that thou didst not avail thyself of the proper helps and remedies, that thou didst not betake thyself to God in prayer, that thou didst not observe thy rules, that thou wouldst not allow thyself to be governed by obedience, that thou wouldst not keep aloof from occasions of sin and from dangerous precipices? Oh, what will be thy frame of mind when thou seest thyself condemned to atone for thy guilt in fiery flames — condemned by Him who shed His blood for thee to the last drop on the cross, and Who all thy life long has never ceased praying and pleading for thee as thy most kind-hearted Advocate!

WEDNESDAY IN THE FOURTH WEEK AFTER PENTECOST.

Si moram fecerit, expecta illum; quia veniens veniet, et non tardabit.—Habac. ii. 3.

If it make any delay, wait for it; for it shall surely come, and it shall not be slack.

I. CONSIDER that one of the greatest difficulties in the service of God would seem to consist in never distrusting His providence, either in adversity or in the midst of aridity and interior darkness, especially when these trials are so severe that they would fain lead us to believe that He has totally withdrawn Himself from us. So long as we enjoy His divine presence good works are easy of performance—but they become well-nigh impossible when we are left, so to speak, in the dark. Shouldst thou find thyself perchance in a like state, thou mayest be sure that Our Lord is trying thy constancy. Hence, He bids thee await patiently His coming, which will certainly follow. By this He means that thou shouldst not at any rate quit thy post, but go on as before in the performance of thy usual good works, such as prayer, Holy Communion, thy wonted mortification, and regular observance—even though in all this thou shouldst no longer feel any pleasure or satisfaction. Oh, how meritorious is constancy of this sort! this is really serving Almighty God for Almighty God's sake!

II. Consider that this constancy must be accompanied by a spirit of great long-suffering, because it is easy enough to practise it for a short time, but not easy to continue in it long. Hence thou art told: *Si moram fecerit, expecta illum—If He make any delay, wait for Him.* It would seem to thee that He is a long time coming, although it appears to thee that thou art not wanting on thy side to fulfil thy duty to the best of thy power by praying and entreating Him, and by shunning all occasions of His withdrawal arising from thy own faults and imperfections—and yet thy Lord favours thee not with His presence. But doubt not, He will at last return, and in proportion as He delays, so also wilt thou enjoy His presence, which will be rendered so much the more delightful as thou shalt have awaited Him with lively faith, and then thou wilt exclaim with all the warmth of thy heart: *Lætati sumus pro diebus, quibus nos humiliasti annis quibus vidimus mala*—Ps. lxxxix. 15—*We have rejoiced for the days in which Thou hast humbled us; for the years in which we have seen evils.*

III. Consider that even though thou hadst to await thy Lord all thy days long in a state of spiritual dryness and desolation—a case that rarely happens—thou wilt find Him most intimately present to thee at the hour of death; and in that dread hour, oh, how will

He not unveil His beauty to thy gaze, assist thee, and let thee know how far more tenderly He has always loved thee than thou didst ever dream of! This is, generally speaking, the reward that is in store for a soul that has faithfully served its God in time of desolation and trial, namely, to die in the midst of the greatest sweetness, *in osculo Domini—in the kiss of Jesus*—and to be able to lay aside in that juncture all the scruples, all the anxieties and doubts that have perplexed it in life. Thy own death may be close at hand, what would become of thee if in the short space that intervenes, thou wert to lose thy constancy?

THURSDAY IN THE FOURTH WEEK AFTER PENTECOST.

Qui spernit modica paullatim decidet.—Eccl. xix. 1.
He that contemneth small things shall fall by little and little.

I. CONSIDER that in these words Our Lord does not say that whosoever commits venial sins shall fall little by little into mortal sin, but He says so of him that despises venial sins, and takes no pains to avoid them, just as though they were of no consequence in the affair of salvation. If thou shouldst perchance discover thyself to be in this deception, oh, how great is the danger thou runnest of losing thy soul! for, bear in mind that these are the infallible words of Almighty God, that whosoever despises little faults shall by degrees fall into great faults: *paullatim decidet*—that is, as S. Thomas says, *a probitate et a statu gratiæ—he shall fall away from uprightness and the state of grace.* What does it matter when a ship is at sea that the leakages are small, if, in consequence of their being overlooked, they by degrees cause it to founder just as effectually as though they had been large? This is a picture of thy own fate if thou despisest little faults.

II. Consider that by making little of small faults thou inflictest on thyself two injuries at one and the same time. The first is, that thou gradually losest that fear which keeps thee back from serious evil, because as venial sins do not, like mortal sins, manifest their sad effects at once, but only, like a blunt file, after they have been at work for some time, they begin to be looked upon as though they were of no consequence at all. Thus it comes to pass that the soul is weighed down with them to such a degree, that they bring it to death's door. We see an illustration of this in the fact that we all shun poison, because it kills outright; but certain slow poisons are greedily partaken of, though capable of causing death after long continuance. The second injury inflicted by venial sin is that, by making little of lesser evils, we keep on seconding that proneness to evil of our unruly passions, which are the more barefaced and noisy in their demands in proportion as more is granted to them—like the fire that becomes fiercer the more fuel is heaped upon it, and is never glutted. Thus the soul, no longer content with the satisfaction it derives from yielding, according to its wont, to lesser faults, seeks a greater license in mortal sin. To succeed in this wile, the devil asks for nothing else at first beyond acquiescence in some slighter negligence, because he knows full well that by this means he will the more easily prepare the way for mortal sin. What, then, pray, art thou thinking about, when thou so readily yieldest thyself to the first preparatory assaults of the devil and of thy own concupiscence, which is unfortunately worse than any demon.

III. Consider that it is not, as thou perhaps imaginest, at all a rare thing, even in religion, to pass from little to great, in matter of sin; because not unfrequently Almighty God chastises lesser sins by permitting the soul to fall into greater ones. This comes to pass when He sees that wholesome warnings no longer prove of any avail, but venial faults are constantly on the increase, without being heeded or cared for; or again, when by long continuance they become intolerable in His sight by reason of their accumulation. Say not that thy sins are not very great, though even so it remains true that they are too many. Dry hay is light enough; but when it is piled up, as is wont to be the case in hay-making-time, in excessive quantity, the wagons creak and stagger far more under the hay than under a load of stone. It would almost seem that the Holy Ghost intended to make an allusion to this accumulation of so many venial faults when He said by His Prophet Amos: *Ecce, strideo subter vos, sicut stridet plaustrum onustum fœno*—Amos ii. 13 —*Behold, I will screak under you as a wain screaketh that is laden with hay.* If, then, Almighty God complains at being overtaxed by thee to such a degree, what matter of wonder will it be if He deprives thee of His protection and takes away that especial help of His, without which thou wilt soon come to lose His grace, and fall into mortal sins?

FRIDAY IN THE FOURTH WEEK AFTER PENTECOST.

Id quod in præsenti est momentaneum et leve tribulationis nostræ, supra modum in sublimitate æternæ gloriæ pondus operatur in nobis.—2 Cor. iv. 17.

That which is at present momentary and light of our tribulations, worketh for us above measure exceedingly an eternal weight of glory.

I. CONSIDER that the Apostle calls momentary and light what thou at present sufferest, because if thou lookest at thy trials which are past, they no longer give thee any pain, and if thou considerest thy present woes—well, after all, what are they? They are not pleasures, it is true, but they are momentary—that is, of very short duration in themselves, and shorter still by far if compared with eternity; so also are they in reality light in comparison with the debt thou hast to pay in satisfaction for thy sins: light also when thou takest into account the grace that is given thee to bear up against them: light, finally, in comparison with the reward that is awaiting thee if only thou endurest them with patience. Endeavour to reflect on these truths amidst the tribulations thou hast at present to undergo, and thou wilt thus more easily come to look upon them, as they really are, momentary and light.

II. Consider what great benefit thou wilt reap from thy own little share of sorrow. It will be a benefit *supra modum—above measure*, because far above and beyond thy own deserts; *in sublimitate—exceedingly*, because not liable to the reverses of this wretched world, but unruffled, unchangeable, and eternal. The glory of heaven is called *pondus gloriæ—a weight of glory*, not as though it could become to any blessed soul a cause of tedium or a burden; but the delights it contains are so exceeding great, that the faculties of our human nature would be overpowered by them were they not strengthened by the light of glory. Raise up thy mind, then, frequently to consider those attributes peculiar to the state of glory, if thou wouldst encourage thyself to suffer in patience; and remember that the glory that awaits thee is lavish, is unchangeable, and solid.

III. Consider what is said of tribulation, viz., that it actually is working out in thee thy future glorification, not as a physical and efficient cause, but as a moral cause, and in the order of merit. Hence thou mayest gather that the glory of heaven is not a mere gift—it is a reward, abundant though it be; and therefore imagine to thyself that just as Almighty God placed Adam in the earthly paradise, *ut operaretur illum*—Gen. ii. 15—*to dress it and to keep it*, so also has He placed in thy midst trials, abasement, and ailments, with a view to preparing in thee a still nobler paradise. Let, therefore, thy Lord work in thee according to His good pleasure: the more merit thy trials bring thee, the greater reward wilt thou obtain. Would not he be a stolid landlord that would find fault with his steward for illtreating his land because he breaks it up with plough and harrow?

SATURDAY IN THE FOURTH WEEK AFTER PENTECOST.

Stulte, hac nocte animam tuam repetent a te; quæ autem parasti cujus erunt ?—Luc. xii. 20.

Thou fool, this night do they require thy soul of thee ; and whose shall those things be which thou hast provided ?

I. CONSIDER that Christ Our Lord called by the appellation of fool that rich man whom the world would have enviously lauded as wise and prudent, because after having gathered in a plentiful harvest, he was pondering within himself how he might best store it up, and enjoy it for a long time to come—*in annos plurimos*. But by Our Lord he was called a fool, because he did not recognise that all his substance came from God, nor did he return Him thanks for having granted it to him, but thought only of how to turn it all to best account for the advantage of his body, being meanwhile entirely forgetful of his soul. Reflect, now, how far more foolish is the soul that, after having entirely renounced and given up the things of this world, in order to attend wholly and solely to the things of heaven, is nevertheless engrossed and taken up with the goods of this fleeting life, which are worth nothing, and overlooks its eternal interests, which alone are of importance. Beware lest thou be found to be amongst these fools who are but too often to be met with: *Stultorum infinitus est numerus*—Eccl. i. 15—*The number of fools is infinite.*

II. Consider the woeful plight of this foolish man of the Gospel, who the very night he was planning more anxiously than ever how to turn his income to best account, was doomed to hear the notice that his soul had to quit his body : *Hac nocte animam tuam re-*

petent a te—*This night do they require thy soul of thee.* Mark that the Latin word is not simply *petent*, but *repetent*, to denote that warning had been previously given to him over and over again, by interior presentiments, and the repeated lessons given him in the unprovided deaths of those amongst whom he lived—all of which forewarned him to be in readiness for death. How many hast not thou also seen or heard of amongst thy acquaintance, friends, and companions that have died unawares; and these are so many warnings for thee to put thyself in readiness for death: and yet thou heedest them so little, and payest not the slightest attention to them!

III. Consider the reproach that was made to this rich man: *Ea quæ parasti cujus erunt?*—*Whose shall those things be which thou hast provided?* This reproach proved doubly bitter to him: firstly, because he beheld all those goods fail him which he had stored up for the benefit of his body with so much pains and toil; and secondly, and much more, because he beheld himself empty-handed and void of those goods he had neglected in his lifetime, and which would have proved so serviceable to him at the hour of death for the benefit of his soul. Do thou begin at least to turn thy serious attention to what is alone of any importance, if thou wouldst avoid incurring a like reproach. What will all thy studies, thy labours, thy toilings, avail thee, if they are not directed to God, but to the acquisition of some temporal advantage? What will those posts of honour avail thee which thou hast obtained to the loss of observance? What will those comforts and conveniences avail thee which thou hast sought after with so much dissipation of heart? What will those friendships avail thee which thou hast formed either at home or outside thy monastery, to the prejudice of thy soul? Would to God that even now thou wert not expending thy labour on thy own impoverishment! That which is of no avail for the salvation of the soul is worth nothing at all. One thing alone there is which is of consequence—the thought of hell.

FIFTH SUNDAY AFTER PENTECOST.

Nisi abundaverit justitia vestra plus quam scribarum et pharisæorum, non intrabitis in regnum cœlorum ?—Matth. v. 20.
Unless your justice abound more than that of the Scribes and Pharisees, you shall not enter into the kingdom of heaven.

I. CONSIDER that Our Lord deservedly exacts greater perfection in the observance of the law of the Gospel than in the observance of the Mosaic law, which was an imperfect code and given to a people that lived in a state of servile fear, and to whom promises of earthly rewards only were held out: *Nihil ad perfectum adduxit lex*—Hebr. vii. 19—*The law brought nothing to perfection.* On the other hand, the Gospel law is of greater excellence and perfection, and offers clearer lights and bestows greater helps of grace; consequently it very justly exacts higher perfection, not only in exterior works, but in interior dispositions also. Now if all Christians under the law of the Gospel are bound to greater perfection than the Jews under the law of Moses, with how much greater reason are religious obliged to practise higher perfection than seculars, having, as they do, so many more lights and aids? Hence the low standard of virtue which will be enough for a secular to attain in order to save his soul, will certainly not be enough for thee who art a religious. Dost thou not blush at beholding so many lay people who far outstrip thee in the exercise of Christian virtues ? Tremble lest Almighty God should punish thy ingratitude.

II. Consider in what point it is chiefly that the Evangelical law requires greater perfection in Christians. It is in the love of one's neighbour, because whereas the Mosaic law forbade injuring one's neighbour in his life and substance, the Evangelical forbids not only displeasing him by injurious and wrathful words, but it even disallows the nourishing in one's heart of any kind of ill feeling or anger. *Qui irascitur fratri suo, reus erit judicio*—Matth. v. 22—*Whosoever is angry with his brother shall be in danger of the judgment.* Now if all this is demanded of seculars, how much more rigorously is it not required of religious ? Oh how thou deceivest thyself, shouldst thou be of the number of those who have no misgivings about, and think little of, faults against the love they owe their neighbour, by fostering feelings of bitterness in their hearts and not laying them aside entirely.

III. Consider what stress Our Lord lays on His command that thou shouldst pluck out from thy heart every sort of unkindly feeling towards thy brethren, and shouldst maintain perfect charity in their regard, seeing that it is His will that wert thou about to offer Him some gift on His altar, or perhaps the Holy Sacrifice, and didst remember having done thy brother some wrong, or wert conscious of entertaining any spite against him, thou shouldst leave the sacrifice and go to effect a reconciliation with him, not only interiorly in thy heart, but exteriorly also, and shouldst then return to offer up thy gift to Almighty God on His altar. He thus gives thee to see how much more earnestly He desires that thou shouldst not remain at variance with thy brother than that even thou shouldst offer Him the tribute of honour which is due to Him. Let this then suffice to cause thee to hold concord and love of thy neighbour in higher esteem than any other virtue.

MONDAY IN THE FIFTH WEEK AFTER PENTECOST.

Venit hora in qua omnes qui in monumentis sunt, audient vocem filii Dei, et procedent qui bona fecerunt in resurrectionem vitæ, qui vero mala in resurrectionem judicii.
—Joan. v. 28.

The hour cometh when all that are in the graves shall hear the voice of the Son of God. And they that have done good things shall come forth unto the resurrection of life; but they that have done evil unto the resurrection of judgment.

I. CONSIDER how mightily that great trumpet of S. Michael the Archangel will resound which will make itself heard by all, and awake the dead in their tombs, summoning them to appear in the valley of Josaphat. The trumpet is wont to be made use of for two purposes, namely, to solemnise high festivals and to call to battle in time of war. So also will the trumpet of the Archangel fulfil this twofold office. It will be the signal of war for the reprobate, and of festivity for the elect. For those who are now unwilling to listen to the voice of their Lord with which He addresses them by His inspirations, or to hearken to the words of His ministers, the trumpet will on that last day be a declaration of war? For those who do not now stop their ears to the voice of God, it will be a trumpet announcing joy unspeakable. Truly art

thou to be pitied if now thou despisest the voice of thy
Lord; too awful will be the fear that the sound of that
trumpet will strike into thy poor heart!

II. Consider that at this summons all the dead will
come forth from their graves; great and small, rich
and poor, learned and unlearned. But with what a
difference between one another! The elect will come
forth with their bodies no longer feeble or bowed down
by dint of austerity, but resplendent with glory and
beauty! The reprobate will come forth with their
bodies so hideous and noisome that the mere re-entering them will constitute a great part of their punishment. Then, again, on beholding this great change
that has come over their bodies, how different will be
the sentiments that will take possession of their souls?
How heartily will the reprobate curse that unbridled
love which they had for their bodies during life! How
the elect will rejoice at the austerities they made theirs
undergo! But far more dreadful still will the separation be that the Angels will make of the reprobate
from the elect. *Exibunt angeli, et separabunt malos de
medio justorum*—Matth. xiii. 49—*The Angels shall go out,
and shall separate the wicked from among the just;* the
good being borne aloft to the skies to meet Jesus Christ
—*obviam Christo in aera*—Thess. vi. 26—and the wicked
remaining below with the refuse of the universe. Oh
what wailing, what gnashing of teeth, what groans and
sighs will be heard by those who though accustomed
to command and lord it over others whilst on earth,
will see themselves brought down so low in that day of
woe! How canst thou then not esteem it the greatest
happiness to lead now a life of humility and austerity,
in order to play the bright part that will be assigned
to the elect on the stage of that great theatre, and
escape that which will fall to the lot of the reprobate!

III. Consider that no other reason is assigned for
this great diversity of fates than the difference of the

works performed during life. Those who were intent on doing good—*qui bona fecerunt*—whether ignorant or poor or simple-minded, will come forth unto the resurrection of life — *procedent in resurrectionem vitæ:* those who have done evil—*qui mala fecerunt*—whether wealthy or noble, princes or monarchs, will come forth unto the resurrection of judgment—*procedent in resurrectionem judicii*—under the sentence of eternal punishment. What sayest thou to this, thou that perchance hast thy heart fixed on anything but good works? On that last day thou wilt understand of how far greater worth is one single act of virtue than all the grandeur, all the learning in the world, because on that day nought else will be taken into account but good works, and nought else will be punished but evil deeds. Learn hence what thou oughtest alone to value and alone to fear.

TUESDAY IN THE FIFTH WEEK AFTER PENTECOST.

Amplius lava me ab iniquitate mea, et a peccato meo munda me; quoniam iniquitatem meam ego cognosco, et peccatum meum contra me est semper.—Ps. l. 4, 5.

Wash me yet more from my iniquity, and cleanse me from my sin; for I know my iniquity, and my sin is always before me.

I. CONSIDER that when David had repented of his fall he heard the pardon accorded to him by Almighty God from the lips of the Prophet Nathan, who announced to him: *Dominus quoque transtulit peccatum tuum*—2 Reg. xii. 13—*The Lord also hath taken away thy sin ;* so that he might have counted on forgiveness. And yet after an assurance even of this sort he never ceased from bewailing his fall, and continually asking Almighty God for pardon. And what, pray, is thy line of conduct who not only art not certain, but art perchance very uncertain whether Almighty God has pardoned thee thy sins? How many tears hast thou shed up to the present time over thy crimes in order to wash away their stains? What penance hast thou done for them? See how many tearful nights the evil of one single night cost David, sure as he was of forgiveness—*Lavabo per singulas noctes lectum meum*—Ps. vi. 7; and wouldst thou persuade thyself that thou hast entirely cancelled thy debt by asking for forgiveness once in a way at the feet of thy confessor for so many sins, which thou canst not know for certain if they have been duly absolved?

II. Consider that David continued in the detestation of his sin even after it had been forgiven, saying, *amplius lava me—wash me yet more ;* because to be perfectly cleansed from sin, it is not enough that the guilt only should be forgiven; it is moreover necessary that the evil consequences of previous infidelity should be destroyed, and, at the same time, the danger of a future relapse should be removed. Oh, didst thou only realise what a host of evil inclinations each individual sin leaves behind it, even though it has been confessed and forgiven, thou wouldst not be satisfied at having bewailed it once in a way, but wouldst continue to bewail it and detest it from thy heart, from the persuasion that sin, though forgiven, may still do thee great harm by consequence of its direful effects! *De propitiato peccato noli esse sine timore*—Eccl. v. 5—*Be not without fear about sin forgiven.* Dost thou not see how many evil consequences original sin has left behind it in thy own soul, although thou hast been cleansed in the laver of Baptism? just as many does every one of thy own actual sins leave behind it, even though blotted out by the sacrament of confession.

III. Consider that the penitent David, lest he should ever cease to bewail his sin, and cleanse his soul more and more, applied himself in good earnest to consider and turn over and over again in his mind the heinousness of the sin he had committed: *Quoniam iniquitatem meam ego cognosco; et peccatum meum contra me est semper*—Ps. l. 4—*For I know my iniquity, and my sin is always before me.* As it is impossible to have a clear knowledge of a supreme good and not to love it most ardently, so also is it quite impossible to have a clear insight into a supreme evil and not detest it most heartily. Wouldst thou know how it comes to pass that thou feelest no further grief for sin when thou hast once confessed it? It is because thou has not yet arrived at a full knowledge of its heinousness. Begin and think in good earnest of the great malice thy sins contain, and thou wilt not cease to hate them and weep over them. David's sin was ever before his eyes, constantly upbraiding him for the ingratitude he had shown to God in preferring a brutal pleasure to His holy will; but thou, on the contrary, throwest the remembrance of thy sins behind thy back, and thus failest to derive from them sentiments of either sorrow or humility.

WEDNESDAY IN THE FIFTH WEEK AFTER PENTECOST.

Confundetur Israel in voluntate sua.—Ps. x. 6.
Israel shall be confounded in his own will.

I. CONSIDER that the chief reason for which even spiritual people are so fond of having their own way, is because they hope thus to find peace and quiet; and yet it turns out to be just the reverse. There is no one thing that is better calculated to upset thee than to follow the dictates of thy own will. Thou wilt continually be in doubt as to whether it is better to act in this way or in that way, whether to go to rest or to watch and pray, whether to fast or to eat; and the more thou thinkest about it, the more wilt thou hesitate. If thou wouldst live a life of peace and quiet, make up thy mind not to live after thy own fashion, but to subject thyself in everything to the will of thy director and superior.

II. Consider a second reason why all are fond of doing their own will, which is, that they may find, not only their own quiet, but their own satisfaction also and credit; just as though the carrying out the will of another was a mark of meanness and servility, and the fulfilment of their own a mark of large-mindedness and nobility. Yet it happens that it is just the other way. *Confundetur Israel in voluntate sua—Israel shall be confounded in his own will*. Because when Almighty God sees that any one is too apt to follow up his own whims, that bear him onwards like an unbroken horse to the brink of a precipice, what He does is this, He makes the horse stumble, and the rider is thrown over the horse's head and comes heavily to the ground. Thou art, perhaps, bent on obtaining some professorship, some employment, some honourable post, in the hopes of acquitting thyself of its duties with credit and honour. If Almighty God shows His love for thee, He will cause it to turn out otherwise than thou wishest, because it would do thee too great harm if thy plans should succeed; thou wouldst perhaps be so attached to thy own will that thou mightest even lose thy soul. Allow thyself, therefore, to be guided by those whose duty it is to do so: *Obedite præpositis vestris et subjacete eis* – Hebr.

xiii. 17—*Obey your prelates, and be subject to them.* *Obedite—obey*, by readiness of execution; *et subjacete eis—and be subject to them*, by the submission of thy intellect, persuading thyself that what they command is the best thing for thee. However learned or clever thou mayest be, never depart one tittle from this spirit of subordination; if thou wilt persist in guiding thyself by the dictates of thy own will, thou wilt certainly come to misfortune: *Confunderis in voluntate tua.*

III. Consider the great happiness of thy religious state, by virtue of which it is thy good lot to live in perpetual obedience; by this means thou art safe to escape all disappointment and to enjoy real peace and quiet, provided only thou art obedient to those who govern thee. Whether thou practisest but little austerity, or whether thou art occupied in hard study; whether thou art chanting in choir, or preaching or hearing confessions; whether thou art engaged in the kitchen or in the professor's chair, thou art always sure of doing what is most pleasing to God and what is the source of greatest gain for thyself. Now is not this a state of most wonderful freedom from care and anxiety? *Qui custodit præceptum, non experietur quidquam mali*—Eccl. viii. 5—*He that keepeth the commandment, shall find no evil.*

THURSDAY IN THE FIFTH WEEK AFTER PENTECOST.

Cunctis diebus quibus nunc milito, expecto donec veniat immutatio mea.—Job xiv. 14.

All the days in which I am now in warfare, I expect until my change come.

I. CONSIDER that thou art placed in this world to fight like a soldier against those three far-famed foes, the devil, the world, and the flesh, which though they do not make a continuous assault upon thee, oblige thee nevertheless to be always with thy arms in thy hands; for if they seem to grant thee a little truce, they return to the attack fiercer than ever. Thus thou hast to live in fear and trembling, with a fierce engagement ever threatening thee, and without ever having any hopes of peace. *Cunctis diebus milito.*

II. Consider that thou must not on this account be dismayed or lose courage, because it is merely a question of a few days. A warfare like this appears to thee burdensome, because thou imaginest, as most men do, that thou hast to live a long life of many and many a year. Imagine, rather, just the opposite, as Job did, who in every occurrence called to mind the shortness of his life, comparing it at one time to a shadow that flits by, at another to a leaf that is whirled away by the wind, or to a flower that after a little time withers and decays. By thus thinking that thy warfare will soon be all over, thou wilt gain courage to put up with the trials that surround thee, with an unconquerable courage. But, unhappily, thou art wont to do just the contrary, and therefore thou gettest to be more disheartened than thou oughtest to be. Oh, how much shorter will thy life, perhaps, be than thou imaginest! *Ecce venio cito, tene quod habes—* Apoc. iii. 11—*Behold, I come quickly; hold fast that which thou hast.*

III. Consider that in order to animate thyself more effectually to endure thy present trials, thou oughtest not only to call to mind the shortness of life, but thou must also remember what a change of condition will come about in thy regard when thou wilt pass from warfare to the possession of a princedom, and to the enjoyment of a throne which thou wilt have won by thy bravery in thy Lord's service. *Expecto donec veniat immutatio mea—I expect until my change come.* Oh how this change, for which thou mayest look forward if only thou behavest like a brave soldier, will give thy heart courage when thou considerest the great difference it will entail in thy state of existence; for if now it is a state of toil, of fear, and of weariness, it will then be a state of rest, of security, and of joy—joy only such as the glory of Paradise can impart! It is quite certain that didst thou well understand the bliss of so happy a state of existence, thou wouldst impatiently look forward to its attainment. But if thou wouldst truly say with Job: *Expecto donec veniat—I expect until my change come*—how holy and excellent a life thou oughtest daily to lead, since death may daily come to summon thee. Examine how thou livest, so that thou mayest not be of the number of those who, though they fear death, do not look forward to it, because they have no hopes of bettering themselves hereafter.

FRIDAY IN THE FIFTH WEEK AFTER PENTECOST.

Sicut exaltavit Moses serpentem in deserto, sic exaltari oportet Filium hominis; ut omnis, qui credit in eum, non pereat, sed habeat vitam æternam.—Joan. iii. 14.

As Moses lifted up the serpent in the desert, so must the Son of man be lifted up ; that whosoever believeth in Him may not perish, but may have life everlasting.

I. CONSIDER that Christ Our Lord, hanging on the Cross, is like the brazen serpent in the desert. That serpent was neither responsible for, nor indeed capable of inflicting, the many deaths caused by the venomous bites of real serpents, but was a serpent only in appearance, formed of molten bronze, and yet it fell to its lot to be fastened to the cross in order to cure those serpent-bitten Israelites who looked upon it. So also Christ, Who was not Himself capable of guilt, but took merely the appearance of a guilty sinner by being moulded in our human nature by the fire of His exceeding love, hangs on the cross, in order that we poor creatures that have been poisoned by the venom of our sins, may be healed by fixing our gaze upon Him. Keep, then, thy eyes turned towards this thy Saviour, in the firm hope of being cured of thy ailings. If thou art not completely cured, it is a sign that thou dost not keep thy gaze continuously fixed on Jesus, Who hangs on the cross for thy sake, naked, despised, and in an agony of pain and grief.

II. Consider that Jesus called His hanging on a cross, like a guilty felon, His exaltation, inasmuch as His being raised aloft on that infamous gibbet resulted in glory and honour, instead of shame and confusion: *Exaltari oportet Filium hominis—The Son of man must be lifted up.* But why this word *oportet—must be?* Would Christ perchance have lacked some degree of greatness and glory had He not endured so great shame and pain for thee? or would He, perhaps, not have been equally blissful if thou hadst been lost? How comes it then to pass that thou art not taken aback with astonishment at this excess of love? How comes it that thou art not ashamed and confused at seeing how thy God and Redeemer deems it honourable to Himself to suffer so much for thy sake? And yet how little anxious art thou to undergo any little suffering for the love of a Saviour Who glories in dying on a cross for thee!

III. Consider that it is said of the brazen serpent that it was exalted in the desert, as a sign: *Pone eum pro signo*—Numb. xxi. 8—*Set it up for a sign.* So also Christ is nailed to the cross—*pro signo—as a sign*, to which we have all to look for hope of salvation; and again, because He is there as a sign which serves as a badge and glorious ensign to all the faithful who make profession of fighting under His standard. A good soldier never loses sight of his colours, nor hesitates to follow them wheresoever his general leads him. In thy character of religious, thou hast made profession in a most especial manner to be a soldier of Christ crucified, and thou must keep thy eyes constantly fixed on the glorious ensign of the Cross, and follow up as closely as thou canst in the footsteps of thy crucified Jesus, if thou wishest to be a religious in reality, and not in name and appearance only.

SATURDAY IN THE FIFTH WEEK AFTER PENTECOST.

Fili accedens ad servitutem Dei, sta in justitia et timore, et præpara animam tuam ad tentationem.—Eccl. ii. 1.

Son, when thou comest to the service of God, stand in justice and fear, and prepare thy soul for temptation.

I. CONSIDER that liability to temptation is common to all in the religious state, but especially to beginners. It is these that Ecclesiasticus particularly exhorts to prepare themselves, because, as regards those who are more advanced, it is to be supposed that they are already prepared; and if such as these are liable to suffer even the most grievous temptations, after being established in their state of life, beginners are still more exposed to the assaults of temptation by reason of the fury of the devil at seeing them in the act of turning their backs on his thraldom. As, therefore, even advanced religious ought to live in fear and in readiness against temptation, with much greater reason ought beginners to entertain a wholesome fear, in order to remain firm in the resolution they have made of serving Almighty God. *Sta in justitia et timore—Stand in justice and fear; in justitia—in justice*, by the performance of good works to merit for thyself the protection of Almighty God; *in timore—in fear*, by a complete distrust of thyself.

II. Consider that the first preparation thou must make for these conflicts against temptation, consists in discovering the wiles of the tempter, and which are. generally speaking, like those with which the evil spirit assailed Christ in the desert. He first of all suggested to Jesus Christ the commission of a smaller sin, and then a greater one, and finally a great crime.

For seeing Him weak and emaciated by His long fast, he exhorted Him to provide Himself with food by means of a miracle. Then being disappointed in his first assault, he tempted Him in his second attack to manifest by an act of presumption how great was his trust that God would give Him a helping hand in His straits, by casting Himself headlong as though he had no care or anxiety for His own life. Lastly, he tempted Him for the third time with ambition by offering Him the possession of the whole world if He would fall down on His knees before him and adore him. This is precisely the method with which the devil assaults one who has left the world and is beginning his new life in the cloister: he represents to him his weak and feeble state of health and the rigour of the religious life, and tempts him to pusillanimity, making him believe that he cannot possibly persevere without a manifest miracle. If his fervour of spirit enables him to think little of bodily austerities, he urges him to ill-treat his body without any discretion, tempting him to presumption, so that his strength may fail under the weight. When these stratagems do not succeed, he places before the eyes of the young religious in golden colours the liberty and ease he might enjoy in the world, the dignities and promotion he might look for there, and tempts him to apostatise. This is the tempter's method of proceeding—he aims at inflicting the greatest of evils—but makes his way little by little. If thou hast stood firm against his first attacks be not too self-confident, but prepare thyself for fiercer assaults.

III. Consider that it is from Christ thou must also learn the art of rejecting the assaults of the evil one. Christ did not begin disputing with the evil spirit, but rejected him each of the three times, powerfully, promptly and quickly. So do thou also; do not begin disputing with these imaginations of thine, behind which thy wily foe shelters himself to fight the battle against thee. When he tempts thee with pusillanimity to get thee to relax the rigour of religious discipline in undue ways, say to him: *Non in solo pane vivit homo*—Deut. viii. 3—*Not in bread alone doth man live*—I am content with what the Lord will provide for me. When he tempts thee to presumption by rushing headlong into singular and indiscreet fervour with sudden and dangerous leaps under the colour of being confident of receiving extraordinary aids, say to him: *Non tentabis Dominum Deum tuum*—Deut. vi. 16—*Thou shalt not tempt the Lord thy God*—and allow thyself to be guided by thy director. And when he tempts thee with ambition and lying hopes, send him whence he came: *Vade Satana—Be off with thee, Satan.* He will picture to thee all that is beautiful and seemingly good in the world, with many a promise of what it is not in his power to bestow, and all this to entice thee: but he takes good care to keep out of sight all the bitterness, the heart-aching and the long train of other evils which the malicious father of lies, and thy most deadly foe, would wish to see come upon thee, and into which he strives to make thee fall.

SIXTH SUNDAY AFTER PENTECOST.

Misereor super turbam, quia ecce jam triduo sustinet me.
—Marc. viii. 2.

I have compassion on the multitude, for behold they have now been with Me three days.

I. CONSIDER the devotion of the crowds of believers that for three continuous days were intent on following Christ without giving a thought to providing themselves with the necessary food, and without any misgiving about perishing of hunger, although they had had no promise from Christ of being provided for, nor did they see any signs of preparations to satisfy their needs. Thou, on the other hand, hast heard the promises of Almighty God repeated over and over again in the Holy Scriptures, and seen them ratified by numberless examples as to the care He has of those that follow Him and how He will provide for the wants of those that serve Him—and nevertheless thou livest with so much solicitude about thyself, and placest so little trust in Divine Providence. Thus, for example, when thou seest thyself assigned by obedience to this or that place, or office or charge, thou becomest fearful lest thy strength or health may fail thee, or something or other be wanting that is requisite for thy happiness, just as though the Providence of Almighty God would fall short of the mark in thy regard. Oh, what an injury thou dost thy Lord! Begin straightway to lay aside such great anxiety about thyself and to trust in the loving care of God, as S. Peter exhorts thee: *Omnem solicitudinem vestram projicientes in eum quoniam ipsi est cura de vobis*—1 Pet. v. 7—*Casting all your care upon Him, for He hath care of you.*

II. Consider how attentively and tenderly Jesus undertook to provide for the wants of the devout crowd. *Misereor super turbam—I have compassion on the multitude.* He sympathises with them with a father's heart, and He is loath that they should return to their houses fasting, lest they should suffer on the way: and therefore by means of a miraculous multiplication of bread He gives them a plentiful meal in the desert. So much will thy Lord do in thy regard, if only thou wilt forget thyself and be intent on following and serving Him in earnest. Jesus once said to S. Catherine of Sienna: *Do thou think about Me, and I will think about thee;* and henceforward the Saint put aside all care for her own interests, her health, her reputation and her life itself, and applied herself solely to do her utmost to serve Him and please Him, to her own great advantage, living as she did under the special protection of Jesus. Dost thou not consider that this is a sufficient motive for thee to do the same?

III. Consider that all that crowd of people regaled and satisfied themselves on nothing else but the bread which had been so wonderfully multiplied; *Saturati sunt—they were filled.* They were refreshed in spirit by His heavenly doctrine and the marvels and wonders He wrought; refreshed in body with this bread that contained in itself every kind of taste, because it was made by the omnipotence of God. A like refection and consolation is in store for all who place their trust in God, and endeavour to serve Him without giving a thought to themselves, but depend wholly and entirely on Divine Providence. Turn, therefore, all thy attention to try and live according to the disposition thy Lord makes of thee by means of thy superiors, and then nothing will be wanting to enable thee to lead a happy and contented life.

MONDAY IN THE SIXTH WEEK AFTER PENTECOST.

Statutum est hominibus semel mori, et post hoc judicium. Hebr. ix. 27.

It is appointed unto men once to die, and after this, the judgment.

I. CONSIDER that the law by virtue of which man is subject to death is called a decree, because it is not in his case a natural law as in the case of other animals, but a positive law; for he was created by Almighty God immortal by virtue of the state of original justice to which he was elevated. However, when the first man lost this privileged state for himself and all his posterity, the decree of death is universal and embraces all. Do what thou wilt, use every imaginable industry to prolong life—but in the end die thou must. Hast thou not heard of Lamech, how he reached seven hundred years, and then *mortuus est?* of Malaleel, how he lived eight hundred years, and then *mortuus est?* of Mathusalem, how he survived nine hundred years, and then *mortuus est?* The same story will be told of thee—and remember that after the lapse of a few years thou must die. Why then live so attached to earth? Think rather of thy departure hence, and think well on it.

II. Consider that *statutum est semel mori—it is decreed once to die.* If once this deed is performed ill, there is no remedy for it; thou canst not possibly make good the fatal mistake of dying in sin. Whatever then art thou about, seeing that as yet thou hast not busied thyself in good earnest about taking this step well, this step which is taken but once only? Look and reflect where this all-important step will place thee—it will place thee in the house of thy eternity;

that is to say, in a mansion of eternal glory, or a dungeon of eternal woe.

III. Consider that the step from life to death is awful, more on account of what comes after it than on account of what it puts an end to. *Et post hoc judicium—and after this the judgment.* In that very spot, at that very instant, in which thou diest, thou wilt behold before thee the vision of that dreadful tribunal, the anticipation of which has caused so many saints to make the grave their text-book. At this judgment-seat, all alone, without attendants, without friends, without thy very body itself, thou wilt behold thyself a naked spirit in the presence of an all-mighty Judge, who will pass sentence on thee according to thy deserts without any personal regard. What wilt thou do? There will be no hope of appeasing Him, or of entreating Him, because the very moment thou breathest thy last, the whole process will be already drawn up against thee, and sentence passed either of eternal reward or eternal punishment—and all this in the twinkling of an eye. But every individual survives, so to speak, after death, in a more or less limited sphere, and in different ways: he continues to live in the memory of men, some esteeming him good, others bad; he continues to live in his literary works, which are productive of different results, some good, some bad; and therefore, the privacy of the particular judgment will be supplemented by the universal judgment, at which the truth will be made known to all as it is, and each one will be awarded publicly according to his deserts, even so far as regards the reward or punishment of the body. If thou wilt keep this great truth before thy mind's eye, thou wilt come to fear death and judgment much less.

TUESDAY IN THE SIXTH WEEK AFTER PENTECOST.

Omne quod tibi applicitum fuerit, accipe, et in dolore sustine et in humilitate tua patientiam habe : quoniam in igne probatur aurum, et argentum, homines vero receptibiles in camino humiliationis.—Eccl. ii. 4.

Take all that shall be brought upon thee, and in thy sorrow endure, and in thy humiliation keep patience. For gold and silver are tried in the fire, but acceptable men in the furnace of humiliation.

I. CONSIDER that there are three classes of sick people. Some are most desirous of being cured, but are unwilling to submit to disagreeable or painful remedies. Others are willing to undergo medical treatment, but only so far as it suits their own whims. Others, lastly, there are, who are ready to submit to any remedy whatsoever, and say to their divine Master, Burn, cut, do with me what seems good to Thee; I am entirely in Thy hands. Now, the last manner of proceeding is the only way in which thou canst hope to be cured of thy maladies. Leave it to thy God to apply what remedies He chooses, for He only knows which amongst so many possible remedies will be most beneficial to thee. *Quod tibi applicitum fuerit accipe—Take all that shall be brought upon thee.*

II. Consider that thou dost not experience such very great difficulty in putting up with any distasteful remedy—such as bodily illness or an interior trial—that comes to thee straight from Almighty God; but thou findest much greater difficulty in undergoing patiently some trial or humiliation which Almighty God sends to thee, either by means of thy superior, or even through the instrumentality of those that wish thee ill. But art thou not aware that the physician does not always apply the remedy to the sick man with his own hands, and that very frequently he avails himself of the services of either a surgeon or a mere assistant? So also does God Almighty. It is His wish that that trial which is destined to be thy remedy, should not come immediately from Himself, but that it should come to thee through some one else, who may even be thy inferior; and therefore thou must not consider who applies the remedy, but who it is that has ordered it, and that is no other than Almighty God; especially, too, since in this case it is He that guides the hand of the operator, in order that it should not do more than its duty. Why, then, dost thou so completely lose sight of the heavenly Physician that prescribes the medicine, and art solely intent on looking at the person that mortifies thee or bids thee act in this or that way? No wonder, surely, that thou gettest impatient and disturbed!

III. Consider what a useful remedy any calamity is that befalls thee in the shape of either pain or humiliation, whether it comes immediately from the hand of the heavenly Physician or by means of men. Until God tries thee with tribulation, how often it happens that thou art quite satisfied with thyself! Thou placest full reliance on those good desires, those firm resolutions, those pious sentiments, that thou experiencest in prayer; but when the time comes to test them, then also thou comest to know thyself, and to find out how far short thou fallest of the standard thou hadst pictured to thyself; for thou suddenly breakest out into complaints, thou gettest disturbed, and losest all thy resignation to God's holy Will. Until the gold and silver is put to the test of the crucible, it cannot be ascertained what alloy they contain; neither can it be ascertained in thy case until thou art tried *in camino humiliationis—in the fire of humiliation*. Thank thy Lord, therefore, if He not unfrequently places thee in trying circumstances, because there is no surer road to heaven than the road of humiliation and trial; but beg Him also to strengthen thee to withstand bravely these troubles.

WEDNESDAY IN THE SIXTH WEEK AFTER PENTECOST.

Obsecro vos ut digne ambuletis vocatione qua vocati estis, cum omni humilitate et mansuetudine, supportantes invicem in charitate, solliciti servare unitatem spiritus in vinculo pacis.—Ephes. iv. 1.

I beseech you that you walk worthy of the vocation in which you are called, with all humility and mildness, with patience, supporting one another in charity, careful to keep the unity of the Spirit in the bond of peace.

I. CONSIDER that thy vocation is the most perfect of all, because it is that which is professed in religious communities. Now the perfection of a religious community, if thou takest notice, is grounded entirely on unity of spirit; because as a community is, morally speaking, one body, so also this body ought to be animated by one spirit: *Unum corpus et unus spiritus*— Ephes. iv. 4—*One body and one spirit.* Hence the distinctive mark of a true religious is not either piety or mortification, or modesty of gait, but sincere brotherly union. Yet thou wilt persist in making greater account of any other virtue than this, on behalf of which the Apostle even goes so far as to entreat thee: *Obsecro vos*—*I beseech you.*

II. Consider that the faults that most of all run counter to this union, so fitting and so necessary in every religious community, are pride, anger, impatience, and indiscreet zeal. And first of all, pride; because *inter superbos semper jurgia sunt*—Prov. xiii. 10 —*among the proud there are always contentions;* and therefore thou art recommended to practise humility, both interior and exterior : *Cum omni humilitate—with all humility.* The next hindrance is anger, because *homo iracundus excitat iras*—Prov. xxvi. 21—*an angry man stirreth up strife.* Hence thou art recommended to show meekness in words and actions. Then comes impatience, which cannot brook any, even the slightest, offence ; and therefore, in the third place, patience is proposed for thy imitation, because it extinguisheth wrath. Lastly, there is an indiscreet zeal that criticises and finds fault with the actions of others ; and therefore thou art warned to put up with the defects of others as thou wouldst have others put up with thy own : *Supportantes invicem—Supporting one another.* Examine thyself to discover if any of these vices lurk in thy heart, and endeavour to correct them to the utmost of thy power by the practice of the four virtues just enumerated.

III. Consider that there are wont to be various kinds of unions in religious houses. There is one kind that is positively vicious—the union of party-spirit and clique ; and this may be called the plague of a community. There is another kind that is natural, by reason of connection, of relationship, or of birthplace ; or again, arising from companionship in office or in studies ; and this is not blameworthy, provided it does not damage religious union. But these kinds of union do not embrace all, nor are they stable, and hence it is only that holy union of religion which binds all together from a superhuman motive, viz., because God so wills it : *Hoc est præceptum meum—This is My precept.* Happy art thou if thou art in possession of this bond that binds thee to thy community ! But if thou wouldst have the bond to be a peaceful bond—*in vinculo pacis*—attend to thy own business, and on no account interfere with what does not concern thee, for peace can never exist where good order is disturbed. *Pax est tranquillitas ordinis*, says S. Augustine—*Peace is the tranquilness of good order.*

THURSDAY IN THE SIXTH WEEK AFTER PENTECOST.

Esto consentiens adversario tuo cito dum est in via; ne forte tradat te adversarius judici.—Matth. v. 25.

Be at agreement with thy adversary betimes, whilst thou art in the way with him, lest perhaps the adversary deliver thee to the judge.

I. CONSIDER that the adversary here spoken of is thy conscience. Thou hast to act with thy conscience as thou wouldst with a powerful enemy who has just claims against thee, by seeking to give him due satisfaction by means of payment, or by coming to terms with him before he has thee up before a court of justice. In like manner must thou act towards the dictates of thy conscience if thou wouldst escape being condemned by the Supreme Judge to pay thy debt to the last farthing. If thou reflectest seriously on this truth, thou wilt not so easily despise thy remorse of conscience, which is often so well grounded.

II. Consider that thy conscience is here called thy adversary, not as though it were thy enemy, but because, though friendly to thy real good, it is opposed to thy disorderly whims. Thy real enemy is thy inclination to evil. Therefore, *esto consentiens cito*—*come to an understanding betimes;* settle the qualms of thy conscience, and strive to satisfy its claims as quickly as thou canst—*dum est in via*—*whilst thou art in the way*—without loss of time, as it may be that thou art near thy journey's end, because *post viam*—that is, after death thy conscience will become an adversary and plaintiff, that will prefer most serious and grievous claims against thee before thy Judge, Jesus Christ, against Whose sentence there is no appeal, and Who, in the judgment He will pass on thee, will give especial heed to the accusations of thy conscience, which thou hast so slighted during thy lifetime. At that tribunal it will help thee little to be sorry then that thou didst not effect an understanding with this thy adversary during life.

III. Consider that there are some who, in order not to hear the troublesome reproofs of this adversary, instead of giving him speedy satisfaction, seek to lull him to sleep, or to drag him to humour their disorderly whims by arguments and garbled pretexts, so that the voice of conscience may be stifled. Woe to thee if such be thy manner of proceeding. If thy conscience be silent now, it will make itself heard and will raise its voice in a terrific manner at the tribunal of thy Judge, Who will condemn thee to prison, a prison of fire, whence *non exies donec reddas novissimum quadrantem*—*thou shalt not go out till thou repay the last farthing*. This prison will have to be either hell or at least purgatory, and the punishment will be either eternal or for a time, accordingly; but in any case it will be far more grievous and severe than anything thou wouldst have had to put up with, hadst thou come to terms with thy adversary, with thy conscience, betimes.

FRIDAY IN THE SIXTH WEEK AFTER PENTECOST.

Patior, sed non confundor. Scio enim cui credidi, et certus sum quia potens est depositum meum servare in illum diem.—2 Tim. i. 12.

I suffer, but I am not ashamed. For I know Whom I have believed, and I am certain that He is able to keep that which I have committed unto Him against that day.

I. CONSIDER that the most grievous temptations in the spiritual life are temptations to diffidence, under the influence of which it would seem that all that one does or suffers for God is useless and in vain. Against such temptations as these let the words of the Apostle be a remedy: *Patior, sed non confundor—I suffer, but I am not ashamed.* He admits that he suffers much, but with all his suffering he is not disconcerted. Dost thou perhaps imagine that the Saints, with all their ardent love of God, did not feel the sharp edge of sufferings? Such is not the case. They felt them most keenly; but they did not lose their courage, because they well knew Who that Lord was to Whose care they had committed themselves. *Scio cui credidi.* But thou wilt say, thou art so extremely sensitive to any suffering of mind or body. Well, what then? That is no argument: if thou didst not feel them, thou wouldst not suffer. Be content, therefore, to suffer, and not lose courage, by maintaining a lively faith and trust in Almighty God.

II. Consider what this deposit is of which the Apostle makes mention: *Certus sum quia potens est depositum meum servare in illum diem—I am certain that He is able to keep that which I have committed unto Him against that day.* It consisted of the many sufferings he underwent for God's sake, because he had entrusted them all to the keeping of God, and he was therefore sure that they would be all hoarded up for him, one by one, with the greatest exactness, to his own future advantage. Seek to do the same thyself; exert thyself, toil and endure for love of God, and tell Him that thou wishest to depend entirely on Him, and to leave thy whole self under His complete control. *In manibus tuis sortes meæ*—Ps. xxx. 16—*My lots are in Thy hands.* In this way thou wilt be far surer of reaping all the fruit of thy sufferings.

III. Consider that the Apostle says that his sufferings were hoarded up not for this world, by receiving a reward for them on earth, but *in illum diem—against that day*—that is to say, for that last day of the particular judgment, and of the universal judgment, because there can be no day in this life like unto that, so pregnant of good for the holy and of evil for the wicked. It is this day thou must ever keep present in thy memory to encourage thee; and remember, that at the particular judgment thy heavenly Master will repay thee, as far as thy soul is concerned, for all thou hast undergone for His sake, and on the day of the universal judgment He will, moreover, return to thee that very body in which thou hast suffered. In this, then, consists that deposit of which the Apostle was truly able to say: *Potens est depositum meum servare in illum diem—He is able to keep that which I have committed unto Him against that day.*

SATURDAY IN THE SIXTH WEEK AFTER PENTECOST.

Lava a malitia cor tuum, Jerusalem, ut salva fias: usqueque morabuntur in te cogitationes noxiæ ?—Jer. iv. 14.

Wash thy heart from wickedness, O Jerusalem, that thou mayest be saved; how long shall hurtful thoughts abide in thee ?

I. CONSIDER how few there are that wash their hearts from wickedness. Many rinse their hearts, as it were, in the laver of confession, and so rid themselves of the sins with which they had defiled their consciences; but very few wash their hearts in such a manner as to leave behind no attachment or affection to their sins. Thou accusest thyself, for instance, of having sought after the vain applause of others; but thou makest no effort to detach thy heart at the same time from the affection thou still retainest to the good opinion of others. Thus thou cleansest thy heart, to a certain extent; but thou dost not wash it thoroughly. It is the same story over again, as regards certain friendships that are not altogether praiseworthy—the love of certain distinctions and pastimes. If it were as easy a matter to wash thy heart as it merely is to rinse it out, it would not have been said to Jerusalem —that is, to the soul consecrated to God: *Lava cor tuum ut salva fias*—*Wash thy heart that thou mayest be saved.*

II. Consider that thy thoughts are the criterion by which to ascertain whether thy heart is washed from wickedness or not. If the thoughts that are fostered there are tainted with grievous sin, thy heart would not be cleansed in any degree at all: and if they are less guilty, but still are such as may little by little incite thee to grievous sin, such as thoughts of worldly pleasures, and greatness, and amusements, it is a clear sign that thy heart, if partially cleansed, is not certainly washed. But note well that bad and wicked thoughts will frequently pass through the minds of all—and that affords no proof of attachment to sin. The proof of this is the dwelling on those thoughts: *usquequo morabuntur in te cogitationes noxiæ?—how long shall hurtful thoughts abide in thee?* All the harm consists in this wilful dwelling on the thought: just in the same way as the most delicate balm is not spoilt by the flies merely passing over it, but by their settling on it. Examine thyself, and see how far thou keepest thy mind free, not only from sinful thoughts, but even from such as are hurtful, and thou wilt thus know from what affections thou must endeavour to wash thy heart.

III. Consider how thou hast to set about cleansing thy heart from wrong affections, and thus effectually washing it. Endeavour, in the first place, to conceive an intense hatred of sin, because if thou wouldst avoid being again entangled by the love of objects that have a great tendency to drag our corrupt nature after them —any weak sort of a hatred is of no good—thy hatred must be deep-seated. It was in this way that Esther acted, who to avoid growing attached in her heart to the diadem she wore on her brow, accustomed herself to hold it in detestation: *Tu scis quod abominor signum superbiæ meæ*—Esth. xiv. 16—*Thou knowest that I abominate the sign of my pride and glory.* She was well aware that if she had not conceived a lively dislike to her worldly greatness, it would have engaged her little by little to love it more than was right. We have another illustration of this in the case of the Israelites, who by reason of their entertaining so strong a liking for the onions of Egypt came at last to commit a sin that they never committed in Egypt itself—that of bowing down in adoration before the idols of Egypt. Thou who hast gone forth from the Egypt of the world, be on thy guard against retaining any affection to the things of the world, if thou wouldst avoid running the risk of worshipping them.

SEVENTH SUNDAY AFTER PENTECOST.

Attendite a falsis prophetis, qui veniunt ad vos in vestimentis ovium, intus autem sunt lupi rapaces.—Matth. vii. 15.
Beware of false prophets who come to you in the clothing of sheep, but inwardly they are ravening wolves.

I. CONSIDER who those are that would seem to be innocent lambs, but are in reality wolves that seek to devour thee. They are those unruly desires that thy self-love engenders and nurtures in thy inmost soul, and which artfully strive to draw thee over to seek for honour and ease, and to be continually humouring thy every whim by flying from humiliation and suffering. Then again, outside of thee they are those friends and inobservant companions, who by their bad example and their ill-counsel invite thee and entice thee to a more remiss manner of life, to pay little heed to the bidding of thy superiors, and to give thyself up to an easy-going style of conduct. Instead of avoiding and hating the like of these as so many wolves, thou hast hitherto welcomed and entertained them as faithful and innocent friends !

II. Consider that it is a very difficult thing to discover the wiles and deceit of these desires that are the offspring of self-love and of these bad companions, because they invite thee to evil under the appearance of good. They urge thee to procure for thyself esteem and reputation, in order thus to labour with greater fruit for the good of thy neighbour; they represent to thee the necessity of thy seeking further comforts and relaxation in order not to wear out thy health and strength; they induce thee to perform thy spiritual exercises perfunctorily, not to tire thy mind by excessive application. By these and similar sham pretexts which have a plausible appearance, and are flattering to self-love, how many are allured to abandon the practice of virtue and contract vicious habits! If thou wouldst escape being deceived any longer by these ravening wolves disguised as sheep, it is needful that thou shouldst apply thyself to recognise them, and to discover their deceitful guile by the light of faith and of the gospel truths, and that thou shouldst seriously consider the great harm thou hast inflicted on thyself in the past, by seconding the whims of self-love and following the example of mischievous companions.

III. Consider—to be the more effectually on thy guard against the snares of bad example and of thy own unruly appetites—that if thou wouldst escape eternal damnation and obtain eternal salvation, it is not enough to make merely outward profession of a religious life without the practical realisation of solid virtue; just as in the case of a tree, the mere display of showy leaves without any fruit is not enough to make it escape the fate of being cut down and cast into the flames. *Non omnis qui dicit, Domine, Domine, intrabit in regnum cœlorum, sed qui facit voluntatem Patris mei qui in cœlis est*—Matth. vii. 21—*Not every one that saith to Me, Lord, Lord, shall enter into the kingdom of heaven, but he that doeth the Will of My Father Who is in heaven.* Do not regulate thyself, therefore, in thy method of life and in thy manner of acting by the bad example of others—much less allow thyself to be guided by the one-sided tendencies of self-love; but in everything thou must regulate thy conduct by the Will of Almighty God, manifested to thee by His precepts and the Evangelical counsels, and by the commands of thy superiors, who hold the place of God in thy regard. In this consists the real carrying out of thy religious profession.

MONDAY IN THE SEVENTH WEEK AFTER PENTECOST.

Gaudete in illa die et exultate, ecce enim merces vestra multa est in cœlo.—Luc. vi. 23.
Be glad in that day and rejoice, for behold your reward is great in heaven.

I. CONSIDER that not without reason does Our Lord expect thee to be glad and rejoice amid the trials thou endurest for His sake, because by means of them thou earnest for thyself so exceeding a reward in paradise, where thou wilt possess and enjoy all the good which God enjoys, and the possession of which constitutes the happiness of God Himself: *Ego ero merces tua magna nimis*—Gen. xv. 1—*I will be thy reward exceeding great.* The husbandman takes great delight in the toil and labour he undergoes in sowing his seed, on account of the yield he hopes to gather from it; and oughtest thou not with much greater reason to be glad to have something to suffer for the love of God in the trials He sends thee, in the shape of sickness and pain, mortifications and persecutions? And why? because from all of these thou wilt reap so abundant a harvest of glory in heaven, that the possession of even its lowest grade would so far outweigh all the pains of the damned, that it would cause them to forget all the torments of hell. If thou art not yet able to rejoice in suffering, it is because thy thoughts are riveted only on thy present trouble and affliction. Rather set thyself to think on the reward thou art earning, if only thou endurest them for the love of Jesus, and thou wilt have great reason to be glad and rejoice, not only *in illa die—in that day*, but even in the very act itself of suffering like the Saints, of whom it is said: *Ibant et flebant mittentes semina sua; venientes autem venient cum exultatione, portantes manipulos suos*—Ps. cxxv. 6—*Going they went and wept, casting their seeds; but coming they shall come with joyfulness, carrying their sheaves.* *Flebant—they wept*, through the keen sense of their sufferings and by the instinct of nature, which cannot but recoil from the trials it encounters; but *cum exultatione—with joyfulness*, because they rejoice with their mind and in spirit through the hope of reward.

II. Consider that the glory of paradise is called in the Gospel by various names, such as a reward, a wreath, a crown, an inheritance: but in this passage Our Lord made use of the appellation reward—*merces vestra copiosa est in cœlis—your reward is great in heaven*—to let thee know how certain it is of attainment and that thou canst never have any safer grounds for being sure that thou art earning for thyself the glory of paradise, than when thou sufferest willingly in this life for love of God, and makest thyself like unto Jesus, Who for love of thee was weighed down by suffering and was nailed to the cross: *Conformes fieri imaginis filii Dei*—Rom. viii. 29—*To be made conformable to the image of His Son.* In other good works there may be a certain admixture of self-love, but in the endurance of suffering it is quite certain that self-love has no share. There is no surer claim to recompense than that which is put forward as being due as wages, and such a claim as this is always recognised even amongst men. Why then wouldst thou at times almost doubt as to whether Almighty God may possibly refuse thee the wages, the reward He has promised thee? *Promisit qui non mentitur, Deus*—Tit. i. 2 —*God, who lieth not, hath promised*. *Non est Deus quasi homo, ut mentiatur*—Num. xxiii. 19—*God is not as man, that He should lie*. Is not then a reward that is so certain and so magnificent, enough to give thee courage to suffer willingly and cheerfully in this life?

III. Consider what hardships are endured by people living in the world, whether in military service or at court or elsewhere, in the hope of a reward that, generally speaking, they do not succeed in obtaining. But even though they do obtain the object of their desires—and as abundantly as they can wish—after all it is only an earthly reward, and only for so long as they are on this earth. In other words, it is a reward that is unreal, unsafe and unstable. It is unreal, because it is not capable of contenting the heart, and is always accompanied by an admixture of bitterness. It is unsafe, because it is so easily lost; and it is unstable, because it comes to an end with the end of life. On the other hand, thou hast doubtless to put up with many a hardship, and it may be not slight ones, for a short time in religion, but thy reward will have no end: it will far surpass in degree all that thou sufferest now; it will be complete, and contain in itself every good thou canst desire. *Satiabor cum apparuerit gloria tua*—Ps. xvi. 15—*I shall be satisfied when Thy glory shall appear*. In the midst of thy trials apply thyself to reflect on the happiness of that other life which will very shortly overtake thee, and in this reflection thou wilt find greater reason to rejoice and to be glad on account of the reward, than to be grieved and sorrowful at thy trials. *Ecce merces vestra*—here is thy reward; look at it, and consider it well! just as though it were actually present before thee.

TUESDAY IN THE SEVENTH WEEK AFTER PENTECOST.

Indicabo tibi, O homo, quid sit bonum, et quid Dominus requirat a te: Utique facere judicium, diligere misericordiam, et solicitum ambulare cum Deo tuo.—Mich. vi. 8.

I will show thee, O man, what is good, and what the Lord requireth of thee: Verily, to do judgment, and to love mercy, and to walk solicitous with thy God.

I. CONSIDER that in these words Our Lord requires of thee three things, for thy own greater good. The first concerns thyself: *facere judicium—to do judgment*: that is, that thou shouldst judge thyself with severity, by a careful examination of thy actions, by a just sentence on them, and a vigorous infliction of punishment for them. Beware of a heedless way of living, but carefully search into thy deeds, thy words, thy thoughts, and the most secret motions of thy heart. In the next place, pass sentence on thyself, without any bias or leaning to self. Oh, how easy a thing it is to flatter oneself, and to lay all blame of one's own shortcomings on those who do not deserve it. Lastly, thou must inflict severe punishment on thyself, by performing a penance that bears some proportion to the fault committed, and will serve thee as a check for the future. If thou wouldst only judge thyself in this wise, thou wilt not be judged severely by Almighty God.

II. Consider the second thing required of thee, which concerns thy neighbour, and is that thou shouldst show mercy in his regard, never examining into his shortcomings, but sympathising with him, forgiving him and rendering him assistance in every circumstance to the best of thy power. Notice, too, that the words are *diligere misericordiam—to love mercy ;* because if thou art really fond of showing mercy, thou wilt be sure to discover thy neighbour's wants, and to render him ready assistance according as thy state of life allows thee.

III. Consider what Our Lord requires of thee in His own regard, to wit, that thou shouldst be careful to walk in His presence : *Solicitum ambulare cum Deo tuo—To walk solicitous with thy God.* All through the course of this thy short-lived pilgrimage, thou must beware of ever parting company with Him, but ever keep close to His side, and, whithersoever thou goest, keep Him company even on the road to Calvary. Follow not the example of those who, like base cowards, forsake Him on Calvary in times of suffering and only follow Him to Thabor in the hour of consolation and glory. Examine therefore and see if thou art earnest in imitating Him, in obeying Him, in seeking to honour and please Him, and examine especially what pains thou takest not to lose Him on thy journey through life, in the midst of so many treacherous foes, who are always on the alert to rob thee of His grace. This careful anxiety is praiseworthy, and is also necessary, but it must be accompanied by an entire trust and assurance that thy Lord will never fail to give thee strength to follow Him and to withstand all these that would tear thee away from Him.

WEDNESDAY IN THE SEVENTH WEEK AFTER PENTECOST.

Regnum cœlorum vim patitur et violenti rapiunt illud.
—Matth. xi. 12.

The kingdom of heaven suffereth violence, and the violent bear it away.

I. CONSIDER that the kingdom of heaven is not a mere gift, but it has to be won by dint of fighting, and therefore it is that Job said: *Militia est vita hominis*—Job vii. 1—*The life of man is a warfare.* Why, then, dost thou fondly imagine that thou wilt gain it without toiling for it? This is an impossibility! See what efforts, what penance, what blood even, it cost every one of the Saints: look at the King of Glory Himself, what did He not do and suffer in order to merit heaven, not indeed for Himself, for it was His already, but for all of us. *Nonne oportuit Christum pati, et ita intrare in gloriam suam*—Luc. xxiv. 26—*Ought not Christ to have suffered these things, and so to enter into His glory?* Pray, what hast thou hitherto done in imitation of Christ, Whose intention it was to encourage thee to set about the conquest of so great a kingdom, by the example of His own excessive sufferings.

II. Consider that the kingdom of heaven has to be acquired by dint of war, and indeed by fierce war, by assault: *violenti rapiunt illud—the violent bear it away.* Thou must use this violence with thyself, and at the same time with God: with thyself by a thorough self-denial, in withstanding and overcoming thy unruly inclinations: with God, by means of prayer, just as though thou hadst to wrest the title-deeds of paradise by main force from His hands. It is only by prayer that violence can be offered to Almighty God.

Hast thou ever beheld a soldier charging the enemy? He does violence to himself by pushing forward and straining every nerve, and he struggles with his foe that seeks to drive him back from the trenches. In like manner must thou seek to do violence to God in prayer, and to thyself, by fighting against thy unruly passions.

III. Consider that in the event of thy not feeling courage enough to generously offer all that violence which is needful to thyself and to God, still paradise may be thine, provided thou allowest thyself to be driven and pushed into it by the efforts of others: this has to be effected by peacefully bearing for love of God the violence that is offered thee in the shape of reverses, of persecutions, of bodily ailings, all of which are arranged by Our Lord to get thee into paradise somehow or other. If on entering a church or other place where there is a great press of people, a person allows himself to be carried along by the pressure of the crowd, he makes way with pretty nearly the same success as another who makes violent efforts to gain admittance. If thou art weak in the spiritual life, and art not equal to offering to thyself the violence that is necessary to gain admittance into paradise, at any rate allow the indispositions, the trials, the persecutions that crowd on thee and hem thee in on all sides—allow these to supply thy own want of strength and to help thee to enter into the glory of paradise.

THURSDAY IN THE SEVENTH WEEK AFTER PENTECOST.

Beatus vir qui suffert tentationem; quoniam cum probatus fuerit accipiet coronam vitæ, quam repromisit Deus diligentibus se.—Jac. i. 12.
Blessed is the man that endureth temptation; for when he hath been proved he shall receive the crown of life, which God has promised to them that love Him.

I. CONSIDER the reason why Almighty God allows the devil to assault thee, and all sorts of trials to beleaguer thee. It is to prove whether thou lovest Him or not. It is easy enough for thee to say that thou lovest God when all goes on smoothly and to thy own liking. But when thou art put to the test by means of some impure temptation, some sickness, or some disgrace or interior desolation, oh, then unfortunately thou art another man altogether. The devil sneered at Job with all his virtue until it was tried: how then canst thou reckon on thine? No, allow Our Lord to try thee and prove thee as He chooses: the present life is a time of trial. *Tentatio est vita hominis super terram*—Job vii. 1—as the Septuagint version reads—*The life of man on earth is a temptation.*

II. Consider that if thou remainest firm under this test or trial of temptation, thou wilt be blessed and wilt receive the crown of life—*accipiet coronam vitæ*—With what glory wilt thou be encompassed when Our Lord places thy crown on thy head on thy coronation day! They used to fight of old to win a wreath of laurel, or ivy, or pine, though it was doomed presently to fade and wither: and hast thou not the heart to fight against the passions of the flesh, against the maxims of the world, and against the assaults of the devil, to win a crown of glory that can neither fade nor wither: *Immarcescibilem coronam gloriæ*— 1 Pet. v. 4—*A never-fading crown of glory*; a crown that is styled *corona vitæ—a crown of life*, because not liable to the ravages of death.

III. Consider that this wondrous crown of life is secure and cannot fail thee, because Almighty God has promised it to thee over and over again in every page of the Scriptures: *repromisit Deus.* Thou wouldst be willing enough to take a prince at his word when he promises thee a handsome reward for a race or the like, even though thou hadst not seen the reward itself; and wilt thou distrust Almighty God? If Our Lord but once showed thee the crown that is in readiness for thee, oh, what courage thou wouldst take! what determination, what joy thou wouldst conceive! But this He does not choose to do for thy own greater gain. He wishes thee to trust in Him. And, then again, how couldst thou wish Him to show thee thy crown when it is not yet wholly wrought and finished? The greater thy sufferings and endurance, the richer and more beautiful will thy crown be; but remember that this crown is not to be a simple gift—it has to be the reward of merit.

FRIDAY IN THE SEVENTH WEEK AFTER PENTECOST.

Quæ mihi fuerunt lucra, hæc arbitratus sum propter Christum detrimenta. Verumtamen existimo omnia detrimentum esse, propter eminentem scientiam Jesu Christi Domini mei; propter quem omnia detrimentum feci, et arbitror ut stercora, ut Christum lucrifaciam.—Philip. iii. 7.

The things that were gain to me, the same I have counted loss for Christ. Furthermore I count all things to be but loss for the excellent knowledge of Jesus Christ my Lord: for whom I have suffered the loss of all things, and count them but as dung that I may gain Christ.

I. CONSIDER how bright was the light of faith and of the Gospel teaching that shone in the mind of the Apostle S. Paul when we see how, under the influence of this light, those very objects which he at one time looked upon as the greatest gain, came to appear to him no longer any gain at all, but a loss. The same change is brought about in any one else that is in possession of a similar interior light. Oh how such a one stands amazed on thinking that he could ever have so blindly adhered to the maxims of the world and made so much account of useless competition, of precedence over his equals, of the empty applause of men! If in thy own case, after having embraced the religious life, thou dost not feel ashamed of thyself for having once upon a time gone in search of those temporal advantages thou hast now abandoned for Christ's sake, it is a sign that thou dost not guide thy life by this heavenly light. *Justitiæ lumen non luxit nobis*—Sap. v. 6—*The light of justice hath not shined unto us.*

II. Consider that the Apostle not only reckoned as

loss what he before looked upon as gain, but he went further still, and counted as loss everything else that was not Christ; that is to say, nobility of birth, eloquence, talent and other such endowments; because whosoever would set his heart on these must either give up all idea of aspiring after the imitation of Christ Our Lord, or else must abandon His service altogether. It was this frame of mind, that, namely, which causes a soul to reckon as loss all those temporal advantages which are held in such high esteem by the world, it was this that made an Apostle of S. Paul on account of the true and great knowledge he acquired in the school of Jesus Christ, where he learnt that no one can be His follower who does not make a complete renunciation into His hands of all that he has and of all that he is. *Qui non renuntiat omnibus quæ possidet, non potest esse meus discipulus* — Luc. xiv. 33 — *He that doth not renounce all that he possesseth, cannot be my disciple.* This is that eminent degree of true knowledge to which thou must strive to attain. If thou succeedest, not only will all the temporal advantages thou didst possess in the world appear to thee no loss, but not even all thou possibly couldst enjoy; and Jesus hanging naked on the cross will be thine in their stead, and satisfy thy cravings more thoroughly than the possession of all of them together.

III. Consider what was the esteem the Apostle formed of all the possible advantages the world can confer. He looked upon them all as dung *Arbitror ut stercora;* because he was aware of the difference there is in value between the goods of this world and Jesus Christ. If we examine the advantages and pleasures which the world proffers, we shall discover that those which have reference to the concupiscence of the flesh are tainted with the stench of sin; those that belong to the concupiscence of the eyes — in other words, to avarice — are sordid and vile; and those, in fine, that belong to the pride of life—that is, to ambition—are full of rottenness and corruption; and therefore did the Apostle say of all these: *Arbitror ut stercora—I count them but as dung.* What a pitiable state of things would it not then be, if instead of imitating the Apostle, thou shouldst forget thy vocation and forsake Christ to go in guest of these fulsome and corruptible goods and pleasures of earth, which S. Paul cast away from him as so much dirt, in order to possess Jesus crucified.

SATURDAY IN THE SEVENTH WEEK AFTER PENTECOST.

Labora sicut bonus miles Christi.—2 Tim. ii. 3.
Labour as a good soldier of Christ Jesus.

I. CONSIDER that every true Christian ought to be a soldier of Jesus Christ, fighting the good battle either, as in the case of the martyrs, against tyrants; or against error, like the doctors of the Church; or against the passions of the flesh and the attacks of the devil, as is the common lot of all the faithful. Thou wouldst, perchance, persuade thyself that no one of the three sorts of warfare just enumerated meets thy own case, but this is not true. They are applicable to every one, because, although it is not necessary to be always actually engaged in combat, there is always great need of being in readiness for an engagement. Hence the Apostle does not employ the word *certa—wrestle*, but *labora sicut bonus miles—labour like a good soldier.* Even in time of peace soldiers do not live in idleness. So also thou, though not actually engaged in holding thy own against tyrants, must imitate the martyrs by wrestling with thy passions, by accustoming thyself to maintain the lustre of thy faith just as though thou hadst to make profession of it before a public tribunal; by habitually despising this fleeting life and persecuting and mortifying thy body as though thou hadst to be handed over to a cruel executioner. But if thou art bent on seeking thy own ease and pampering thy flesh, how canst thou boast of being a soldier of Christ Jesus?

II. Consider that although it does perchance fall to thy lot to combat error, as is the office of the doctors of the Church and of the preachers of the Word of God, yet for all that in thy quality of soldier of Christ thou oughtest to render thyself expert in combating and refuting so many maxims and customs that one hears and sees amongst Christians, but are in open contradiction to the practical teaching of the Gospel; as for instance that it is dishonourable to pardon an enemy, to yield one's views and opinions, to refrain from giving way to anger, to humble oneself, and many other like falsities. How, then, canst thou make profession of being a soldier of Jesus Christ and not show thyself eager to condemn these false maxims, which worldlings sow broadcast wherever they go, in opposition to the teaching of the Gospel? *Labora sicut bonus miles Christi*—labour like a good soldier of Christ Jesus.

III. Consider that thy duty as a true soldier of Christ does not consist even in battling against thy passions and their accomplices, the devils, only when they actually assault thee; but even if they happen to give a short truce, thou must always be on the look out with thy weapons at hand. It is just when thou deemest thyself in the greatest security that there is the greatest need of watchfulness, for it is just at that time that Almighty God will sometimes allow them to attack thee more fiercely in punishment of thy heedlessness. No soldier is ever called upon to be always actually fighting, but every soldier has continually to endure hardships. Moreover, in order to conduct thyself as a true soldier of Christ, thou must fight, not like a mercenary whose end in view is his pay-money, but like a volunteer who fights for his king only; thy only aim and object in fighting against the enemies of God must be to please Him as He watches thee from His throne in heaven to see how thou deportest thyself in difficulties; *ut ei placeat qui se probavit*—2 Tim. ii. 4—*that he may please Him to Whom he hath engaged himself.*

EIGHTH SUNDAY AFTER PENTECOST.

Filii hujus sæculi prudentiores filiis lucis in generatione sua sunt—Luc. xvi. 8.

The children of this world are wiser in their generation than the children of light.

I. CONSIDER how the dishonest steward of the Gospel, through fear of being discharged on account of his bad management, and of being persecuted by his master, set himself to think in good earnest about his own interests, and to contrive how he might provide for his own future: yet thou, who hast squandered so many benefits received at the hands of God, hast no misgivings about the direful calamity and irreparable loss that awaits thee when thou wilt have to balance thy accounts. Alas! how many of the great natural and supernatural gifts God Almighty has bestowed on thee, to be expended in His service and employed for His glory—how many of these, I say, hast thou squandered and misapplied for the benefit of thy own body, of thy perverse inclinations and of thy own self-love? And though thou knowest full well that very shortly thou wilt have to render a most rigorous account of the shameful wrongs thou hast done to Almighty God, yet thou hardly givest it a thought and makest no effort to offer Him any amends! Oh! how true it is that—*filii hujus sæculi prudentiores sunt—the children of this world are more prudent.*

II. Consider that the shrewd artifice made use of by the steward was entirely to his own advantage and the loss of his master, who nevertheless praised his shrewdness in having contrived betimes to make himself friends amongst his debtors by reducing the amount of their bills in order that they might afterwards supply him with the necessaries of life. *Quantum debes? . . . Centum cados olei: scribe quinquaginta—How much dost thou owe? . . . a hundred barrels of oil: put down fifty.* It is just the reverse in the case of Almighty God, on Whom thou canst inflict no injury by providing for thy own real interests. The only way in which thou canst wrong Him is by injuring thyself. Why, then, dost thou overlook so many means within thy reach by which thou mightest well secure thyself against thy own utter penury, and thus at one and the same time procure thy own advantage and the good pleasure of God? Reflect a while on the studious care with which men of the world seek to sharpen their wits, and how they apply themselves to further their own temporal welfare; how cautious they are not to lose what they already possess; how they toil to obtain that on which they have set their hearts, and how provident they are for their future or possible wants. Yet these are all temporal objects that perish within the span of a century, and come to an end at death. Happy wouldst thou be if thou didst take as great pains to acquire and ensure the goods of heaven, that will last for ever!

III. Consider that life is short, death uncertain—it may overtake thee at any minute; and then, indeed, it will be said to thee: *Jam non poteris villicare—now thou canst be steward no longer.* Thou wilt then have no more time to put thy accounts straight, or to amass the merit of good works in order to compensate for the waste of so many gifts received from God in the religious state, in the shape of so many interior lights, so many secret inspirations, so much good example— for all of which thou wilt have to render a most rigorous account at the hour of death. This is only in accordance with that assurance of the Gospel: *Omni cui multum datum est, plus requiretur ab eo*—Luc. xii. 48 —*Unto whomsoever much is given, of him much shall be required.*

MONDAY IN THE EIGHTH WEEK AFTER PENTECOST.

Estote misericordes, sicut et Pater vester misericors est. —Luc. vi. 36.
Be ye merciful, as your Father also is merciful.

I. CONSIDER that real mercy—the mercy by means of which thou hast to become like unto thy heavenly Father—is not that which springs merely from a certain feeling of tenderness and compassion for the misfortunes of thy neighbour, but it is that which has its origin in the virtue of charity, and which urges thee to come to the assistance of thy neighbour for the love of God. When this is the motive that awakens in thy heart a feeling of compassion, then is thy mercy full and perfect, because in that case its desire is not only to relieve the misfortunes of thy neighbour, but furthermore to share them, and grieve over them, together. Such is the mercy which God Almighty has shown in thy regard, inasmuch as He has not only been good enough to aid thee in thy poverty, but He has chosen, by becoming man, to show thee also the tenderness of His compassion: *Debuit per omnia fratribus assimilari, ut misericors fieret.*—Hebr. ii. 17—*It behoved Him in all things to be made like unto His brethren, that He might become a merciful High-priest.* Such, also, is the full and perfect mercy thou oughtest to show towards thy neighbour, succouring him for the love of God, and feeling his misfortunes as though they were thy own.

II. Consider that this mercy and compassion has not to be restricted to thy friends and acquaintance only, but must be shown even to the unworthy, to strangers and enemies, towards whom thou wouldst not naturally be drawn to show compassion. If practised after this fashion, thy mercy will be more perfect and more like unto the mercy of God, Who excuses the failings of the sinner and lends abundant assistance to His enemies. Take notice also, how, in proposing for thy imitation the example of the mercy of God, Christ calls Him on this occasion by the title of Father: *Estote misericordes, sicut et Pater vester misericors est— Be ye merciful, as your Father also is merciful*—because He knows how to make allowances for the shortcomings of His children, and most tenderly comes to their assistance, even though they be undutiful and wayward. How often, instead of feeling either compassion or sorrow at beholding an enemy or an undeserving fellow-creature overtaken by some calamity or misfortune, thou art even pleased rather than otherwise! In such cases, if thou dost not feel thyself equal to sympathising with them with real feeling of heart, endeavour at least to help and succour them; if not materially, at least by prayers poured forth in their behalf. Do this for the love of that Saviour Who has shown such boundless mercy in thy own regard, though thou wert so ungrateful and unworthy, for He has made thy misfortunes His own, and has come to the rescue even at the cost of His own blood.

III. Consider that amongst all the virtues that are attributable to the Eternal Father, Our Lord never proposes to us throughout the whole Gospel any other one in particular, except this of mercy, because it is this that will render us most like unto God. The attribute of mercy, both as it exists in God and as it is manifested in its effects, is the greatest of all His attributes, because it was mercy that moved Him to ransom mankind with His own blood: *Secundum misericordiam suam salvos nos fecit*—Tit. iii. 2—*According to His mercy He saved us.* So also is mercy the greatest of virtues in thy own case; because the exercise of mercy towards thy neighbour for God's sake is true charity, which binds thee to God as well as to thy neighbour, and opens out a large field before thee for the exercise of many different acts of virtue, in which self-seeking will have no share, especially when performed on behalf of the destitute. Foster, therefore, in thy heart an ardent love of mercy, and so liken thyself to thy heavenly Father.

TUESDAY IN THE EIGHTH WEEK AFTER PENTECOST.

Si ceciderit lignum ad austrum aut aquilonem, in quocumque loco ceciderit, ibi erit.—Eccl. xi. 3.

If the tree fall to the south or to the north, in what place soever it shall fall, there it shall be.

I. CONSIDER that thou art that tree which is here spoken of. If when thou hast been cut down by the axe of death, thou shalt fall to the right hand—to the south—in the south shalt thou remain; if thou shalt fall to the left hand—to the north—to the north shalt thou remain. There will never be the faintest hope of changing thy position. Thou wilt be for ever either a prince on his throne or a slave in chains—for ever honourable and honoured, or for ever branded with ignominy. Is not this great diversity of lots a matter that interests thee? Is it not worth thinking about? How comes it then that thou who art always building castles in the air, and art so intent on acquiring or maintaining some post of honour, or procuring some convenience which will all come to an end after a few short days—how comes it that thou thinkest so little about which of these two fates will very shortly be thine?

II. Consider that if thou art anxious to know to which side thou wilt fall, thou hast only to see to which side thou leanest. When the saw has cut the tree through, it is certain to fall on that side to which it leans. If it leans to the south, it will fall to the south; if it leans to the north, it will fall to the north. If when thou art cut down by death thou leanest to the north, do not think for an instant that thou wilt fall to the south. It is the weight of the tree that makes it lean on one side; so also the cause of thy tendency to either side are thy inclinations and affections; if these drag thee over to the side of the north, oh what great reason hast thou not to fear thy fate! The number of those religious is by no means small, who, by having turned their affections towards the good things of this earth, and the esteem of the world, have in death met with a most lamentable fate.

III. Consider that, if thou choosest, thou art still in time to take a favourable bend, by doing violence to thy vicious propensities and disorderly affections. But delay not. A habit once contracted is like a tree, that, the older it gets, the less pliant it becomes. Begin, then, in good earnest to turn thy heart to God and thy thoughts to eternity, and heed not this fleeting world, and thus thou mayest with good reason hope for a happy lot after death. Didst thou not embrace the religious state to make sure of a happy eternity ? Why, then, give so much attention to what is unbecoming to thy state of life, and makes thee run the risk of being lost ? Thou canst not form an adequate idea of what the force of habit—either good or bad—will do at the hour of death.

WEDNESDAY IN THE EIGHTH WEEK AFTER PENTECOST.

Ecce ascendet Dominus super nubem levem, et ingredietur Ægyptum, et commovebuntur simulacra Ægypti a facie Domini.—Isa. xix. 1.

Behold the Lord will ascend upon a swift cloud, and will enter into Egypt, and the idols of Egypt shall be moved at His presence.

I. CONSIDER that when our divine Saviour entered Egypt, concealed under the cloud of His humanity, all the idols of that country trembled and fell to the ground, as the Prophet Isaias foretold. Thy heart is just such another Egypt, where as many idols are set up as are the vicious inclinations to which thou payest homage. Yet thy divine Lord graciously condescends to make His entrance into this Egypt of thine under the cloud of the sacramental species, not in order to save Himself and His own life from Herod's sword, but to save thy life for thee, every time thou receivest Holy Communion. How, then, canst thou remain so apathetic on the loving entry of Jesus into thy heart? Why dost thou not bestir thyself, and offer Him thy sincere homage?

II. Consider that no sooner had Jesus entered Egypt, than all the idols bore witness to His sovereignty, and quivered and trembled at the presence of the Lord of the universe: *A facie Domini.* How far more fitting it is, therefore, that the vices of thy heart should stagger and fall to the ground at the presence of thy Saviour, and when they are brought face to face with the example of the divine virtues He gives thee in the sacrament of His love! Then, again, how many idols there are in thy heart! Such an idol is the vice of pride; another such is thy hastiness and impatience; another the excessive love of thy own reputation and of thy own will. How, then, comes it to pass that all these idols remain unmoved, and do not fall to the ground, on beholding thy God humbled to such a degree for love of thee, in the sacred Host; enduring with such unconquerable meekness, for thy sake, the affronts He receives under the sacramental veils, and submitting Himself to the behest of His ministers, however unworthy; at the words of consecration, coming down from His Father's bosom at their sheer bidding, whensoever He is called? Is it not reasonable that these idols of thine should be all cast to the ground, and that Jesus should gain in thy heart the same victory that erst He won in Egypt?

III. Consider that the Prophet Isaias does not say that the idols of Egypt were struck by lightning, or felled to the ground by violence, but that they tottered and fell of themselves at the presence of the true God. Such is the process which thy vices ought to undergo in thy heart. Thou must not wait for thy Saviour to cast them down by main force, but thou must prevail on them to give way and collapse of their own accord, and render Him this spontaneous act of homage from love rather than constraint. See, therefore, that thy vicious affections fall to the ground, in the presence of thy Saviour, of themselves, otherwise these idols of thy heart will prove to be more stubborn and less amenable than those idols of stone which rendered Him so glorious a testimony in Egypt.

THURSDAY IN THE EIGHTH WEEK AFTER PENTECOST.

Qui certat in agone non coronabitur nisi legitime certaverit.— 2 Tim. ii. 5.
He that striveth for the mastery will not be crowned, except he strive lawfully.

I. CONSIDER that in order to be crowned thou must fight against thy rebellious appetites, because the crown of glory which awaits holiness of life and religious perfection is not to be won by devotions or disciplines, or fasting performed at caprice, but is won by a perfect victory over self; all things else are but aids and means for arriving at this victory over self. What can all the exterior virtue thou practisest avail thee, if meanwhile thy interior failings thrive so wonderfully, if thou thinkest more of thyself than of others, if thou art so ready to find fault with thy brethren and art so easily ruffled at the slightest remark, if thou showest thyself so slow to obey and so eager to seek thyself and thy own ease in everything? Assuredly this is not the way to win the crown!

II. Consider that if thou wouldst be crowned, it is not even enough to fight and strive, thou must needs strive lawfully; that is, as S. Augustine says, unweariedly, so long as the soul finds itself in the arena of this life. Thou must never cast thy arms aside;

and if now and then thou sufferest a partial defeat, thou must put up with it patiently. Our Lord does not bid thee triumph over thy passions to such an extent that they should never presume to show themselves again. He bids thee only to fight without coming to any parley or truce with them: *Usque ad mortem certa pro iustitia*—Eccl. iv. 33—*Even unto death fight for justice.*

III. Consider that thou must not be dismayed at this continual struggle against thy passions, because after all this is the easiest method of combating them, both because they lose strength by giving them no peace, and also because this spiritual combat is not at all the same thing as an ordinary combat; in the latter, the more one exerts oneself the more wearied one gets, whereas in the former the more thou strivest the greater strength thou gainest in proportion as grace, thy only source of energy, grows within thee. The arms with which thou hast to fight are distrust of thyself, and trust in God, and prayer. Distrust of thyself will cause thee to avoid presumption, to go cautiously and, in case of a fall, to humble thyself, but not to be disturbed in consequence, from the firm conviction that of thyself thou canst do nothing. On the other hand, trust in God will enable thee to gain the victory which Our Lord is able and even anxious to confer on thee; and, lastly, prayer will ensure thy obtaining all the help thou requirest. In the Olympic games of old, a wreath used to be awarded by the judges to the victor, but no assistance was given to the combatants. Almighty God does both. He promises thee a crown of glory, and He also gives thee the help of His grace, provided only thou askest Him for it with confidence and perseverance.

FRIDAY IN THE EIGHTH WEEK AFTER PENTECOST.

Beati mortui qui in Domino moriuntur. Amodo jam, dicit Spiritus, ut requiescant a laboribus suis.—Apoc. xiv. 13.

Blessed are the dead who die in the Lord. From henceforth now, saith the Spirit, that they may rest from their labours.

I. CONSIDER how although death lays low all equally without distinction, there is nevertheless so great a difference between the death of a fervent religious and that of a remiss religious, that in the case of the latter death is styled a vigil or watch : *Cum dormierit . . . aperiet oculos*—Job xxvii. 19—*When he shall sleep . . . he shall open his eyes:* and in the case of the former it is called a rest and repose : *Ut requiescant a laboribus suis*—*That they may rest from their labours,* The death of the unobservant religious is a vigil, because in the act of dying he opens his mind's eyes and beholds all those gratifications he has allowed himself vanished like a dream, all the liberty he has taken contrary to holy obedience disappeared, and all that applause he sought after, to the frequent displeasure of his Lord, gone like smoke. *Aperiet oculos et nihil inveniet*—Job xxvii. 19—*He shall open his eyes and find nothing.* On the other hand, the death of the fervent religious is a repose, because it will put an end to all his penances, his poverty, his mortification, and his crosses, and he will behold himself stripped in death of nothing but what he had long since despised for God's sake, and will see it all changed into a treasure of merits : *opera illorum sequuntur illos* —Job xiv. 13—*their works follow them.* What will death prove to be in thy regard?—vigil or repose? If thou desirest to die the death of a fervent religious, thou must also lead the life of a fervent religious.

II. Consider that the death of a remiss religious is a vigil, not only in virtue of what he sees vanish from before him, but much more so by reason of what he sees appear before him to torment his mind in the most dreadful manner. To whatever side he turns, all is fear and fright: within him his troubled conscience disturbs him on account of his sins: around him he finds a legion of devils that assail him, and only increase his confusion of mind, by their suggestions: above him he descries his Judge already on the point of summoning him before his tribunal, and below him he sees the chastisements and torments he deserves. Oh what a woeful and terrible vigil! On the other hand, the fervent religious feels little or no concern about his sins, because he knows he has bewailed them and made satisfaction for them over and over again: he has very little fear of the devil, on account of his being under the fatherly care of Almighty God: he awaits with great longing the coming of his Judge to receive at His hands the reward of his faithful service, saying with the Apostle: *Bonum certamen certavi, cursum consummavi, fidem servavi. In reliquo reposita est mihi corona justitiæ*—2 Tim. iv. 7 —*I have fought a good fight, I have finished my course, I have kept the faith. As for the rest, there is laid up for me a crown of justice.* Were death to overtake thee at this moment, couldst thou speak in this strain?

III. Consider that the most painful watch in the case of the remiss religious, as also the sweetest repose of all for a fervent religious, is that which follows after they have breathed their last. The fervent religious will behold himself borne along to rest in the bosom of God, and to receive the congratulations of all the choirs of saints and angels, at having triumphed over the flesh, the world, and the devil. The relaxed religious, if he dies in the displeasure of Almighty God, will behold himself condemned to an eternal vigil of torments and misery, which in intensity are inconceivable and infinite in duration; and if he dies in grace, what a long and dreary vigil he will have to undergo, until he has paid his debt to the last farthing in the fiery furnace of Purgatory, to endure pains which far exceed in acuteness any pain that has ever been experienced in this world, and this for years and years! Reflect now a while, whether for the sake of the momentary satisfaction the unobservant religious procures for himself, it is worth thy while to undergo such a vigil at the hour of death, or rather if it be not desirable, by means of a mortified life, to enjoy the repose peculiar to the death of the observant religious.

SATURDAY IN THE EIGHTH WEEK AFTER PENTECOST.

Beatus vir cujus est nomen Domini spes ejus; et non respexit in vanitates et insanias falsas.—Ps. xxxix. 5.

Blessed is the man whose trust is in the name of the Lord; and who hath not regard to vanities and lying follies.

I. CONSIDER how properly the man is styled blessed that places all his hope and trust in Jesus, Who is our Saviour not merely in name but in reality; He is blessed because He relies on One Who is infinite power itself, infinite wisdom, infinite goodness; and Who has therefore not only the power and the knowledge necessary to confer every benefit upon us, but is moreover most anxious to do so. Not equally blessed indeed is he who reposes his trust in men. Such a one is truly to be pitied, for it is a rare occurrence to find persons who are anxious to heap favours on us: besides, even when they have the will, they frequently either know not how to set about it, or are not able to do so. Do thou, therefore, once for all have recourse to Jesus thy Saviour, and place in Him all thy hope, and in this way thou wilt be blessed; thou hast hitherto but too often run after men in the hope of obtaining some worthless favour, and hast but too often been disappointed.

II. Consider that it is not such an easy matter to have this entire hope and trust in God; and therefore he who is fortunate enough to succeed in attaining it is called *vir—a man* by excellence; because it demands strength to begin the exercise of hope, and strength not to give it over. Many never even so much as begin to hope, because they are dismayed by their own misery, and think they are not capable of receiving great graces at the hands of Our Lord: many begin but do not persevere, as though their hope were useless, either because Our Lord makes them sue for His favours a long time, or because He grants them without their knowing anything about it. Do not imitate these, but remain steadfast in the exercise of hope, and make recourse with equal confidence both in time of desolation and in time of consolation, in prosperity and in adversity, and thou will be sure of obtaining every good gift that will render thee blessed. There is no one thing that gives so much pleasure and honour to our divine Redeemer, as to make our own worthlessness the measure of our trust in Him : *Ego autem semper sperabo et adjiciam super omnem laudem tuam*—Ps. lxx. 14—*But I will always hope, and will add to all thy praise.*

III. Consider that it is the peculiar privilege of a soul that has placed all its trust in God, to despise the goods of this world. To such a one, Jesus crucified is all-sufficient: He stands him in good stead on all occasions, He does for everything, supplies every want, and affords more consolation than aught else. Consequently when any one has this true and firm confidence deeply rooted in his heart, he despises all earthly pleasures to such a degree that he will not deign even to cast a glance on them; he regards them all as mere shams, as sheer folly. What account dost thou make of the goods of this world? If thou hast really placed thy hope in Jesus crucified, as every religious ought to do, make up thy mind not to cast even a side-glance at such objects, lest they should seduce thee, as they seduce so many others who deceive themselves, but will find out their mistake when it is too late. How such as these will exclaim in the anguish of their souls: *Ergo erravimus a via veritatis; et sol intelligentiæ non est ortus nobis*—Sap. v. 6 —*Therefore we have erred from the way of truth, and the sun of understanding hath not risen upon us.* What folly to lay the blame of their own deplorable darkness on that Sun of Justice, of whose light they have irreparably deprived themselves!

NINTH SUNDAY AFTER PENTECOST.

Non relinquet in te lapidem supra lapidem, eo quod non cognoveris tempus visitationis tuæ.—Luc. xix. 44.

They shall not leave in thee a stone upon a stone, because thou hast not known the time of thy visitation.

I. CONSIDER that the ruin over which Jesus so bitterly wept in the case of the unfortunate city of Jerusalem, was occasioned by its not having taken advantage of His goodness in coming purposely to sanctify it. This same ruin is renewed in the case of, and to the great loss of, such souls as refuse the secret visitations of their Saviour which He makes with the express view of enriching them with His gifts. These gifts consist in inspirations and whisperings to the heart, in interior lights and impulses by which He urges souls to abandon vice and embrace virtue. *Ecce sto ad ostium et pulso*—Apoc. iii. 20—*Behold I stand at the gate and knock.* Blessed is the soul that accepts these gifts, and equally to be pitied is the soul that rejects them and makes no answer to the invitation of heaven. How hast thou welcomed the many visits with which thy Lord has favoured thee in His desire of bringing about thy salvation?

II. Consider the great loss thou incurrest if thou neglectest to entertain thy Lord. In the first place, He will no longer visit thee with His powerful inspirations, or at least He will do so less frequently and less sensibly. Now, if thou failest to profit by His more loving visits, what good canst thou hope for when thou art deprived of these more special helps, and when His visitations cease altogether, since without them thou art unable even to conceive a good thought in thy mind? A second loss that thou incurrest, when once deprived of these special aids, is that Our Lord will leave thee in the power of thy disorderly passions, and a prey to thy infernal foes, who emboldened at seeing the unarmed and no longer protected by the mighty succour of heaven, *circumdabunt te—will hem thee in* with violent and continual temptations; *ad terram prosternent te—they will beat thee flat to the ground*, causing thee to fall most lamentably and go from bad to worse, beginning with wilful venial sins and ending with mortal and most grievous sins. Alas! how many instances of similar ruinous downfalls have been witnessed even in the cloister!

III. Consider, on the other hand, the great advantages to be gained by welcoming the visitations of God and giving a speedy answer to His inspirations, resigning oneself entirely into His hands and conforming one's will to that of Almighty God, like the spouse of the Canticles who said: *Anima mea liquefacta est ut dilectus locutus est*—Cant. v. 6—*My soul melted when my beloved spoke*. In this wise the soul allows itself to be guided in all things by the voice of Almighty God, without keeping back any kind of attachment to its own will. If only thou wilt do the same, thou wilt have thy Lord in the midst of thy heart: *Si quis audierit vocem meam, et aperiet mihi januam, introibo ad illum*—Apoc. iii. 20—*If any man shall hear my voice and open to me the door, I will come in to him*, and by His presence He will defend thee against temptation and all hostile assaults; He will feed thee with spiritual consolation; he will refresh thee with enlightenment of mind, and enable thee to spread for him a banquet of good works and choice virtues: *Introibo ad illum et cœnabo cum illo, et ipse mecum—I will come in to him and will sup with him, and he with Me*. Oh, what privileges does he enjoy that gives ear to the calls of his Saviour, and quickly lays himself open to His visitations! How many there are, like a S. John Gualbert and numberless others, that have arrived at sublime sanctity by having in the first instance obeyed the voice of God that invited them to perform some act of heroic virtue!

MONDAY IN THE NINTH WEEK AFTER PENTECOST.

Omnes nos manifestari oportet ante tribunal Christi ut referat unusquisque propria corporis, prout gessit, sive bonum, sive malum.—2 Cor. v. 10.

We must all be manifested before the judgment-seat of Christ, that every one may receive the proper things of the body, according as he hath done, whether it be good or evil.

I. CONSIDER that the universal judgment has been ordained chiefly to let each one know what is the reward or punishment awarded to every one else. Therefore is it decreed that all should appear before that great judgment-seat and discover whatever may at present be secret and hidden within our bosoms, either in thought, word or deed. What shame and confusion will not the worldling experience at this dread disclosure of the fatal blunders he made during life in overlooking or even running down what he ought to have upheld, and in upholding what he ought to have opposed! But meanwhile, as regards thyself, why art thou so fearful of the judgment of the world? What does it matter if the whole world should blame thee, provided God Almighty commends thee?

II. Consider that this disclosure of our whole selves will be made by our being subjected to a scrutiny which will search us through and through, just as a clear mirror exposed to the light of the sun reflects even the smallest particle of dust that lies upon it. Then, indeed, will falsehood and truth, human wickedness and divine goodness, man's ingratitude and God's bounty, be brought face to face. What shame will overwhelm thee at beholding thyself exposed to the gaze of all, so utterly different to what others believed thee to be in life! Now thou art wont to estimate the guilt of thy sins by the judgment which the generality of mankind form of them and, but too often a sin is thought lightly of because oft repeated. But on that day thou wilt learn to form thy estimate of thy sins from what they are in the sight of God, Who is truth itself,—*ante tribunal Christi:* and then the shame and confusion thou wilt witness in others will serve at the same time to make thee realise thy own guilt all the more keenly.

III. Consider that on the occasion of this universal judgment, each individual will receive the award of punishment or recompense which is his due, and this not only as regards the soul but as regards the body also: *Ut referat unusquisque propria corporis, prout gessit, sive bonum, sive malum—That every one may receive the proper things of the body, according as he hath done, whether it be good or evil.* Oh, what an anxious sentence! Either unalloyed happiness without admixture of evil, or unalloyed misery without admixture of good! Can it be that thou dost not give this matter a thought? seeing that there is so much at stake as regards thy personal interests? At this judgment-seat of Christ no account is taken of nobility of birth, nor of learning, nor of wealth; it is only our works that are taken into account. He that has done well, shall fare well; he that has done ill, shall fare ill, for all eternity: *Secundum opera manuum eorum tribue illis*—Ps. xxvii. 4 —*Give them according to their works.* Why then dost thou not apply thyself in good earnest to what is alone of any importance ?

TUESDAY IN THE NINTH WEEK AFTER PENTECOST.

Venite ad me omnes qui laboratis et onerati estis, et ego reficiam vos.—Matth. xi. 28.
Come to Me all you that labour and are burdened, and I will refresh you.

I. CONSIDER who are they that labour, and whose only reward is to feel the weight of their burden. They are all those who seek consolation in the pleasures and riches of the world, because they toil only to become rich and are never content with what they have gained, and because—which is worse still—after all their exertions they do not succeed in obtaining what they crave after : *Laborant et onerati sunt—They labour and are burdened.* Not a few of these unhappy souls are to be found even in the cloister, and such as these labour, one to win a great name and reputation, another to procure greater ease and comfort, or to carry out his own schemes and fancies; and then after all they find themselves burdened with secret misgivings, disappointments, and remorse of conscience, entangling themselves meanwhile in a maze of faults, in consequence of which they come to lose all relish for their spiritual exercises and feel the religious life to be an intolerable burden. Woe to thee, shouldst thou ever be of the number of these unhappy ones !

II. Consider that as the only means of freeing ourselves from this miserable condition, Jesus invites us to have recourse to Him, and He will relieve us and refresh us : *Venite ad me omnes qui laboratis, et onerati estis, et ego reficiam vos*—*Come to Me all you that labour and are burdened, and I will refresh you.* Oh, loving words that ought to make thy heart burst with tenderness ! Since Jesus Himself calls thee, and promises to console thee, where is there room for doubt ? Dost thou fear that He will not, perchance, console thee, when He invites thee so lovingly ? or art thou afraid, perhaps, that He cannot console thee, He who is the fountain-head of all consolation, of all strength ? If only thou wouldst make up thy mind once for all to give over running after worldly consolation, and to go straight to Jesus, thou wouldst very soon be relieved of thy burden : *Auferetur onus de humero tuo*—Isa. x. 27 —*The burden shall be taken away from off thy shoulder.* Look around thee and see who amongst thy brethren in religion leads the most quiet and contented life ; is it he that is all anxiety to procure for himself worldly consolations, or is it he that neither desires nor seeks consolation elsewhere than at the feet of Jesus crucified ?

III. Consider that the alleviation and refreshment Our Lord will bestow on thee is of two kinds—one negative, the other positive. The former consists in relieving thee of the weight of the toil and disappointment of seeking after consolation which cannot be found in the pleasures of this world because it exists in Him alone. The latter consists in making thee experience just the contrary effects to those produced by the vain search after worldly consolation ; for whereas this fruitless search only served to embitter and disquiet thee, only compromised thy conscience and put thee in danger of losing thy soul, the mere fact of not seeking other consolation but that which is to be found at the foot of the crucifix will give thee the peace of a good conscience, will strengthen thee with the aids of grace, and will fill thy heart with the joyful hope of that reward which is prepared for thy complete refreshment in paradise. Surely this ought to be enough to engage thee to accept Jesus' invitation and to betake thyself speedily to Him.

WEDNESDAY IN THE NINTH WEEK AFTER PENTECOST.

Væ vobis qui ridetis nunc; quia lugebitis et flebitis.—Luc. vi. 25.

Woe to you that now laugh; for you shall mourn and weep.

I. CONSIDER that Our Lord justly chides all those who give themselves up entirely to the enjoyment of pleasure, and who make it the main object of their lives to be merry and comfortable; because they are making merry *in valle lacrymarum*—in the tearful valley of this world, where nothing else is to be found but misfortune, and sin, and misery, all which ought with good reason rather to make them sad. This is not the time for laughing: the future rather than the present is the fitting time for rejoicing. *Tempus flendi, tempus ridendi*—Eccl. iii. 4.—*A time to weep, and a time to laugh.* Moreover, Our Lord rebukes such as these because they laugh at those very things which ought to be to them a cause of bitter wailing: *Lætantur, cum mali fecerint, et exultant in rebus pessimis*—Prov. ii. 14—*Who are glad when they have done evil, and rejoice in most wicked things.* Do thou at least learn to pity these poor creatures, and thank thy God for having enabled thee to leave the world and placed thee out of the way of its follies. But at the same time ponder seriously, and beware lest the too great liberty and excessive indulgence thou perhaps allowest thyself, do not render thee also liable for thy own share of weeping and sorrow.

II. Consider the punishment with which Jesus Christ threatens these poor creatures, that are all intent now on their own amusement. *Væ vobis..... quia lugebitis et flebitis—Woe to you .... for you shall mourn and weep.* The soul mourns, the body weeps; and they will take both body and soul with them into the depths of hell. Reflect, therefore, first of all on the unspeakable regret that they will suffer in their souls by reason of the pain of loss. If the privation of an inheritance, or of a property, or of an office, is in this life looked upon so often as a just cause for most bitter heart-rendings, what will it be when these thoughtless souls will behold themselves deprived for ever of an infinite good such as Almighty God is, and when they bring home to themselves the fact that they have lost Him for a foul pleasure which was gone in a moment? Oh, how their anguish, their agony and despair will be aggravated by the clear insight they will have of the immense bliss of the happy denizens of heaven—a bliss that far surpasses in degree even the extremity of their own woe! Think seriously on this, and thou wilt then be glad to have no share in their merriment so as to escape being the partner of their ravings hereafter.

III. Consider the wailing and weeping that these pleasure-seekers will have to undergo in their bodies by reason of the pain of sense. Hast thou never witnessed or experienced the agony of pain a person undergoes that is suffering from a severe hurt, and how it makes the tears stream from his eyes ? Yet who is there, pray, in the whole world that has ever had to undergo the tortures that each and all of the damned endure ? *In ventre impii ignis ardebit*—Eccl. xl. 32—*In the bowels of the wicked there shall burn a fire.* This fire will cause them to experience at one and the same time all sorts of pains, although in their own nature contrary to each other—the scalding of fire, the aching of cold, the faintness of swooning, the tortures of gout, the weakness of consumption, the agonies of internal diseases, and the inexplicable phenomena of nervous derangement. *In uno igne omnia tormenta sentient,* says S. Jerome—*They will experience in the same fire every kind of torment.* Oh, with what torrents of bitter tears, with what shrieks and yells will these hapless wretches give vent to their agony when they feel the demons disjointing their bones, and racking and torturing their limbs in a thousand ways; then, again, their sufferings will be all the more dreadful when they reflect that their short-lived folly and laughter has drawn down upon them this weeping and wailing that will never come to an end. How much better then it is for thee to deprive thyself in this life of the pleasures of the world, and weep over thy own sins and the sins of thy neighbour, so as not to have to bewail them fruitlessly and hopelessly in the next world, where the measure of this life's enjoyment will have to become the measure of the grief and torment to be endured there ? *Quantum glorificavit se, et in deliciis fuit, tantum date illi tormentum et luctum*—Apoc. xviii. 7—*As much as she hath glorified herself and lived in delicacies, so much torment and sorrow give ye to her.*

THURSDAY IN THE NINTH WEEK AFTER PENTECOST.

Spiritus ubi vult spirat ; et vocem ejus audis, sed nescis unde veniat aut quo vadat : sic est omnis qui natus est ex Spiritu.— Joan. iii. 8.

The Spirit breatheth where He will; and thou hearest His voice, but thou knowest not whence He cometh or whither He goeth : so is every one that is born of the Spirit.

I. CONSIDER that the progeny that is begotten of human parents is like unto the parents that begot it, although it does not attain but by degrees their perfection ; so also he that is begotten by the supernatural generation of the Spirit is like unto the Spirit of the Lord that begot him, although he is not equal in perfection, but remains a far way behind even when he has reached the full growth of the spiritual life in heaven. Hence all the actions of a really spiritual man have something divine about them, pourtraying to a certain extent those properties which Our Divine Lord attributes in the words just cited to the inspirations of Almighty God. The first property is, *Spiritus ubi vult spirat—The Spirit breatheth where He will*, with complete liberty of action, being subject to no law, to no rule. Such also is the line of conduct of every really spiritual man—*sic est omnis qui natus est ex Spiritu.* It is enough for such a one to know the Will of God, and he will instantly put it into execution, heedless of all the opposition of nature and of human respect. Art thou possessed of a like liberty of action in spiritual matters, and in such as belong to the service of Almighty God ? or rather art thou not hampered by a thousand trammels? There is nothing more hateful to the Spirit of God than the conduct of one that acts as though under constraint.

II. Consider the second property of the Spirit of God, namely, that He speaks to the heart in such a manner that thou canst not help hearing His voice—*et vocem ejus audis.* Thou canst, if thou choosest, resist and refuse to accept His divine inspiration; but thou canst not but hear His voice even though thou stoppest thy ears. So also with every really spiritual man: he has a certain gravity of manner, a certain calmness and modest reserve, a spirit of humility and obedience, that with a silent language speaks to thy heart and invites thee to good, so that although thou omittest to imitate him thou canst not but hear the silent invitation. Does thy conduct possess this charmed voice? does it speak to all and invite all to good? Happy indeed art thou if such be the case! Beware, rather, lest thy behaviour be such that it should incite to evil rather than good.

III. Consider that there is no knowing whence the voice of the Spirit of God comes nor whither it goes: *nescis unde veniat aut quo vadat.* There is no knowing whence it comes, because at one time it may come from beholding a corpse, at another from hearing a sermon, at another from reading a spiritual book or holding conversation with a holy person. There is no knowing whither it goes. Who is there that can foresee what designs Almighty God has over us when He calls us to a more perfect life? who can say whether He designs us to be apostles or martyrs or models of patience? *Quis poterit cogitare quid velit Deus?*—Sap. ix. 13—*Who can think what the Will of God is?* Such also is the conduct of the spiritual man. Content to have God alone for witness of the motive and end of his good works, he heeds not the idle gossip of others: and although he does not cloak over his virtuous actions, he conceals his intentions and the means he employs from all, except that one person whom he has chosen as his director in this world to fulfil in his regard the place of God. It is a sign that thy virtue is not genuine, if thou art given to make a vain display and boast of thy manner of living to any but those whose duty it is to direct thee.

FRIDAY IN THE NINTH WEEK AFTER PENTECOST.

Deponentes omne pondus et circumstans peccatum, per patientiam curramus ad propositum nobis certamen: aspicientes in auctorem fidei, et consummatorem Jesum, qui, proposito sibi gaudio, sustinuit crucem, confusione contemptâ.—Heb. xii. 1.

Laying aside every weight and sin which surrounds us, let us run by patience to the fight proposed to us: looking on Jesus, the author and finisher of faith, Who, having joy set before Him, endured the cross, despising the shame.

I. CONSIDER that the battle in which thou art called upon to take part, is a battle against those three but too well-known foes—the undue love of riches, pleasure, and esteem. Thou hast to encourage thyself to engage in this battle by means of a determined resolution to suffer and to accept with patience poverty, pain, and scorn, under one or another of which heads come all the various hardships that thou hast to encounter during the course of the day. In order, however, to succeed in doing this, thou must, in the first place, not only lay aside the burden of sins already committed, but thou must also avoid the occasions of committing the same sins over again. How canst thou possibly succeed in refraining from all unlawful pleasures, and in not caring about glory and worldly greatness, so long as thou art surrounded by so many worldly enticements which decoy and deceive thee.

II. Consider that after thou hast got rid of these impediments, thou must, in the next place, encourage thyself with the example of Jesus Christ, and He Who has suffered such extremities for love of thee will enable thee to acquire readiness of disposition to undergo suffering, and also patience in enduring the same for love of Him. In order, therefore, to gain courage, fix thy gaze on Jesus, Who purposely refused the temporal glory which was His due, and chose poverty, suffering, and scorn for His share, in order to lead thee after Him by His example: *Proposito sibi gaudio sustinuit crucem, confusione contemptâ—Who, having joy set before Him, endured the cross, despising shame.* What else was the whole life of Jesus but one continued realisation of the cross to which He was nailed by those three executioners—poverty, suffering, and scorn? These were His companions at His birth, during life, and at His death. Fix, then, thy gaze steadily on Jesus, and, like the brazen serpent in the desert, He will give thee strength to overcome thy weakness.

III. Consider that Jesus is here called *auctorem fidei et consummatorem—the author and finisher of faith*, because as He is the author or originator of faith, it is for Him to encourage thee to strive after what He holds out to thee now, and as its finisher or perfectioner to encourage thee with the prospect of what He will bestow on thee hereafter. Jesus is the author of faith whilst thou art on earth, instilling it into thee by His teaching, impressing it on thee by His example, and strengthening it in thee by the many lights He imparts to thy understanding and the many inspirations He lavishes on thy will. He will be here after in heaven the finisher of faith, by rewarding it in proportion to the extent to which thou possessest it here below, by a clear and distinct vision, since faith will resolve itself into vision; but the degree of this blissful intuition will be only according to the degree in which during thy present state of strife and war thou shalt have conformed thyself to His example by embracing poverty, running away from riches, by welcoming sufferings and shunning pleasures, by hailing scorn and contempt, and discarding all kinds of honour and self-conceit.

SATURDAY IN THE NINTH WEEK AFTER PENTECOST.

Ego Dominus Deus tuus docens te utilia.—Isa. xlviii. 17.
  I am the Lord thy God that teach thee profitable things.

I. CONSIDER that Almighty God Himself deigns to be thy teacher in the art of prayer, in order to instruct thee in it and make thee an adept in it. When He speaks to thee by means of His ministers from the pulpit, He gives thee lessons as the teacher and master of all the faithful in common, but when thou communest with Him in prayer He is teacher to thee alone. What love hast thou for these private lessons? how dost thou frequent them? It is the aim of thy divine Teacher to make thee learn in this school not subtle and high-flown theories, but what is useful, *docens te utilia*—and what will enable thee to root out vice and acquire virtue and an intimate union with God. The surest sign by which thou mayest know if thy prayer is good, is not the amount of light thou gainest nor of the tears thou sheddest, but the fruit it produces in a more mortified life, a greater energy and fervour in the practice of virtue. When thy prayer has no beneficial influence on thy actions, be suspicious of it, because prayer is a school that aims at practical reality.

II. Consider that thy divine Master teaches thee not only by word of mouth, but also by the force of example : *Ego ipse qui loquebar, ecce adsum*—Isa. lii. 6 —*I Myself that spoke, behold I am here.* There is no need of straining thy imagination in order to find a good and practical rule of action : thou hast only to look at Christ and see how He acted in that particular circumstance in which thou actually findest thyself. Every other rule of action is faulty: the quickest and safest rule for thee is to keep an eye on the actions of thy divine Master : *Erunt oculi tui videntes præceptorem tuum*—Isa. xxx. 20—*Thy eyes shall see thy teacher.* No occasion can present itself but thou mayest at once have at hand, by meditating on the life of Christ, the very model thou needest on which to regulate thy own conduct under the particular proof by which Almighty God wishes to test thee, whether at one time it be in the shape of prosperity, or at another by means of persecution or the assaults of the devil.

III. Consider that not only does this divine Master give thee lessons of practical utility in the school of prayer, but He furthermore confers on thee the capability of understanding them and the strength to put them into practice. See, therefore, with what earnestness thou oughtest to frequent such an excellent school as is that of prayer. Many a simple-minded peasant girl has, by purity of life, succeeded in attaining in prayer a knowledge of truths altogether unknown to the most learned divine. How many souls feel themselves braced up in time of prayer to apply themselves in earnest to the exercise of those great virtues of humility, patience, and charity, which until then seemed too difficult for them to realise! Learn, therefore, to appreciate the teaching of so great a Master, Who, in the very act of propounding His principles, gives thee also the capability and the strength to sanctify thyself by their means: *In scientia sua justificabit ipse justus servus meus, multos*—Isa. liii. 11—*By His knowledge shall this My servant justify many.*

TENTH SUNDAY AFTER PENTECOST.

Duo homines ascenderunt in templum ut orarent; unus Pharisæus et alter publicanus.—Luc. xviii. 10.

Two men went up into the temple to pray; the one a Pharisee and the other a publican.

I. CONSIDER in this Pharisee of the Gospel the exact likeness of a haughty and proud spirit, and first of all in his outward gait, for he does not deign to bow his head or knees, even in the very presence of God: *stans orabat.* Prouder still in his interior dispositions, he boasts and he extols himself on the strength of the little good he had performed, without giving a thought to his vices and to his pride. When his neighbour is in question his attention is turned solely to his faults, and he looks on every one but himself in the worst light; he prefers himself before all: *Non sum, sicut cæteri homines*—*I am not like the rest of men.* In his prayers he asks Almighty God for nothing; he does not recommend himself in any way to His mercy and goodness, just as though he said: *Sufficiens mihi sum*—Eccl. xi. 26—*I am sufficient for myself*. Turn now thy eyes on thyself and see whether in thy dealings with God and man thy exterior behaviour be that of a haughty man of the world, or of a humble religious. Examine if thou art vainglorious and art loud in thy own praises about the good thou performest, and givest little or no heed to thy faults. See if thou art given to censuring the shortcomings of thy neighbour and considerest thyself superior to him; because if this spirit of pride was so displeasing to God in a Pharisee, how much more so will it not be in a religious?

II. Consider in the poor publican the deportment of a truly humble soul. He enters the temple conscious of his lowliness in the sight of God, and in the estimation of men: *stans a longe—standing afar off*, like one that is excommunicated and deemed unworthy of holding intercourse with any one: *nolebat nec oculos ad cœlum levare—he would not so much as lift up his eyes towards heaven*—overpowered by a sense of shame, and bowing his head he did not presume even to raise his eyes to heaven: *Percutiebat pectus suum— He struck his breast*—from a sincere sorrow for his sins, and acknowledging himself to be the worst of sinners he implored Almighty God to have compassion on him: *Deus propitius esto mihi peccatori—O God, be merciful to me, a sinner*. Here is a true model for thee to imitate when thou presentest thy petitions to Almighty God for mercy and pardon: *Oratio humiliantis se nubes penetrabit*—Eccl. xxxv. 21—*The prayer of him that humbleth himself shall pierce the clouds*.

III. Consider how in this proud Pharisee and in this humble publican these words of Our Lord are verified: *Qui se exaltat humiliabitur, et qui se humiliat exaltabitur*—Luc. xviii. 14—*Every one that exalteth himself shall be humbled, and he that humbleth himself shall be exalted*—because pride is of all vices the most hateful to heaven, and the one that places the greatest distance between God and the soul, and humility is of all virtues the most acceptable to heaven, and draws the soul nearer to God than any other virtue. Almighty God will put up far more readily with men full of all kinds of vices than with men puffed up with pride. A guilty conscience, but which is accompanied with humility, is less hateful in His sight than innocence itself if coupled with pride: *Deus superbis resistit, humilibus autem dat gratiam*—1 Pet. v. 5—*God resisteth the proud, but to the humble He giveth grace.* Hence, just as humility drives away sin and cleanses its stains, so also does pride poison virtue and change it into vice. Use, therefore, thy best endeavours to acquire a great horror of the vice of pride, and an ardent love of the virtue of humility. It is humility that Jesus has taught us in a most especial manner by His own example, in order that we might correct that first of all vices, pride, of which Lucifer set the first example, and which he began to propagate in the very beginning in the earthly paradise, and which has been inherited by all of us from our first parents. Apply thyself seriously to consider and examine the example of humility which thy Saviour has given thee, and very soon thy highest ambition will be to become a disciple of Jesus, the great teacher of humility, in preference to remaining a disciple of Lucifer, the master of all pride.

MONDAY IN THE TENTH WEEK AFTER PENTECOST.

Qui se existimat stare, videat ne cadat.—1 Cor. x. 12.
He that thinketh himself to stand, let him take heed lest he fall.

I. CONSIDER that S. Paul does not say *qui stat, videat ne cadat—he that is standing, let him take heed lest he fall;* but *qui se existimat stare, videat ne cadat—he that thinketh himself to stand, let him take heed lest he fall.* For, in reality, who is there that is so firm on his feet as never to stagger nor ever to be in danger of falling? Wouldst thou fain persuade thyself that by virtue of thy religious state thou art now safe? O how thou deceivest thyself! Call to mind the example of Lucifer, who fell from heaven, of Solomon, of David, and do not imagine that falls in the path to heaven are to be met with only in the case of beginners; there are but too many instances on record in the case of even the most far advanced. This wholesome dread of falling must not only be entertaiued in youth, but must be preserved in old age as well, according to the saying of Ecclesiasticus ii. 6 : *Serva timorem Domini et in illo veterasce—Keep the fear of the Lord, and grow old therein.*

II. Consider that S. Paul says *videat—let him take heed;* that is, thou must watch and keep an eye on thyself, and find out where thy greatest danger of falling lies ; if, perhaps, in thy overweening self-assurance of not falling, or in too great reliance on thy own strength; or, again, if it is to be found in thy great negligence in performing thy spiritual exercises, and in having recourse to God ; or in the excessive tenderness with which thou treatest thy body, and in a want of sufficient guard over thy senses; or again, in the dangerous occasions thou oughtest to avoid, and the example of bad companions whom thou oughtest to shun; or lastly, if it is to be found in thy sloth and negligence in resisting the attacks of the temptations of the devil and of the unruly appetites of the flesh. If thou wouldst escape either actually falling, or the dangerous state of believing thyself safe, thou must keep a watchful eye on all these dangers, in the midst of which thou must necessarily spend thy whole life.

III. Consider that if thou wouldst secure thyself against falling, it is not enough merely to note the dangers to which thou art exposed, but thou must also ward them off with the utmost diligence. However, with all thy diligence, thou wilt never succeed in guaranteeing thyself against falling over these stumbling-blocks unless thou provide thyself with a guide and with a support. Thy guide must be a good spiritual father, to direct thee along a safe route. Thy support is God's help, which thou must ask for perseveringly; in this way only wilt thou escape all dangers, whereas, without a guide and without support, thou canst not take a single step on the road to heaven without running most serious risks.

TUESDAY IN THE TENTH WEEK AFTER PENTECOST.

Tollite jugum meum super vos, et discite a me, quia mitis sum et humilis corde.—Matt. xi. 29.

Take up My yoke upon you, and learn of Me, because I am meek and humble of heart.

I. CONSIDER that it is the Evangelical counsels which are, properly speaking, the yoke of Christ. They are called a yoke, because they oblige one to lead a life not in accordance with one's own whims, but under the rule and guidance of him that holds God's place. They are, moreover, here called Christ's yoke—*jugum meum*—*My yoke;* because, as God, He is the origin of this yoke, and has sanctioned it, and as man He carried this yoke for three and thirty years, passing His days in the greatest poverty, the greatest mortification, and the greatest subjection. This is a yoke that is not meant for brute beasts, but for men endowed with reason; and it has therefore to be carried of one's own accord and free will. For this reason Our Lord says: *Tollite jugum meum super vos*—*Take up My yoke upon you*—to give thee to understand that thou must not place this yoke on thy shoulders sullenly, or with resistance, or only materially and mechanically, but thou must submit thy superior faculties which thou enjoyest as a man: *Rationabile obsequium vestrum*—Rom. xii. 1—*Your reasonable service.* Reflect now for a while if thou carriest the yoke of religion unwillingly, and even restively, like a beast of burden; or if, as a rational being ought to do, thou submittest thyself to this yoke with a good will, not only as far as thy exterior is concerned, but as regards thy interior dispositions also: *Collum vestrum subjicite jugo, et suscipiat anima vestra disciplinam*—Eccl. li. 34 —*Submit your neck to the yoke, and let your soul receive discipline.*

II. Consider that there are two vices which are generally the cause of a religious carrying the yoke of religion unwillingly; to wit, impatience and pride. Impatience, because it makes this yoke appear too heavy; pride, because it makes it appear too full of scorn and disgrace. For this reason it is that Christ bids thee learn of Him patience and humility, because if thou art patient and humble in imitation of Christ, the burden of His yoke will become light, and thou wilt enjoy rest. Go, therefore, to Jesus' feet, and learn true meekness and true humility, and so thou wilt feel no trial or hardship too burdensome.

III. Consider how everything that is capable of weighing thee down and disturbing thy peace of mind, comes to thee either from outside of thee or from inside thee. From outside come contempt, harsh treatment, misfortunes; from inside come all thy shortcomings, both moral and physical. The strongest and most necessary weapons to contend with these evils, whether inside or outside of thee, are humility and meekness; meekness against contempt and other evils that are inflicted on thee by others; humility against thy own imperfections, either physical or moral, that proceed from thyself. With these two virtues to support thee, thou wilt be enabled to remain calm and firm, like a rock in the midst of a storm.

WEDNESDAY IN THE TENTH WEEK AFTER PENTECOST.

Non habemus hic manentem civitatem sed futuram inquirimus.—Hebr. xiii. 14.
We have not here a lasting city, but we seek one that is to come.

I. CONSIDER that this woeful earth is by no means the city where thou hast a lasting residence. Thy real abode is Paradise, and the idea of comparing earth with heaven would be like comparing some miserable hut to the palaces of ancient Rome. Under how great an obligation, then, thou liest of thanking Almighty God for having caused thee to abandon thy own earthly home by means of thy vocation to the religious state, that in religion thou mightest recognise no other home than heaven: *civitas perfecti decoris*—Thren. ii. 15—*the city of perfect beauty*. S. Francis of Assisi experienced great delight in making the renunciation of all right to his father's inheritance, in the presence of his bishop, because, thus stripped of everything, he would no longer have any occasion to recognise any other father than his Heavenly Father. Do thou in like manner congratulate thyself on not having, in the religious state, to recognise any other fatherland than Paradise.

II. Consider that it is thy duty, consequently, to deport thyself in this world as a stranger does in a town where he is making no permanent stay. He takes no interest in its affairs, he is not attached to it, he looks upon it as something that does not concern him. In the same way must thou also act so long as thou livest in this world. This is not thy own town;

thou art a stranger here. Yet thou art so anxious to settle down here, thou takest such lively interest in the affairs of thy relations, of thy home and native place, just as though thou hadst never to leave them altogether. Oh, this is truly a great disorder, and of the greatest harm and injury to thy own real interests.

III. Consider that thou art not only a stranger on this earth, but thou art also a pilgrim : *Futuram inquirimus—We are in search of a future home.* A pilgrim that passes through different places on his pilgrimage, is careful not to take anything beyond what is absolutely necessary for his maintenance ; he goes as unencumbered as may be, with as little burden as possible, and he tries to discover the shortest and quickest way to his destination. This is the way in which thou also oughtest to act during the pilgrimage of this life. Thou must, indeed, be here below in body, but in mind thou must soar aloft, just as the pilgrim is bodily present in the place through which he passes, but is in thought and desire in the place he is yearning to reach. Alas, how different is thy manner of acting, seeing how little thou thinkest about heaven, just as though it were not thy real home and fatherland !

THURSDAY IN THE TENTH WEEK AFTER PENTECOST.

Quæ seminaverit homo, hæc et metet.—Gal. vi. 8.
What things a man shall sow, those also shall he reap.

I. CONSIDER that the present life is the time for sowing the seed, and the next life for reaping the harvest. The seed consists in our works, the harvest in the return made for these works. Whoever shall have sown wheat, or, in other words, shall have lived well, shall fare well; and he that shall have sown cockle, that is, shall have lived ill, shall fare ill. This is a law which suffers no exception; it is binding on all. Whether prince or beggar, no distinction will be made. Why, then, dost thou give so little heed to the sort of life thou leadest ? Thy works are so many seeds that must produce their respective fruits in the eternity that awaits thee; pay attention, therefore, as to whether they are good or bad, because, if they are bad, oh thou art truly to be pitied! What a harvest of woe awaits thee! If they are good, go on scattering thy seed with a light heart, for thou wilt reap eternal weal.

II. Consider that in order to ensure a good harvest, it is not enough simply to sow good seed, but it must be sown in good soil also; because a barren soil may well be the cause of a bad harvest. *Seminaverunt triticum, et spinas messuerunt*—Jer. xii. 13—*They have sown wheat, and reaped thorns.* Thou hast within thyself two soils—one good, which is the spirit, the other bad, which is the flesh. Hence the apostle tells thee: *Qui seminat in carne sua, de carne et metet corruptionem; qui autem seminat in spiritu, de spiritu et metet vitam æternam*—Gal. vi. 8—*He that soweth in his flesh, of the flesh also shall reap corruption; but he that soweth in the spirit, of the spirit shall reap life everlasting.* He sows in the flesh that works on behalf of the flesh; he sows in the spirit that works on behalf of the spirit. It is not, however, enough that thy works should be good in themselves only; it is needful that thou shouldst direct them and make them tell to the advantage of the spirit and not of the flesh. When thou toilest in the charge that obedience has entrusted to thee, when thou art studying, or preaching, or teaching, thou sowest good seed; but if all this toil be directed to some ambitious end, thou sowest in the flesh, and therefore *metes corruptionem—thou shalt reap corruption.* If thou wouldst fain reap a profitable harvest, sow thy seed to thy spiritual advantage, and not with a view to flatter the inclinations of thy unruly flesh.

III. Consider that if the doer of good or of evil were forthwith to receive his meed of good or evil in this world, we should all be far more cautious in our daily dealings. But do not reckon on this being the case, because a man's works are like the seed that is cast into the ground; and as for their reward or punishment, we must abide the harvest season that will come in eternity. If, therefore, thou hast done ill, say not: *Peccavi, quid mihi accidit triste?*—Eccl. v. 4—*I have sinned, and what harm hath befallen me?*—because thou wilt reap but too plentiful a harvest of punishment in due season. If thou hast done well, thou mayest be sure thou wilt reap an everlasting reward. Look how patiently the farmer waits for the harvest; so also do thou have patience: *Quoniam adventus Domini appropinquavit*—Jac. v. 8—*For the coming of the Lord is at hand.*

FRIDAY IN THE TENTH WEEK AFTER PENTECOST.

Christo igitur passo in carne, et vos eadem cogitatione armamini.—1 Pet. iv. 1.

Christ therefore having suffered in the flesh, be you also armed with the same thought.

I. CONSIDER that although Christ suffered so much in His own flesh, it was not from any need of bringing it into subjection, because it was most pure and most obedient to the spirit, but it was on account of the great need thou hast of conquering and bringing under thy own ever rebellious and stubborn flesh. On this account it might have seemed reasonable that S. Peter should have exhorted thee to bring thy flesh into subjection by means of the same sufferings as Christ underwent, namely, by lashes, thorns and nails. Yet, notwithstanding as the apostle knew all about thy frailty, he wishes thee to arm thyself, if not with the actual sufferings that Christ underwent, at least with the thought and remembrance of His sufferings. What excuse, therefore, wilt thou find, if thou art not willing to do even this much?

II. Consider that this armour ought to be of two kinds, one defensive, to ward off the attacks of thy rebellious flesh; the other offensive, to enable thee to attack it and keep it in due obedience. Now, the thought of what Christ has suffered for thy sake is the best armour thou canst have, whether defensive or offensive. It will be thy best defensive armour, according to the words of the Prophet: *Dabis eis scutum cordis, laborem tuum*—Thren. iii. 65—*Thou shalt give them a buckler of heart, thy labour:* because how is it possible that whilst contemplating Christ weltering in His own blood on the cross for thy sins, thou shouldst at one and the same time think of indulging thy own body in unlawful pleasures? It will likewise stand thee in good stead as offensive armour, because it will enkindle in thy heart a holy indignation against thyself, to urge thee on to illtreat and mortify thyself, and so inflict on thy flesh the punishment it deserves. To succeed in this, however, a mere reflection on the Passion will not be enough; it demands thy assiduous and attentive consideration; because as thy flesh is ever on the alert to urge war against thee, it behoves thee never to lay aside an armour that tells so well against it.

III. Consider that if thou desirest to derive really great benefit from this thought of the Passion, thou must pay especial heed to Who it is that has suffered so much for thy sake. Even though the Son of God had done nothing further in thy behalf than to taste a little sip of gall, such condescension ought to have been sufficient to cause a miserable worm like thee to spend thy life in a sea of bitter sorrow for love of Him. What then ought to be the result when thou ponderest over the awful tortures which the Son of God endured in His body, and which even necessitated His endowing Himself with superhuman strength. No sooner did Tobias discover that his kind guide was the Archangel Raphael, than he fell to the ground half dead with emotion: such also ought to be the effect produced on thee by the thought that He Who came down from heaven to earth to suffer such torments for thee, is no other than the Son of God Himself. This thought ought to cause thee to live, as it were, dead to thyself, so that thy flesh shall no longer have it in its power to be able to trouble thee. *Memoria memor ero, et tabescet in me anima mea—* Thren. iii. 20—*I will be mindful and remember, and my soul shall languish within me.*

SATURDAY IN THE TENTH WEEK AFTER PENTECOST.

Libenter gloriabor in infirmitatibus meis, ut inhabitet in me virtus Christi.—2 Cor. xii. 9.

Gladly will I glory in my infirmities, that the power of Christ may dwell in me.

I. CONSIDER how S. Paul prayed Our Lord with great earnestness over and over again to be freed from the sting of the flesh: *Ter Dominum rogavi ut discederet a me—Thrice I besought the Lord that it might depart from me*—although he never yielded to the temptation, but chastised his body and kept it in subjection. Yet he was told by Our Lord that it was better for him to be liable to this frailty of human flesh like other men: *Sufficit tibi gratia mea, nam virtus in infirmitate perficitur—My grace is sufficient for thee, for power is made perfect in infirmity;* and no sooner did he hear these words than he gloried in this his very weakness: *Libenter gloriabor in infirmitatibus meis —Gladly will I glory in my infirmities*, because it would prove to be the occasion of establishing in himself the power of Christ. Take a lesson from this example, that thou must not glory in being free from temptations, even from impure temptations, but in deriving from them that benefit which Almighty God designs for thy soul's advantage.

II. Consider what was the power of Christ which S. Paul beheld established in himself by means of his frailty. It was, forsooth, humility in his own regard, and meekness with regard to others. This was the power, these the virtues, taught and publicly practised by Christ above all others: *Discite a me, quia mitis sum et humilis corde*—Matt. ii. 29—*Learn of Me, because I am meek and humble of heart*. Now it was precisely this sting of the flesh that was capable at one and the same time of keeping the apostle humble amidst the many incentives he had to vainglory, and meek in his relations with his neighbours by having compassion on their faults and weaknesses. If only thou didst know how to draw from thy own failings the result of humility and meekness, then mightest thou also begin to glory in them. Thy weaknesses and failings ought to be for thee like so many windows that enable the sunlight to penetrate the chamber of thy soul and thus enlighten thee by a low esteem of thyself, and warm thee by charity towards thy neighbour. Surely thou canst not despise so great a benefit? *Infirmitas gravis, sobriam facit animam*— Eccl. xxxi. 2—*A grievous sickness maketh the soul sober.*

III. Consider that thou hast not the same occasions for getting vainglorious as the Apostle S. Paul had, and yet, notwithstanding this, thou hast not the less need of a remembrancer of thy misery, seeing that thou persistest in being so foolishly proud. If it happens that thou sheddest two or three tears in time of prayer, thou thinkest thou hast reached the third heaven, and thou at once beginnest to ape an air of austerity, finding fault with and correcting others. What else, therefore, canst thou expect, if Our Lord allows certain weaknesses and shortcomings to manifest themselves in thee, to which even great and holy souls are liable?—with, however, this difference, that in the case of holy souls these weaknesses are allowed, in order to keep them steadfast, and in thy case they are also a punishment, because thou art at the same time needy and proud. Reflect, therefore, what a great gain it is to be humble and meek, seeing that in the case of even the saints themselves it is well worth their while to have to put up with the most dreadful temptations of the flesh in order to be possessed of these two virtues.

ELEVENTH SUNDAY AFTER PENTECOST.

Adducunt ei surdum et mutum . . . et apprehendens eum de turba seorsum misit digitos suos in auriculas ejus.
—Marc. vii. 32.

They bring to Him one deaf and dumb . . . and taking him from the multitude apart, He put His fingers into his ears.

I. CONSIDER how in the cure of this deaf and dumb man, Christ teaches thee three different remedies, by means of which thou mayest cure thy vices and lead a religious and fervent life. First of all, then, *apprehendit eum de turba seorsum*—He withdrew him on one side, away from the crowd of people. This is thy first remedy for the emendation of thy vices; begin by withdrawing thyself from the crowd of so many thoughts and affections for the things of the world, from such a frequency of conversation and so many useless recreations which serve only to keep the mind distracted; begin to enter into thyself, and to think in earnest on the state of thy soul, because it is in this state of solitude that thou wilt receive greater help and light from Almighty God to correct thy failings, and take to heart the acquisition of virtue. *Ducam cam in solitudinem, et loquar ad cor ejus*—Osee ii. 14—*I will lead her into the wilderness, and I will speak to her heart.* Rid thyself, then, of all those hindrances that encircle thee, put away from thee all that is so unbecoming to thy state as a religious, if thou really wishest to amend thy life. *Sedebit solitarius et tacebit: quia levavit se super se*—Thren. iii. 28—*He shall sit solitary and hold his peace: because he hath taken it up upon himself.*

II. Consider the second remedy indicated in those

words : *suspiciens in cœlum—looking up to heaven.* Jesus raised His eyes to heaven to teach thee that thou must not only withdraw thyself from undue concern and affection for the things of the world, but must also give thyself up to the serious study and pursuit of what concerns heaven and eternity. This was the wont of the holy King David, who said : *Annos æternos in mente habui*—Ps. lxxvi. 6—*I had in my mind the eternal years;* because by dint of continually keeping his attention fixed on eternity, he came to disregard utterly and not care for the fleeting, short-lived goods of this world, all of which disappear and melt in smoke after the lapse of a few short days. If thou also wouldst fix thy thoughts on what is to come, thou wouldst easily learn to make little of the present, and to correct thy evil inclinations by the earnest pursuit of virtue, saying with the same holy David : *Et dixi, Nunc cœpi ; hæc mutatio dexteræ Excelsi*—Ps. lxxvi. 11 —*And I said, Now have I begun; this is the change of the right hand of the Most High.*

III. Consider that thou wilt never succeed in raising thy mind to an habitual recollection of eternity, nor in ridding thyself of the thought of and affection for the present, with all its adjuncts, unless thou enjoyest the especial and efficacious aid of divine grace. Hence the third remedy consists in having recourse to Almighty God to give thee His aid, and in earnestly begging Him for it in prayer, as Christ teaches thee by His example : *suspiciens in cœlum, ingemuit—looking up to heaven, He groaned.* Thy prayer has not to be a cold, heartless uttering of words, but a fervent outpouring of the heart, accompanied by tears springing from a burning desire of being aided and helped on in the acquisition of virtue. The child does not always obtain its wish of being carried in the mother's arms, by simply asking her to do so, but its wish is always gratified when it pleads for it with tears.

MONDAY IN THE ELEVENTH WEEK AFTER PENTECOST.

Vide bonitatem et severitatem Dei: in eos qui ceciderunt severitatem; in te autem bonitatem Dei, si permanseris in bonitate; alioquin et tu excideris.—Rom. xi. 22.

See the goodness and the severity of God: towards them indeed that are fallen, the severity; but towards thee the goodness of God, if thou abide in goodness; otherwise thou also shalt be cut off.

I. CONSIDER both the mercy and the severity of Almighty God: His mercy in the benefits He confers on us without any merits of our own, His severity in the punishments He inflicts on us on account of our demerits; although Almighty God is never rigorously severe, because He never punishes to the full extent that He might do, but always shows more or less mercy; but He is said to be severe when He makes a greater display of His justice than of His mercy. The consideration of this clemency and severity must be the ladder by which thou wilt be enabled to escape the clutch of thy foes. When thou art tempted to distrust or despair, ascend to the consideration of the goodness of God towards those even who have no claim on it: *Vide bonitatem Dei—See the goodness of God.* When thou art tempted to presumption, descend into the depths and contemplate the severity of Almighty God, even in regard of some of His chosen ones: *Vide severitatem—See the severity of God.*

II. Consider the rigour of Almighty God in the case of so many individuals whom He has allowed to fall from the loftiest heights, whether of holiness or dignity: look at the case of Judas, of Saul, of Solomon, of Origen, and so many others. How many there are who are continually falling from an elevated degree of holiness, and are plunged into the depths of hell—many, perhaps, snatched away on the commission of their first grievous sin! Oh, what an awful thought is this! On the other hand, consider the mercy of God in thy own case, inasmuch as He has borne up with thee after so many oft-repeated crimes, and has even called thee to the religious state. It is quite certain that this result is not attributable to thy own deserts—it all springs from the pure goodness of thy God. But beware! thou art not yet sure of thy salvation: thou knowest not if in consequence of thy ill-correspondence thy Lord will continue to show thee the same amount of mercy. Thou wilt save thy soul if Almighty God continues to favour thee with those especial aids which He is in nowise bound to bestow on thee, *si permanseris in bonitate—if thou abide in goodness.* But who can assure thee that this will be the case?

III. Consider that were Almighty God to withdraw from thee the enjoyment of the favours of His mercy, thou wilt for a certainty be lost. *Excideris—thou also wilt be cut off* from the tree of life without any regard, and cast into everlasting fire. Therefore, commend thyself earnestly and constantly to Almighty God; take up thy stand between fear and hope, and remember that He is severe as well as merciful.

TUESDAY IN THE ELEVENTH WEEK AFTER PENTECOST.

Superbiam numquam in tuo sensu, aut in verbo dominari permittas : in ipsa enim initium sumpsit omnis perditio. —Job iv. 14.

Never suffer pride to reign in thy mind or in thy words: for from it all perdition took its beginning.

I. CONSIDER how pride, which is an inordinate craving after pre-eminence, was the root of all the woe that befell both Lucifer and Adam, by their aspiring to become like unto God. What a dread we ought, therefore, to have of this vice, which expanded into life in paradise itself—not only in the Garden of Eden, but in the courts of heaven also! Lucifer aspired to become like unto God by exercising sway over the stars : *Super astros Dei exaltabo solium meum*—Isaias xiv. 13—*I will exalt my throne above the stars of God.* So also Adam aspired to become like unto God in his knowledge : *Eritis sicut Dii, scientes bonum et malum*— Gen. iii. 5—*You shall be as gods, knowing good and evil.* Reflect, then, how important it is that thou shouldst know how to keep thyself within the bounds which Almighty God has marked out for thee in whatever sphere it may happen to be, whether of knowledge, of authority, or of position. So soon as thou exceedest these bounds, thou wilt be numbered amongst the proud.

II. Consider the direful downfall which this baneful pride brought about in the case both of Lucifer and Adam. Lucifer was in the twinkling of an eye hurled down to the lowest depths of hell, together with all his followers—those whilom noble spirits, the fairest of God's creatures. Oh, what a great evil must not pride therefore be, when a single sin of pride, though only in thought, has wrought so grievous ruin! Not less sad are the consequences that befell Adam in his earthly paradise: he was deprived of his sway as master of the earth, and stripped of his privileges of original justice, and condemned to all kinds of woe and misery; and this sentence he brought down not only on his own head, but it passed on to all his posterity, without any cessation or diminution in the duration or extent of a penalty entailing irremediable evils. Canst thou allow a vice which is so hateful to God, and so severely punished by Him, to reign in thee even for an instant?

III. Consider that, in the text under consideration, pride is spoken of as of two kinds—viz., *in sensu et in verbo*, that is to say, by thought and by speech, because these are the two means it usually has resort to, and it is from these two faculties that thou must use thy utmost endeavours to keep it at the greatest distance. If thou wouldst keep pride from entering thy mind, and prevent it from infecting thy thoughts, think often who thou art, and who God is, and thou wilt learn how right and proper it is that thou shouldst be subject to Him in all things, and conform thyself entirely to His divine Will. If thou wouldst keep away pride from thy speech, reflect how unbecoming it is, and how ridiculous it seems even to thee, when thou hearest others make use of arrogant language. In a word, fly all kind of pride, whether in thy interior or thy exterior. Moreover, pride is a most subtle vice, that very easily conceals itself even in good works, and it is only too likely that it should sometimes take thee by surprise, and, at least to a certain degree, reign in thee. But as soon as thou becomest aware of its presence, drive it away instantly, either by a contrary act of humility, or else, if it continues to harass thee, by despising it, and turning thy attention elsewhere. If thou art successful in avoiding this vice, thou wilt be spotless in the sight of God; if thou knowingly allowest it to reign in thee, woe betide thee!

WEDNESDAY IN THE ELEVENTH WEEK AFTER PENTECOST.

Recupera proximum tuum secundum virtutem tuam, et attende tibi, ne incidas.—Eccl. xxix. 26.
Recover thy neighbour according to thy power, and take heed to thyself that thou fall not.

I. CONSIDER how great and many are the claims that bind thee to thy Creator and Redeemer, Whose love has reached such a point as to die for thy sake on the hard tree of the cross. Yet as many and as great are the claims that bind thee to thy neighbour, on whose behalf thy Saviour has given up His right to thy services, because as He has no need of anything Himself, so also it is His wish that thou shouldst do on behalf of His servants what thou canst not do for the Master. How, then, canst thou presume to refuse so just a recognition to a Master Who, in return for the many great benefits conferred on thee, expects thee to come to the aid of thy neighbour and ease him of his burden.

II. Consider that by the law of charity thou art bound to love thy neighbour as thyself, and to feel his losses as thy own. Now the losses thou oughtest to feel most keenly are the spiritual injuries of the soul, because these are losses of greater importance, and are less heeded by those who, like abject slaves, allow themselves to be driven to hell without offering the slightest resistance. Everybody takes good care to rid themselves of temporal evils; yet how few there are that strive to free themselves from the evils of sin, and oftentimes how many there are that think nothing of it! Supposing thou wert to behold a dear friend seized as a slave, and put on board a pirate ship, wouldst thou not be moved to compassion, and wouldst thou not exert thyself to the utmost to have him set at liberty? Why, then, art thou not moved to still deeper compassion for those precious souls that have become the slaves of Lucifer? and why dost thou not bestir thyself to free them from that most terrible of all slaveries, and bring them back to Jesus Christ, Who ransomed them and gained the right of possession over them by shedding the last drop of His precious blood?

III. Consider that thou oughtest on no account to withdraw thyself from this work of love, by reason of thy own frailty, or on the plea of not having the necessary talent. Listen to those words which are addressed to thee also: *Recupera proximum tuum secundum virtutem tuam—Recover thy neighbour according to thy power?* Thou canst not, perchance, declaim from the pulpit, nor cross the ocean to bring back souls to God. But souls may well be saved, also, by private advice, by especial reproof, by prayer, by mortification, by good example. Oh, what immense good thou art capable of doing thy neighbour in this way! *Non enim in sermone est regnum Dei sed in virtute*—1 Cor. iv. 20—*For the kingdom of God is not in speech, but in power.* But take heed at the same time of the loving warning that is given thee, namely, *Attende tibi ne incidas—Take heed to thyself that thou fall not;* in other words, look to thyself meanwhile, and beware of losing thy own soul whilst thou art intent on saving others. Be careful lest in endeavouring to extricate others from the morass, thou become exposed to the danger of falling into it thyself. Beware lest in thy eagerness to come to the rescue of others, thou overlook thy own safety by neglecting thy wonted prayers and devotions, or by sacrificing the practice of mortification and religious seclusion. Thou must endeavour to regulate thy conduct by the aid of wholesome rules and fitting precautions : *Attende tibi ne incidas—Take heed to thyself that thou fall not.* How many there are who, after having succeeded in sending many souls to heaven, actually find themselves buried in the depths of hell !

THURSDAY IN THE ELEVENTH WEEK AFTER PENTECOST.

Ventilabram in manu ejus et purgabit aream suam; et congregabit triticum in horreum suum, paleas autem comburet igni inextinguibili.—Luc. iii. 17.

Whose fan is in His hand, and He will purge His floor; and will gather the wheat into the barn, but the chaff He will burn with unquenchable fire.

I. CONSIDER that the fan, or winnower, in Our Lord's hand, is an emblem of the judiciary power He exercises as God and man; as God, in virtue of His supreme power; as man, because He has earned it in several ways, but especially by His having deigned to be treated as a culprit at the tribunals of Pilate and Herod. It is but just that the Saviour of mankind, Who for our sake suffered Himself to be condemned by the most unjust of sentences at the tribunals of man, should be seated on a throne of majesty to judge all mankind. Congratulate Him on the glory which will be His on the day of universal judgment, and at the same time earnestly crave His mercy whilst He still acts as thy Advocate, since on that awful day He will administer rigorous justice only, in quality of Judge. Consider, moreover, that by the threshing-floor is understood the Church of the faithful only, inasmuch as all unbelievers who are outside the Church, will be judged summarily according to those words : *Qui non credit jam judicatus est*—Joan. iii. 18 —*He that doth not believe is already judged*. Wherefore the winnowing-fan will be employed on that last day in regard of the faithful only, to blow away the chaff from the barn floor, and separate the reprobate from the elect. Still more searchingly will this process be applied in the case of religious communities, whose members, good or bad, pass their lives together in this world. Reflect now awhile on the fate that awaits thee on that dread day. Which will be thy lot, that of the grain or that of the chaff?

II. Consider that the good are likened to the grain, by reason of the manifold fruit they yield, and by reason of the wholesome and solid influence they exercise in the world at large. The wicked are likened to the chaff by reason of their unfruitfulness, their levity, and inconstancy. For the present the good are intermixed with the wicked, because as the corn is benefited by its contact with the chaff, so also the good are benefited by the occasions which their intercourse with the wicked affords them of being more modest, more mortified, and more humble. This admixture of corn and chaff, of good and bad, is to be found to a certain extent even in religious communities, and if perchance thou shouldst be mortified and kept under, like the good grain, think not of envying the chaff, that by reason of its very lightness assumes an ascendency over the grain. Before long the chaff will be separated and scattered to the winds : *Dispergam eos ventilabro*—Jer. xv. 7—*I will scatter them with a fan*. Wherefore, shouldst thou be like the chaff, take heed betimes lest thou be cast away into the abyss.

III. Consider the result of this separation: *Congregabit triticum in horreum suum ; paleas autem comburet igni inextinguibili—He will gather the wheat into His barn, but the chaff He will burn with unquenchable fire.* This barn, or granary, is paradise, where the elect will take up their abode in peace and security, full of joy at being all united together by the bonds of love to praise and bless Almighty God, and at being freed from the necessity of intercourse with the wicked, who hitherto had tried them so sorely. Far better is it for thee to secure for thyself, at any cost, the happy lot of the grain, than to be carried away with the chaff and cast into the flames of hell, where the wicked will burn—not, indeed, to be reduced to ashes, but to continue suffering agony in *igne inextinguibili—in unquenchable fire !* Think seriously on the awful reality of burning for ever in the midst of flames so searching and agonising, that the fire of this world is, in comparison, a mere imitation, a harmless feint; and then, indeed, thou wilt strive to be found amongst the grain, and not amongst the chaff.

FRIDAY IN THE ELEVENTH WEEK AFTER PENTECOST.

Recogitate eum, qui talem sustinuit a peccatoribus adversus semetipsum contradictionem; ut ne fatigemini animis vestris deficientes. Nondum enim usque ad sanguinem restitistis, adversus peccatum repugnantes.—Hebr. xii. 3.

Think diligently upon Him that endured such opposition from sinners against Himself; that you be not wearied, fainting in your minds. For you have not yet resisted unto blood, striving against sin.

I. CONSIDER that thou must never be tired of thinking on Christ crucified as a remedy for thy ailings. Wherefore it ought to be thy constant practice—*recogitare*—to think over and over again who it is that suffers: it is the King of Glory, Who, though He suffered in His saints from the first ages of the world, in the person of Abel, of Joseph, of Jeremias, suffers now not only in His chosen ones but in His own Person as well—*adversus semetipsum*. At whose hands does He suffer? At the hands of those very individuals for whose salvation He is nailed to the cross—at the hands of sinners. What does He suffer? A persecution in every respect the most grievous, most shameful and unjust. Master well these three circumstances, and thou wilt find therein a balm for all thy wounds.

II. Consider that if thou wouldst encourage thyself to suffer, nothing will help thee so much as to ponder often on the passion of Jesus. Nothing inspires a soldier with greater bravery than the sight of his king himself, worn out with fatigue and stained with

11—2

his own blood at the head of his troops. Do not for a moment entertain such a thought as that thou dost not need fresh courage! See how easily thou art depressed at every little difficulty, and growest remiss in the service of thy Saviour.

III. Consider what a sense of shame thy want of generosity ought to beget in thee, when thou reflectest on it at the foot of the crucifix. Thy sins could do thy Saviour no harm, and yet see what torments[1] He endured on the cross to rid thee of them. On the other hand, thy sins do harm to thy own self, and that to an infinite degree; and yet what measures hast thou taken to keep sin away from thee? Hast thou ever gone so far on this account as to shed even one drop of blood? The apostle says but too truly: *Nondum usque ad sanguinem restitistis adversus peccatum repugnantes—You have not yet resisted unto blood, striving against sin.* Not only art thou not willing to shed thy blood, but thou art not willing even to put up with any little injury to thy reputation or thy health, not even to deprive thyself of some vain and empty self-satisfaction. This will never do. Thou art bound to resist and fight through thick and thin, *usque ad sanguinem—unto blood.* The point at issue is too important: it is a question of refusing admittance to that deadly foe, sin; to destroy which Jesus has, of His own accord, shed His own precious Blood to the very last drop.

SATURDAY IN THE ELEVENTH WEEK AFTER PENTECOST.

Dixerunt animæ tuæ: Incurvare, ut transeamus; et posuisti ut terram corpus tuum, et quasi viam transeuntibus.—Isa. li. 23.

They have said to thy soul: Bow down, that we may go over; and thou hast laid thy body as the ground, and as a way to them that went over.

I. CONSIDER that when the devil tempts thee to sin, he has a mind to place his foot on thy neck and trample thee under foot as his own vile slave. But since it is not in his power to force thee to this, nor to offer thee violence, but can only persuade and urge thee, he would fain prevail on thee to bow down of thy own accord, and abase thyself by freely consenting to his evil suggestions. What, pray, is thy candid opinion of this abject servility, and which thou hast so often shown the tempter by yielding to sin? Art thou not ashamed of thyself to think that thou hast so often hastened to prostrate thyself under the fulsome feet of those devils upon whom, contrariwise, it was thy duty to have trampled.

II. Consider that the devil has always the worst of designs against thee, and yet he asks thee merely to bend and stoop down just for a moment; because by asking at thy hands only a beginning of evil, which seems inconsiderable in itself, and does not alarm thy conscience very much, he will easily obtain all he wants. So easy is it in the regions of evil to go from little to great, that from a glance of the eye, a hankering after the forbidden fruit as in the case of Eve, he will easily urge thee on to the accomplishment of thy own ruin. Why ever, then, dost thou not set thyself with a bold face at once to reject the suggestions of thy enemy if thou wishest that thy bowing down should not be made the occasion of casting thee to the ground—in other words, if thou art anxious to avoid more grievous sin ?

III. Consider that the result of the soul prostrating itself to be trodden under foot by the devil is that it comes to be, as it were, a thoroughfare by which its enemies are free to pass to and fro at pleasure. Just such is the state at which the sinner at length arrives : from actual sin he passes on to habitual sin, thus making himself by actual sin *ut terram—as the ground*, and by habitual sin, *quasi viam transeuntibus—as a way to them that went over*. What the devil aims at when he asks thee to accommodate him just for one moment is to plant his foot firmly on thy neck, to obtain a hold which, once obtained, he intends to keep, and he will tread thee under foot like a vile slave for endless ages. Be not so foolish as to allow thyself to be thus grievously imposed upon. If thou allowest him to pass he will establish a right of way, and maintain a permanent thoroughfare. Alas, how many souls, even amongst religious, have been in the end victimised after this fashion ; yielding at first in some small matter, till at length they find themselves irremediably involved in far worse guilt than they ever contemplated. Beware of ever allowing thy sworn and treacherous enemy any opportunity of gaining a like hold on thee !

TWELFTH SUNDAY AFTER PENTECOST.

Diliges Dominum Deum tuum ex toto corde tuo.—Marc. xii. 12.

Thou shalt love the Lord thy God with thy whole heart.

I. CONSIDER what is here required of thee by Our Lord. In giving this command it is His behest that thy heart, or in other words thy will, be directed towards God; that thy appetites should recognise no other law but that which comes from God; that thy desires should ignore every other object but union with God; that thy only joy should be the honour of God, thy only sorrow the offence of God; thy only fear to incur the displeasure of God. Moreover, He proclaims His wish that all the members of thy body should be employed in furthering the glory of God, and that all the powers of thy soul should tend towards God, so that all thy studies and all thy aim should be to please God. This precept is above all the rest in importance, inasmuch as it constitutes the end and object of them all, and it surpasses them in excellence inasmuch as it raises thee to a real and intimate friendship with God. Even though Our Lord had not commanded thee to love Him, it would have been a pressing obligation on thee to beg Him to allow thee to love Him—so worthy is He of all love. How then comes it to pass that even at His express command, thou lovest Him so little?

II. Consider that thou wilt never be able to fulfil this precept to perfection on earth, but only when thou shalt be in heaven: nevertheless, thou must do thy best to fulfil it at least in part, by giving Almighty God the first place—as being thy last end—in everything, and under all circumstances. Look at the miser, who loves his money as though it were his last end; first and foremost, under all circumstances, he is anxious to put his treasure in safety, and he never consents to any diminution of it. Nay, more, see how all his plans, all his toils, his every industry, his every longing—all is directed to the hoarding and the safe keeping of his money. Now if for the sake of a false God—as money is—the miser works himself up to such a total concentration of all his energies, because he considers that in his gold he virtually possesses all his happiness, why canst not thou do as much for that true and only God in whom thou really possessest all thy happiness, all thy weal?

III. Consider what are the chief means thou hast to employ in order to possess God. The first is to acquire as thorough a knowledge of Almighty God as thou art capable of, by pondering on His infinite worth. The saints in heaven are enabled to love Him so ardently because they know and see Him *facie ad faciem—face to face;* do thy best to know and recognise Him at least from afar in the many benefits He has conferred on thee in His works in the order of nature, of grace, and of glory. The second means thou hast to make use of is to exercise thyself in frequent acts of the love of God, and to accustom thyself to perform all thy actions for the love of God. Lastly, as a third means, thou must earnestly beg for the grace of the love of God in persevering prayer; for there is nothing better pleasing in the sight of God, Who loves thee with an infinite love, than that thou shouldst love Him in return. As He loves thee without any benefit to Himself, do thou also aim at loving Him without looking to thy own advantage, and avail thyself of the fear of punishment and of the hope of reward merely as helps to enable thee to love Him still more.

MONDAY IN THE TWELFTH WEEK AFTER PENTECOST.

Diliges proximum tuum sicut teipsum.—Marc. xii. 31.
Thou shalt love thy neighbour as thyself.

I. CONSIDER that the precept of loving our neighbour goes hand in hand with the precept of loving Almighty God, because they are twin virtues, born at one birth. The love of God is said to be the first commandment, and the love of our neighbour the second, because we ought to love our neighbour on account of God, and God for Himself, and not on account of our neighbour. Anyhow, these two precepts are so clearly linked with one another that thou canst not truly love thy neighbour if thou lovest not God, nor canst thou love God if thou dost not love thy neighbour. Hence these two kinds of love are even more than twins, because they are not only born together but they necessarily die together. How comes it then that thou makest so little account of this commandment?

II. Consider that the love of thy neighbour consists in wishing him well, both in soul and body, and thou wilt attain to the love of thy neighbour as thyself—*sicut teipsum*—only when thou wishest him this twofold class of well-being in the same manner as thou wishest it to thyself. Thou must wish well to thy neighbour inasmuch as he is thy neighbour, that is to say, inasmuch as he is in a position to obtain eternal bliss together with thyself, and therefore thou must wish well to all, great or lowly, countryman or foreigner, good or wicked, friend or foe, because all are capable of being thy companions in paradise. Hence, so long as thou excludest any one of these from thy love there can never be in thy heart a real love of thy neighbour, just as there can be no real faith in a person that denies a single tenet of dogmatic teaching. And yet how many there are who flatter themselves on possessing this love of their neighbour, but who, in regard of more than one individual, omit that well-wishing they are bound by the law of charity to entertain towards all, without exception, and which is of the same obligation as the love of God Himself.

III. Consider that the love of thy neighbour ought to fulfil three conditions: firstly, thou must never for the love of any one consent to any wrongful or unjust demand on his part; because if thou wert to do so, not only dost thou not wish him well, but thou hatest him as the devil does, by co-operating with or leading him into sin. Secondly, thou must love thy neighbour for his own advantage. When, therefore, thou lovest him either for the sake of the pleasure of his conversation, or on account of mutual interests, if thou art not guilty of an infringement of the precept, at any rate, thou dost not fulfil it; because thou dost not love him for his own sake, as thy neighbour and equal, but for thy own sake and for thy own advantage. Thirdly, thou must not wish well to thy neighbour with merely a cold and inactive good-will, but with an efficacious love: *in charitate non ficta*—2 Cor. vi. 6—*in charity unfeigned*. When thou art bent on obtaining what thou believest advantageous to thyself, what pains thou takest! Just the same painstaking oughtest thou to bestow for thy neighbour's welfare, if thou lovest him *tamquam te ipsum—as thyself*. Oh, how few there are on earth who carry out this beautiful precept! How many love their neighbours with a hurtful love; how many with an interested love! and how very many with a love that is rather dead than alive! Reflect awhile what sort of a love is thine.

TUESDAY IN THE TWELFTH WEEK AFTER PENTECOST.

Hic est Filius meus dilectus, in quo mihi bene complacui ; ipsum audite.--Matth. xvii. 5.
This is My beloved Son, in Whom I am well pleased ; hear ye Him.

I. CONSIDER that Jesus is the Son of the Eternal Father, beloved—in the fullest meaning of the word—on His own account, because He is His Son by nature, whereas the souls of the just are children by adoption only, and are beloved on account of Jesus, Who raised them to the dignity of being His brethren and partakers of the divine nature. Wherefore the Father has conferred on Jesus, as a sign of His love, all power, without limit or reserve of any sort, in order that, as we have been raised by Christ to the dignity of children of God by grace, so also we may receive every other gift suitable to our elevated state from Christ. With what tender affection, then, oughtest thou to love this Divine Son, so well beloved by the Eternal Father, and Who has shown such excess of love in thy regard by becoming thy brother, and raising thee to the dignity of child of God! Congratulate Him on this beautiful appellation of well-beloved, and on the glory He enjoys at the right hand of the Father; but endeavour to keep thyself by means of love, in intimate union with Christ, Who has obtained for thee so great a privilege, and from Whom alone thou hast to look for every real good.

II. Consider that when the Eternal Father said, *Hic est Filius meus dilectus, in quo mihi bene complacui—This is My beloved Son, in Whom I am well pleased,* He not only expressed His satisfaction at having poured all the fulness of His Godhead on the humanity of Jesus, but furthermore, He signified that His good pleasure in His Son was the motive of His conferring all intended benefits on mankind, and that through His merits, *proposuit . . . instaurare omnia in Christo*—Eph. i. 9—*He hath purposed . . . to re-establish all things in Christ*—rescuing man from the slavery of sin, and bestowing on him both grace and glory. Now, is it not a matter of great wonder that the Eternal Father should have been pleased to give us poor wretches His beloved Son to be our Redeemer, without any interest of His own or any deserts of ours ? But this is precisely the peculiarity of divine love. Canst thou refuse, then, to love one who loves thee so truly ? Now, if the love of God on thy behalf has shown itself by what He has done for thee, it is but just that thou also shouldst give proof of thy love for God by thy works.

III. Consider that as the Eternal Father has ordained that all our good should come to us through Christ, made man like ourselves, and become our own brother, with what great confidence oughtest thou to betake thyself to Him in thy needs to obtain what thou desirest. But if thou wishest that Christ should hear thee, it is meet that thou also shouldst listen to Him, and carry out what He teaches thee as thy own master. To obtain any favour from an earthly prince petitions must be presented and continued applications made ; but to obtain favours from Christ our Lord, thou hast to open thy ears rather than thy lips—listen rather than entreat : *ipsum audite*—*hear ye Him ;* because if thou payest attention to what He teaches thee by His doctrine and by His example, and executest what He demands of thee, He will render thee deserving of being quickly heard, and will pour out on thee the fulness of His treasures.

WEDNESDAY IN THE TWELFTH WEEK AFTER PENTECOST.

Uniuscujusque opus manifestum erit; dies enim Domini declarabit, quia in igne revelabitur: et uniuscujusque opus quale sit, probabit.—1 Cor. iii. 13.

Every man's work shall be manifest; for the day of the Lord shall declare it, because it shall be revealed in fire: and the fire shall try every man's work, of what sort it is.

I. CONSIDER that there are three days called in Holy Writ in a peculiar sense days of the Lord. The first is that of the universal judgment: *Dies Domini magnus*—Soph. i. 14—*The great day of the Lord.* The second is that of the particular judgment: *Dies Domini sicut fur veniet*—1 Thess. v. 2—*The day of the Lord shall so come as a thief.* The third is the day of trial, which is itself a sort of judgment that comes before the particular judgment, in which Almighty God tries a man to prove if he is faithful. Now, it is of each and all these three days chosen by Almighty God to put man's virtue to the test, that the Apostle says: *Dies Domini declarabit—The day of the Lord shall declare it.* Reflect awhile what sort of appearance thou wilt make on each of these three days—for all three are days on which thou wilt be judged.

II. Consider how on the day of the last judgment, *Uniuscujusque opus manifestum erit—Every man's work shall be manifest.* All thy most hidden actions will then have to be brought to the light under the eyes of the whole world. It is, therefore, of little avail to employ so many wiles and artful ways to hide thy failings and misdeeds from the eyes of the community of which thou art a member. So also at the particular judgment, *Uniuscujusque opus manifestum erit—Every man's work shall be manifest:* inasmuch as the poor man, so overlooked and forsaken now, will be borne away like Lazarus to rest in Abraham's bosom; the rich man, so fawned upon, flattered, and envied, will be dragged off by devils to the depths of hell, without a shadow of hope of there ever being a change of scene for him for all eternity. Canst thou say what part thou wilt sustain in this act of the play? The third judgment day is the day of trial, when Almighty God sends affliction to prove a man and let him know what sort of a man he is. How often does it not happen that thou showest thyself to be quite a different man in time of trial to what thou didst seem to be in time of prosperity! This is precisely the judgment to which Almighty God submits thee when He sends thee any affliction. If under persecution, disgrace, and sickness, thou remainest not firm and faithful, thou wilt never be of the number of those of whom it is written: *Deus tentavit eos et invenit illos dignos se*—Sap. iii. 5—*God hath tried them, and found them worthy of Himself.*

III. Consider that it is said that these three judgments will be brought about by means of fire: *quale sit ignis probabit*—*the fire shall try of what sort it is*—as real gold is known from false gold by the test of fire. On the day of the last judgment the fire that will envelop the whole world will distinguish the elect from the reprobate; the former will receive no hurt from it, while the latter will suffer most terribly. At the particular judgment the fire of purgatory will be the test of the elect, and the fire of hell the test of the reprobate. Lastly, in the judgment-day of trial, it is by means of the fire of suffering and sorrow that the true gold is known from the false, the good from the bad; because the virtuous man resists and stands firm, the bad man yields and gets worse. True it is that naturally enough the good man cannot but feel the smart; but it will not injure his virtue, provided he be faithful, and do not break out into complaints and vexation. If, therefore, thou feelest keenly that trial by which Almighty God is proving thee, be not discouraged, only manage to remain constant, if not by the strength of poor nature, at any rate by the aid of grace.

THURSDAY IN THE TWELFTH WEEK AFTER PENTECOST.

Si separaveris pretiosum a vili, quasi os meum eris.—Jer. xv. 19.

If thou wilt separate the precious from the vile, thou shalt be as My mouth.

I. CONSIDER the first meaning of these words, which is, that if thou divide in thyself what is precious from what is vile, and attribute to Almighty God what thou holdest from Him—which is all that is precious, and to thyself what thou hast of thyself—which is all that is mean and lowly, thou shalt be like unto the mouth of God Himself, because thou wilt thus always speak the truth. All men are styled liars: *Omnis homo mendax*—Ps. cxv. 11—*Every man is a liar;* because every one attributes to himself more than is his own. What hast thou, pray, of thyself that is worth having? Noble extraction, perhaps — talent or knowledge. But all these are gifts of God. Still more are all spiritual blessings the gift of Almighty God; and thus thou hast not of thyself aught but mere sinfulness. Make, therefore, the rightful division, by attributing to God what comes from God, and to thyself what is thy own handiwork. If there is in thee anything at all that is good, admit frankly that it is not thyself that performest it, but Almighty God, since thou never dost anything of thy own self but evil: and thus wilt thou become like unto the mouth of God.

II. Consider the second meaning of the text, which is, that if thou soberly distinguishest whilst in this world between what is worthy of being esteemed and what is worthy of being despised, thou wilt be like unto the mouth of God. In ordinary parlance, he is called happy who lives in the midst of plenty, who holds power over others, who enjoys every comfort: *Beatum dixerunt populum cui hæc sunt*—Ps. cxliii. 15— *They have called the people happy that hath these things.* Almighty God, on the contrary, pronounces those happy who place all their happiness and contentment in Him alone: *Beatus populus cujus Dominus Deus ejus* —Ibid.—*Happy is that people whose God is the Lord.* How far is thy language in accordance with these maxims? Hast thou yet learnt in the religious state to make this proper choice, and set no value upon aught but the grace of God? All other possessions are valuable only in so much as, by laying little store by them, they may help us to acquire a greater supply of grace. How sad it is to hear a religious with the praises of worldly vanities constantly on his lips! If first of all thou assignest to everything its proper value in thy own mind, thou wilt do so also with thy tongue, and become like unto God's own mouth.

III. Consider the third meaning of the text, which is that if thou labourest to extricate souls from the depths of sin, thou wilt separate what is precious from what is vile, and be like unto the mouth of God Himself, because God Almighty will speak by thy mouth. This is the occupation in which Jesus was engaged on earth. He acted as the mouthpiece of His Eternal Father; in the same way were the apostles employed afterwards, and all those who lawfully follow in their footsteps. Do thou also, therefore, endeavour to discharge this same duty with fidelity, in so far as thy position and thy talents allow thee. If thou art not in a position to hold forth from the pulpit, or to betake thyself to distant missions, to draw souls from sin, at least be careful not to overlook occasions of drawing them to God, by wholesome maxims in familiar intercourse, which oftentimes make a deeper impression on the heart than all the loud eloquence of a sermon.

FRIDAY IN THE TWELFTH WEEK AFTER PENTECOST.

Mihi autem absit gloriari, nisi in cruce Domini nostri Jesu Christi, per quem mihi mundus crucifixus est, et ego mundo.—Gal. vi. 14.

But God forbid that I should glory, save in the cross of Our Lord Jesus Christ; by Whom the world is crucified to me, and I to the world.

I. CONSIDER that the apostle might truly have gloried in wisdom or in godliness, or even in the superhuman power of working miracles, and yet he glories in nothing save the cross. Happy, indeed, wouldst thou be if thou wert ever to arrive at a like wisdom, and entertain a proper esteem for so great a glory. No doubt, as a Christian, and as a follower and disciple of the crucified One, thou dost glory in the cross of Christ to a certain extent. But dost thou make it thy glory to be crucified on the cross, after the example of thy divine Master, in poverty, pain, and disgrace? The world constitutes its glory in riches, comforts, and dignities. The glory of the religious that professes to follow Christ must be just the reverse.

II. Consider what is the precise meaning of those words: *Mihi mundus crucifixus est, et ego mundo—The world is crucified to me, and I to the world.* They mean that thy sentiments and likings have to be the reverse of those of the world. If two persons are fastened to the same cross, they necessarily turn their backs upon one another. Just so has it to be in thy case. The world turns its back on thee, and thou must turn thy back on the world. The world laughs thee to scorn because thou carest not for what it desires so eagerly; do thou in thy turn laugh at the world. The world neither loves thee nor esteems thee, and neither do thou love nor esteem it. This is that complete crucifixion of which the apostle made open profession, and which thou must imitate in thy religious state.

III. Consider that in order to actually arrive at this crucifixion, the world must necessarily be dead to thee, and at the same time thou must needs be dead to the world. The world dies to thee when thou renouncest, in effect, all its riches, because it has nothing else wherewith to entice thee; and it therefore becomes, as it were, dead in thy regard. Thou diest to the world when thou renouncest it, still further, in affection, because then thou art not even open to its enticements; and thus thou art, as it were, dead in its regard. When thou didst embrace the religious state, thou didst undertake to profess openly that thou wert dead to the world, and that the world was dead to thee. Reflect now awhile, and see how far thou hast really and truly renounced the world, with its riches, conveniences, and distinctions, not only externally and in effect, but also interiorly and in thy affections. The fact is that thou wilt never arrive at this happy crucifixion, this happy death, except by means of a real and ardent love of Jesus crucified, which alone can loose thee from the possession and affection of all the world can hold out to thee: *Fortis est ut mors dilectio*—Cant. viii. 6—*Love is strong as death.*

SATURDAY IN THE TWELFTH WEEK AFTER PENTECOST.

Deus superbis resistit, humilibus autem dat gratiam.—Jac. iv. 6.

God resisteth the proud, and giveth His grace to the humble.

I. CONSIDER that just as any one withstands a thief that means to take away what belongs to him, whether it be his property, his good name, or his life, so also Almighty God withstands the proud, because they would fain take away what belongs to Him. In sooth, what a barefaced, villainous thief art thou, when thou thinkest thyself to be something by reason of some natural gift or virtuous quality, and lookest down upon others; when thou boastest and pridest thyself on possessing such things as though they were due to thyself, whereas they are all Almighty God's gifts. *Quid habes quod non accepisti?*—1 Cor. iv. 7—*What hast thou that thou hast not received?* And, if they are all His gifts, why wax vainglorious about them? True it is that thou concurrest in thy virtuous acts by means of thy free will; but this concurrence is also itself a gift of God: *Deus est qui operatur in te velle*—Philip. ii. 13—*For it is God Who worketh in you to will.* Thy body concurs in the various operations of sight, motion, and so on, and yet he would be a madman that would attribute such acts to the body and not to the soul that governs it. So also with thy free will, which without the grace of God is like the body without the soul. It will be well with thee, indeed, if thou canst succeed in thoroughly mastering this truth.

II. Consider that Almighty God willingly bestows on the humble His richest graces, because they are trustworthy holders who do not steal or appropriate to themselves, but employ what is given them to the honour of Him Who gave it. He knows that He is placing His treasures in faithful hands, and that all will come back to Himself, just as, according to the Wise Man, the rivers return whence they took their source. Oh, how right it is that Almighty God should be jealous of His glory, for glory belongs to Him alone. When thou humblest thyself, thou merely sayest the truth, and on this account art pleasing to God; when thou art vainglorious thou art a liar, and art therefore hateful to God.

III. Consider what thou hast to do when thou undertakest any difficult work to the honour and glory of Almighty God; thou must seriously and earnestly avow thy own nothingness and utter helplessness, and then be persuaded that for this very reason Almighty God will deign to co-operate with thee, since thy own incapability will make it all the more evident that it is He alone that does the work with so poor and weakly an instrument. With a lively confidence like this, thou wilt overcome every difficulty, because thou wilt have with thee the Almighty: *Erit Omnipotens contra hostes tuos*—Job xxii. 25—*The Almighty shall be against thy enemies.*

THIRTEENTH SUNDAY AFTER PENTECOST.

Decem viri leprosi steterunt a longe, et levaverunt vocem . . . unus autem ex illis regressus est.—Luc. xvii. 12.

There met Him ten men that were lepers, who stood afar off, and lifted up their voice . . . and one of them . . . went back.

I. CONSIDER that all are wont to make recourse to Almighty God for assistance in any public or private calamity. But these lepers who went to Jesus to be made clean, serve thee as a model of the right way to set about making recourse to obtain any favour. In the first place, then, *steterunt a longe—they stood afar off,* deeming themselves unfit to draw nigh by reason of their loathsome disease. *Levaverunt vocem—they lifted up their voice,* thus showing an eager desire of being cured. *Præceptor miserere nostri—Master, have mercy on us—*thus proving at one and the same time the confidence and resignation with which they made their petition. The same conditions oughtest thou to observe when thou beggest help of God in thy various needs. Thou must own thyself to be unworthy to appear in His divine presence, tainted as thou art with the leprosy of so many sins. Thou must, by thy fervent and continued entreaties, show how earnestly thou desirest to be heard, and whilst thou art filled with confidence thou must be resigned to the Will of Almighty God. If the prayers thou puttest up to God are accompanied by real humility, earnest desire, and entire resignation and confidence, thou wilt be sure to obtain a favourable hearing.

II. Consider how these ten lepers obtained the favour they asked of Jesus, that, namely, of being made clean from their leprosy; and that, too, in the very act of going to the priests as had been enjoined them, to give thee to understand that if thou wouldst obtain what thou askest of Almighty God, thou must do what He bids thee. Thy petitions will be presented, and will most certainly be heard, if thy actions correspond to thy prayers. When thou art engaged in praying Almighty God, thou freely recognisest Him as thy supreme Master and the Giver of all good gifts, and avowest thy readiness to be entirely dependent on His bounty. But if in thy daily actions thou obeyest Him not, and art bent on acting after thy own fashion, thy deeds are in open contradiction to thy requests, and thy entreaties lose their power.

III. Consider that among these ten lepers, there was only one, a Samaritan, that came back to thank Our Lord for the benefit conferred on him. *Nonne decem mundati sunt, et novem ubi sunt?—Were not ten made clean? and where are the nine?* We see here our own conduct depicted; how far more anxious we are to betake ourselves to Almighty God for help in our needs, than to show Him our gratitude after we have been freed from our straits. By how many titles thou art bounden to God, and what scanty thanks hast thou hitherto returned Him! Gratitude opens out fresh channels for further and still greater benefits. Hence this Samaritan who *regressus est cum voce magna . . . gratias agens—went back, with a loud voice . . . giving thanks,* in addition to his bodily health, obtained also the health of his soul: *Fides tua te salvum fecit— Thy faith hath made thee whole.*

MONDAY IN THE THIRTEENTH WEEK AFTER PENTECOST.

O Mors, quam amara est memoria tua homini pacem habenti in substantiis suis.—Eccl. xli. 1.

O Death, how bitter is the remembrance of thee to a man that hath peace in his possessions.

I. CONSIDER how pitiable is the condition of a man that has set his heart on the goods of this world—on honours, on comforts, on riches; he cannot think on death, which is as much as to say he cannot think on that for which alone life itself is given him—namely, to get himself ready for that step on which depends an eternity of reward or of punishment. Mark well, too, it is nòt said that to such a one the awaiting of death is bitter, but the very thought of death: *O Mors, quam amara est memoria tua*—*O death, how bitter is the remembrance of thee.* Because such men as these are never on the look-out for death, and never prepare themselves for it; if they chance to hear of, or see under their own eyes, the death at one time of a friend, at another of a townsman, or a relation, who can describe the bitterness of soul that overwhelms them, as they try and find out some reason to promise themselves freedom from a like death? Bewail the sad condition of so great a portion of mankind, and endeavour not to be, thyself, amongst their number.

II. Consider the indescribable dismay of these souls when they find themselves overtaken by death—death which will forcibly tear them asunder, not only from their bodies, but also from all those possessions they have loved equally well with their bodies, and far more than their souls. Ah! then will these wretched beings cry out in despair: *Siccine separas amara mors?*

—1 Reg. xv. 32—*Doth bitter death separate in this manner?*—repeating to themselves *Siccine separas*—dost thou come to tear us away from all our pastimes, from our travels, our hunts, and our banquets? Dost thou wrench from us all our honours, our dignities, and our riches? Oh, how much better these unfortunate souls would have done to have begun long before to wean themselves of their own accord, little by little, from all these things, and with merit to themselves, from which in the end they are forcibly parted by death, to their own great grief and pain!

III. Consider how grateful thou oughtest to be to thy Lord, for having caused thee to leave all earthly goods and to renounce them for His sake, before the arrival of death, by calling thee to the religious life. Earthly possessions are called sometimes by the name of worldly substance, because worldlings think that without them they could not subsist, and they cannot therefore dream of not losing them. But whoever succeeds in coming to the proof that one can live without them, and live contentedly too, oh how far easier it is to undergo this separation. But meanwhile beware, lest after having renounced them in effect, thou go in search of them again in desire, as is not rarely the case. Be still more on thy guard, lest after having renounced the temporal goods of the world outside, thou grow attached to the goods of the religious world inside the cloister, to honours and offices, to thy own little conveniences, all which will again make death painful to thee. If thou desirest that death should be painless for thee, see that there be nothing of which it can deprive thee against thy own will.

TUESDAY IN THE THIRTEENTH WEEK AFTER PENTECOST.

Diligite inimicos vestros.—Matth. v. 44.
Love your enemies.

I. CONSIDER that this is a very important precept in the cloister, where at times disagreements and antipathies exist that give rise to most lamentable disorders. Bear in mind, however, that although in itself it is a difficult task to love an enemy—because it is contrary to the dictates of nature and self-love—yet in practice it is not so difficult after all, because He who imposes this precept gives also the grace to fulfil it, and grace imparts strength to overcome nature and self-love: *Omnia possum in eo qui me confortat*—Philip. iv. 13—*I can do all things in Him Who strengtheneth me.* Reflect how many there are who have gained the victory over nature by the help of God's grace, to such a degree even as to shed their blood for love of Jesus; and wilt not thou manage, by the help of God's grace, to overcome thy own self-love by freely forgiving thy enemy?

II. Consider that in giving this precept, it is not Christ's intention to command thee to love the ill-will of thy enemy, but that thou shouldst love him as thy neighbour, as a fellow-creature made after the image of God, and as having been washed in the blood of Jesus, Who, though thou wert His enemy, went so far as to give His very life-blood for thee. The precept of loving thy enemy obliges thee to love him in a general way, by not excluding him from the ordinary goodwill thou bearest thy neighbour. Thus thou canst not lawfully refuse an enemy those common signs of intercourse which as a rule thou showest to others in a like position; but it is only a matter of counsel to use in his regard those tokens of special love thou art wont to manifest, not indeed to all indifferently, but only to a few, for some particular reason. Reflect, now, how far thou art disposed to show ordinary goodwill when thou comest across some one who dislikes thee, or has done thee some wrong. Do not say that thou hast forgiven him, that is not enough, if thou dost not show it outwardly in thy behaviour. Our Lord says: *In hoc cognoscent omnes, quod discipuli mei estis, si dilectionem habueritis ad invicem*—Joan. xiii. 35—*By this shall all men know that you are My disciples, if you have love one for another.* So that thou must let it be known by all that thou lovest thy enemy, and bearest him no ill-will.

III. Consider that in giving this command, it is furthermore Christ's intention not only that thou shouldst love thy enemy, but, moreover, that thou shouldst do good to him; so that thou be not like the fig-tree of the parable, barren and cursed. These benefactions are of two kinds: the first merely negative, by avoiding giving him offence: *Dilectio proximi malum non operatur*—Rom. xiii. 10—*The love of our neighbour worketh no evil;* the second, positive: *Benefacite his qui oderunt vos*—Luc. vi. 27—*Do good to them that hate you.* The first kind of benefaction is obligatory, the second is of counsel. But if thou refusest a good turn that it would have been thy duty to do him had he not been thy enemy, thou art taking revenge, and thou offerest him an affront. On whom canst thou confer a benefit with greater advantage to thyself, than to an enemy? No kind action performed on behalf of thy neighbour will afford thee so much merit and consolation as a kindness shown to thy enemy for the love of Jesus. It is one of the most certain signs of being among the true children of God: *Ut sitis filii Patris vestri qui in cœlis est*—Matth. v. 45—

That you may be the children of your Father Who is in heaven; and it is a sure proof that thou lovest Almighty God in good earnest. The farther a fire stretches its flames, the more active and fierce it becomes; so also the love of Almighty God becomes more ardent in proportion as it extends itself further in doing kindnesses, for His sake, to an enemy.

WEDNESDAY IN THE THIRTEENTH WEEK AFTER PENTECOST.

Ignoras, quoniam benignitas Dei ad pœnitentiam te adducit?—Rom. ii. 4.
Knowest thou not that the benignity of God leadeth thee to penance?

I. CONSIDER how hurtful a thing it is that thou shouldst not be aware of the reason why Almighty God bears up with thee so patiently, notwithstanding thy great remissness in the duties of a religious life. He tolerates thee, not as though it were out of His power to abandon thee, and let thee run headlong into perdition, but because He does not wish to do so, in the hope that meanwhile thou mayest come to a better mind and amend thy life. Thou seest, therefore, that the kindness of thy Lord not only invites thee to turn over a new leaf and do penance, but, as far as it depends on Him, He presses thee to do so, He urges thee on, He does thee a sweet violence by means of His interior lights and inspirations. How, then, canst thou resist His call, when thou considerest that a Lord of so great majesty puts up with so many affronts at thy hands, merely in order that thou, vile worm that thou art, may not perish? Is not such wonderful goodness enough to melt a heart of stone ? *Expectat Dominus, ut misereatur vestri*—Isa. xxx. 18—*The Lord waiteth that He may have mercy on you.*

II. Consider the dreadful guilt thou incurrest if thou art emboldened to offend thy Lord with greater license because He shows Himself so kind in having patience with thee. Wouldst thou, then, become worse because He still continues to heap favours on thee, and because He has done so in the past—because, for thy sake, He has clothed Himself with thy flesh, and has undergone so many labours and shed so much blood for thee, and has even died on a cross for thee ? And yet if thou reflectest on thy conduct, such would seem to be the consequence thou drawest, inasmuch as the goodness of thy Saviour does not move thee, *ad pœnitentiam—to do penance*, but rather *ad impenitentiam—to harden thy heart* by multiplying thy sins.

III. Consider that the kindness of thy Saviour is an entirely gratuitous bounty on His part, and He is quite at liberty to abandon thee when He chooses. How, then, comes it to pass that thou tremblest not at this thought ? What would become of thee if He left thee to thyself, as thou but too richly deservest ? Has His patience, perhaps, no limits beyond which it will not go ? Or, rather, has it not, forsooth, a fixed number and a certain time prescribed for its exercise in the unsearchable decrees of Providence ? Who can say whether this fixed number, this certain time, be not already reached in thy regard ? The mercy of God is in itself infinite, but in its acts and in its effects it is limited. Be not, then, so foolish as to abuse any longer the goodness of thy Saviour, Who has borne up with thee until now, but do thy best without delay to avail thyself of it, to make amends for faults committed, and to better thy manner of life in conformity with what the religious state thou professest demands of thee.

THURSDAY IN THE THIRTEENTH WEEK AFTER PENTECOST.

Quis poterit habitare de vobis, cum igne devorante ?—Isa. xxxiii. 14.
Which of you can dwell with devouring fire ?

I. CONSIDER that hell-fire is styled a devouring fire, not as though it consumed or destroyed the damned, but to denote its activity and fierceness. Our fire does its work little by little, and it does not possess itself of its fuel all at once; but hell-fire completes its ravages in an instant, and with the same ferocity with which it attacks its prey on its first entrance into hell, continues to devour it for ever, without relenting one degree in its activity. What an appalling lot for the miserable damned soul to have a never-ending abode in such flames. Wert thou condemned to be confined in a prison of which the walls, the pavement, the ceiling, were molten iron, and the atmosphere all flame, what wouldst thou think? What, then, will it be to have a far more searching fire than this burning the very marrow of thy bones, and to become like a mass of red-hot iron, where the iron becomes fire and the fire becomes one with the iron? Wilt thou be so foolish as to put thyself in danger of dwelling for ever in such a woeful abode for the sake of an empty honour, a whim, a momentary pleasure?

II. Consider what would be thy horror hadst thou to enter a den of ferocious wild beasts; and now reflect what it will be to dwell in hell, where the devils are worse than any wild beasts thou knowest of, and are all on fire and mad with rage; nay, even more, each damned soul will itself become all fire, and with its flames prey upon the others—*Ignis devorans*—like so many flaming brands in a huge fire that burn and consume one another. Go now and say, if thou canst, that after all, if thou goest to hell, thou wilt not be there all alone. Thinkest thou it will bring much relief to have many companions in that flaming dungeon?

III. Consider that this fire is called a devouring fire, because it possesses only the burning power of fire, without its illuminating qualities. *Vox Domini intercedentis flammam ignis*—Ps. xxviii. 7—*The voice of the Lord divideth the flame of fire.* Almighty God has created hell-fire with only one half of the properties of our fire: it burns and torments, but neither comforts or enlightens. Ponder, therefore, what would befall thee were it ever thy fate to burn eternally amidst such dreadful darkness. Dost thou, perchance, fondly imagine that persons living like thyself in the religious state are never damned, that it can never be their fate to be burned in the lowest depths of that abyss? A holy friar once told Blessed Giles that Our Lord had allowed him to see hell opened before his eyes, and that he had not seen a single friar there. "Just so," replied Blessed Giles; "thou hast not descried any of thy brethren that are damned because they are buried in the very bottom of hell, on account of their having abused those more especial aids they had in religion to save their souls and to escape that eternity of woe."

FRIDAY IN THE THIRTEENTH WEEK AFTER PENTECOST.

Charitas Christi urget nos .... ut qui vivunt jam non sibi vivant, sed ei qui pro ipsis mortuus est.—2 Cor. v. 14.

The charity of Christ presseth us .... that they who live may not now live to themselves, but unto Him Who died for them.

I. CONSIDER that when Christ died for thee in frightful agony on the disgraceful gibbet of the cross, it was not His only object to repurchase thee from the slavery of hell—a single tear or a sigh would have been enough to effect that—but He most certainly aimed at winning over thy heart in such a way that thou shouldst no longer live for thyself, but wouldst be constrained to live for Him alone. This is what the apostle means when he says: *Charitas Christi urget nos*—*The charity of Christ presseth us*—because it was this same love that would allow him no rest in toiling in the service of his Lord, and in devoting himself, heart and soul, to win back those souls so precious in his sight. How far dost thou experience this holy impulse in thy own heart? If thou hast not yet felt its force, at any rate seek to obtain it according to the requirements of thy state.

II. Consider that the apostle does not say: *Mors Christi urget nos*—*The death of Christ presseth us*, but *Charitas Christi urget nos*—*The love of Christ presseth us*—because although thou oughtest to be touched at the consideration of all that Christ has suffered for thee, much more oughtest thou to be touched by that love which caused Him to endure all that He did suffer. Whatever Christ vouchsafed to undergo for thy salvation is nothing in comparison with what He was willing to suffer had such been His Father's Will; all that sea of shame and suffering was not enough to extinguish the burning flame of His love. If, therefore, what Christ endured for thy sake ought to be sufficient to move thee to the determination of living for Him alone, the consideration of the love with which He endured it ought to constrain thee to do so. His sufferings had a limit, His love had none; and to this very day that love which brought Him down from the bosom of the Eternal Father to clothe Himself with our human flesh and hang on the cross as His own sacrifice for thy ransom—that love maintains itself still in all its ardour and intensity in thy regard. *Christus heri et hodie*—Hebr. xiii. 8—*Jesus Christ yesterday and to-day.*

III. Consider what it is to live for one's self. It means living according to one's own will, for one's own glory and comfort. All this ought to have ceased in thee since Christ has gone so far as to die for thee with so great love; and the reason of this is that if He has actually given His own life of infinite worth for thee, what great thing is it if thou shouldst make up thy mind to give Him thine in return, so lowly in itself and worthy of death? But even though thou dost not go so far as actually to lay down thy life for Him, thou art bound at least to live for Him, that is, to live in order to love Him, and to make others love Him, and to promote His glory to the utmost of thy power.

SATURDAY IN THE THIRTEENTH WEEK AFTER PENTECOST.

Humiliatio tui in medio tui.—Mich. vi. 14.
Thy humiliation shall be in the midst of thee.

I. CONSIDER that if thou wouldst find matter for self-humiliation thou needest not seek it outside of thyself, but within thee—*in medio tui*—*in thy midst.* If thou considerest thyself from without, thou mayest perchance rather wax proud than not, because thou wilt haply behold thyself in some position of authority, applauded, esteemed and loved; but not so if thou lookest well at thyself in thy own interior. It will be quite enough for thee to reflect seriously on what, as a matter of fact, thou hast been, on what thou art, and on what thou wilt be. Each one of these three considerations is of itself quite enough to keep thee humble; apply thyself therefore to whichever of the three thou preferrest.

II. Consider then, the wickedness of thy past life, and in what a deplorable state thou wert when, whilst living in the world, thou hadst fallen into the power of Satan and become his vile slave, and liable to be punished in those flames which thy sins had prepared for thee in hell. Now that thou art in religion we will suppose thee to be already out of such a sad plight: and yet in thy present state reflect how little gratitude thou showest towards Him Who has freed thee from so great evils. How dost thou correspond with the designs of that good God Who has so mercifully called thee to the religious state? See how intent thou art on pandering to thy whims, how vain, unmortified, and impatient thou art, and how prone to even the most shameful sins. Then again as regards the future, canst thou, perhaps, foretell what will become of thee with thy weak and unstable will? If even the columns of the firmament have crumbled away, what will happen to thee who art but a supple reed? may not a violent attack of passion be sufficient to lay thee prostrate? and once laid low, who knows if thou wilt be able to rise again, or how thou wilt die? Surely there is matter here to keep thee humble!

III. Consider that even though thou do possess any good at all, it does not take its rise from thee as its source, but all has come to thee from above—*Desursum est*. The soil of thy own heart is capable of producing nothing of itself but briars; thus, *in medio tui—in thy midst*, thou hast only wherewith to humble thyself. However, this self-humiliation ought not to be merely speculative, but it must be practical, so that in thy own heart thou shouldst foster a low esteem of thyself, and not appropriate to thyself any of that esteem which may come from outside, but give it all back at once to God in thought, in word and in deed.

FOURTEENTH SUNDAY AFTER PENTECOST.

Nemo potest duobus dominis servire.—Matth. vi. 24.
No man can serve two masters.

I. CONSIDER that this saying of the gospel is true for all Christians, but most especially in the case of those religious who would fain serve Almighty God and the world also, which is an impossibility, for *quicumque voluerit amicus esse sæculi hujus, inimicus Dei constituitur*

—Jac. iv. 4—*Whosoever will be a friend of this world, becometh an enemy of God.* Christ has declared war against the world and the world against Christ, nor is it possible for any one to be on good terms or come to an understanding with both the one and the other. This is a truth well worthy of notice, since Christ will not be served by halves; He claims our whole selves. Whosoever, therefore, would give a share of his affections to the world, will serve the world and not Christ. As for thyself, by embracing the religious state thou madest profession of serving Christ, and didst engage to abandon the service of the world. Leave the world then to be served by the friends of the world, and attend only to the service of Jesus Christ, without mixing thyself up with the world, and so become the friend of Jesus Christ, and say to Him —but from thy heart—*Servus tuus sum ego*—Ps. cxviii. 125—*I am Thy servant.*

II. Consider what opposition there is between Christ and the world: Christ wishes that thou shouldst serve Him in poverty, in humiliation, in self-hatred and self-denial. The world, on the contrary, wishes to be served by thee by thy going in pursuit of pleasures and delights, by thy seeking after honour and greatness. How, then, is it possible for the service of Christ to go hand in hand with the service of the world? But though Christ expects thee to embrace His cross, He also at the same time makes it sweet for thee by interior consolations, and by the aids of His Grace, by peace of heart, and by the hope of an eternal recompense; whereas the world holds out promises of pleasures, but really gives only anguish, for it mingles with any advantage it confers such an amount of remorse of conscience that one of its trials alone is enough to embitter all its happiness. Consider any one of thy companions that serves Jesus in good earnest, and thou wilt see how much more contentedly he passes his days with his cross than does another who goes in pursuit of worldly goods.

III. Consider the reward that the world bestows on its followers, and that which Christ bestows on His. After having afflicted and illtreated its followers in this life, the world is the cause of their finding nothing but punishment and fire in the next life. Christ, on the contrary, causes His followers to enjoy in the midst of the crosses of this life, a continual flow of peace and consolation, which softens down all their trials, and in the next world He bestows on them a never-ending kingdom, and so great bliss that they will live for ever, plunged, as it were, in an ocean of every conceivable happiness. Does not, then, Christ's service seem to thee more desirable than that of the world? Abandon, therefore, altogether any engagement with the world, and consecrate thyself to the service of Christ; thank Him for having enabled thee, by means of thy religious vocation, to leave the world in order the better to embrace and practise a closer imitation of Him.

MONDAY IN THE FOURTEENTH WEEK AFTER PENTECOST.

Ibit homo in domum æternitatis suæ.—Eccl. xii. 5.
Man shall go into the house of His eternity.

I. CONSIDER that the house in which thou dwellest is not thy own; it is but a lodging where thou abidest only for a short time. Thy own house will be the grave: *Sepulchra eorum domus illorum in æternum*

—Ps. xlviii. 12—*Their sepulchres shall be their houses for ever;* whence thou shalt not depart until the general destruction of the world, when all that thou now makest so much account of and admirest, on this earth, shall be reduced to ashes. However, the house of thy eternity is not, properly speaking, the grave, for thou wilt not thyself walk into thy grave nor remain there thyself, but it is only thy corpse that will be carried there when it is already beginning to decompose. The real house of thy eternity will be either heaven or hell. Oh, what a vast difference there is between these two abodes! Canst thou tell me which of the two will fall to thy lot? Mayest thou never, please God, have reason to reply: *Infernus domus mea est*—Job xvii. 13—*Hell is my house.*

II. Consider that it is now in thy power to choose for thyself either of these abodes, for every one goes where he lists. *Ecce do coram vobis viam vitæ et viam mortis*—Jer. xxi. 8—*Behold, I set before you the way of life and the way of death.* Wilt thou be so senseless as to choose to go rather to hell than to heaven? But before making such a foolish choice, make up thy mind to ponder seriously on the one hand what it means and what it entails, to have to remain burning in hell in the midst of such fire for an eternity; so that when thousands and millions of ages shall have passed away thy punishment will be only beginning over again. Art not thou bewildered at the consideration of the incomprehensible torments of an eternal hell?—thou that art so faint-hearted and cowardly in enduring the trifling and short-lived pains of this world. On the other hand, raise thy mind's eye to heaven and contemplate the eternal peace and continual joy that each of the blessed enjoys in that abode of bliss. *Lætitia sempiterna super capita eorum*—Isa. li. 11—*Joy everlasting shall be upon their heads*—and after comparing these two so widely differing abodes, choose by all means the one that pleases thee the better.

III. Consider how many there are that toil and exert themselves a great deal more to gain hell than thou needst toil and suffer to gain heaven. What folly, then, it is on thy part, if when it is a question of two such different houses of eternity as are heaven and hell, thou dost not strive to gain possession of heaven, especially when it is to be had with less trouble than many others put themselves to, to purchase hell! Reflect for an instant on the amount of toil that so many people undergo—one to sell his goods, another to satisfy a disorderly passion, and compare it with the hardships of the religious state, and thou wilt quickly see how much lighter is thy burden than theirs. And if still it seems a great hardship to thee to live in the observance of thy rule, and to be subject to the obedience of others, reflect on the eternal torments from which by this means thou settest thyself free; reflect on the eternal rewards thou art laying by for thyself by means of this subjection, and by bearing the cross of religion: in this way thou wilt not feel thy cross so heavy, but it will become light and an object of love.

TUESDAY IN THE FOURTEENTH WEEK AFTER PENTECOST.

Væ vobis divitibus : quia habetis consolationem vestram.
—Luc. vi. 24.
Woe to you that are rich: for you have your consolations.

I. CONSIDER that this most terrible word, *Væ*, not only denotes a dreadful calamity which it at the same time deplores; but it holds out a threat, and foretells its infliction on the rich; not because they steal, not because they oppress the poor, nor because they are given to murder, but because they have their comfort and consolation in this life — *quia habetis consolationem vestram.* And wouldst thou fain envy the greatness of the rich, instead rather of feeling pity and compassion for them? When, therefore, thou beholdest the splendour of their palaces, the magnificence of their equipage and of their suite, do not go admiring them, and thinking them fortunate; but say: *Væ vobis divitibus—Woe to you that are rich!*

II. Consider for what reason it is that the rich deserve thy compassion: it is because the having their consolation here below is the worst possible sign—it is a sign that they will not have it hereafter; as was said to the rich man in the Gospel: *Memento quia recepisti bona in vita tua*—Luc. xvi. 25—*Remember that thou didst receive good things in thy lifetime.* Moreover, this sign has a special significance in the case of the rich: inasmuch as the many extra opportunities their riches afford them of giving vent to their passions, and satisfying the disorderly appetites of corrupt nature, are the occasion of their falling into a great many sins and running headlong to perdition. How far better, then, it is not to have here below the consolation of having one's own way! it is an inviolable law that we cannot enjoy ourselves both in this world and in the next. Oh, then, pour out thy heartfelt thanks to Almighty God, for having drawn thee out of this danger, and caused thee to embrace in holy religion that evangelical poverty, by virtue of which, in proportion as thou hast less of the comforts of this world, thou wilt enjoy a greater abundance of happiness in the next! *Væ vobis divitibus! Beati pauperes —Woe to you rich ones! Blessed are the poor.* What a difference between these two sentences—both of them uttered by the lips of the Uncreated Wisdom Himself!

III. Consider that when Christ called the rich unhappy, He referred to those whose hearts are attached to their riches, and who place their consolation in them as a means of satisfying their every whim. He did not mean that *væ* for those whose hearts are not attached to their riches, and who employ them for such purposes as Almighty God allows or commands. So also when He styles the poor blessed, He meant those that are poor of their own accord—*beati pauperes spiritu*, and not those that are poor against their will, and that love and long after gold. Dost thou practise poverty voluntarily, or is thy heart attached to gold, and dost thou envy those that possess it? If thou art poor against thy will, that dreadful threat of Our Lord—*Væ vobis*—is more applicable to thee than to many wealthy Christians who live in the world with their affections more detached from riches than thou who art in the cloister, and who in order to have thy own conveniences and comforts, lovest and seekest after money in ways unworthy of thy profession. If such be thy condition, thou art truly to be pitied: the words that Christ addressed to Judas may well be applied to thyself: *Melius erat tibi si natus non fuisses* —it had been better for thee that thou hadst never been born to the religious life at all; for thou wilt not enjoy either the reward that is promised to the poor in the next world, or the consolations of the rich in this.

WEDNESDAY IN THE FOURTEENTH WEEK AFTER PENTECOST.

Confiteor tibi, Pater, Domine cœli et terræ, quia abscondisti hæc a sapientibus et prudentibus, et revelasti ea parvulis.—Luc. x. 21.

I confess to Thee, O Father, Lord of heaven and earth, because Thou hast hidden these things from the wise and prudent, and hast revealed them to little ones.

I. CONSIDER what was the subject-matter of this outpouring of praise and thanksgiving that Christ made to His heavenly Father. It was that He had hidden from the wise ones of this world those wonderful truths and doctrines which regard the intellect, and which they proudly turn to scorn, because they are above their intellectual capacity ; and also because He had hidden from the prudent ones of this world those truths and doctrines which regard the will, and which they arrogantly despise because they are at variance with their own crooked views. Moreover, He thanks and praises His heavenly Father for having discovered these speculative and practical truths to the humble and lowly, who willingly and eagerly embrace them. Learn, hence, what great good accrues from the practice of humility in the school of Christ ; and, on the other hand, what injury pride inflicts. True wisdom, real prudence, such as is acquired in the school of Christ, is nothing else but Christian humility—it consists in becoming one of Christ's beloved little ones ; not indeed by lack of common sense, but by absence of guile. Many a pious old woman will be found in heaven to have had more real wisdom than an Aristotle or a Tacitus ; inasmuch as such a one will have known what was her last end, and will have succeeded in attaining it. Reflect, meanwhile, how necessary it is for thee to acquire that humble simplicity which is opposed to that vain self-conceit, which is in reality the most foolish and hurtful of all ignorance.

II. Consider in what manner God hides His truths and His teaching from the proud and reveals them to the humble. He reveals them to the humble by bestowing on them special lights and great penetration to know and appreciate them. He hides them from the proud by refusing them any such special lights, and by allowing them just that amount of light which would suffice to arrive at a knowledge of them if they applied themselves in good earnest, and is enough to render them inexcusable. This is the reason why Christ praises and thanks His Eternal Father, for having showed His mercy towards the humble and His justice towards the proud. Oh, what great reason hast thou, therefore, to keep thyself humble! Of thyself thou art not able to perform a single action that is worth anything, unless God Almighty deals with thee mercifully in bestowing on thee that light and special help He is wont to give to the humble, and to refuse to the proud; but which He is not bound in justice to bestow on thee.

III. Consider that Our Lord in this instance calls His Father by the joint title of Father and Lord: *Pater, Domine cœli et terræ*—*Father, Lord of heaven and earth.* He styles Him Lord on account of the justice which He exercises towards the proud, and Father on account of the mercy He displays towards the humble. *Deus superbis resistit*—1 Pet. v. 5—*God resisteth the proud* in His character of Lord and Master; *humilibus autem dat gratiam*—*but to the humble He giveth grace,* in His character of tender Father. If thou desirest to find in Him the kindness of a loving Father in all thy needs, thou must have humble and confiding recourse to Him, just as the little child runs to the arms of its parent.

THURSDAY IN THE FOURTEENTH WEEK AFTER PENTECOST.

Si non in timore Domini tenueris te instanter, cito subvertetur domus tua.—Eccl. xxvii. 4.

Unless thou hold thyself diligently in the fear of the Lord, thy house shall quickly be overthrown.

I. CONSIDER what an amount of toil and labour is requisite to build up a spiritual edifice: how many acts must be elicited of self-denial, of obedience, and of humility, as well as of mortification and penance! And yet this edifice, the result of so many years' patient toil, and of so oft-endured sufferings, may fall to the ground at a moment's notice. One single mortal sin, though in thought only, is enough to work the mischief; and if at such a conjuncture Almighty God should allow death to overtake thee, or did not come to thy aid with an abundance of grace to raise thee up again, it is all over with thee. Alas, how many noble structures far more beautiful than thine, have been utterly ruined in this way! Reflect on the terrible falls of so many souls who at one time were so fervent! How justly, then, mayest thou not fear for thyself, who hast not wrought anything like the good that they did!

II. Consider what is the origin of so formidable a danger. It arises from the fact that Almighty God can at any moment, and without doing thee any wrong, deprive thee of that especial assistance of His grace, which thou needest continually in order not to fall into mortal sin. Whatever may be the amount of good thou hast done in the past, thou canst never place Almighty God under any obligation not to refuse thee that fresh supply of grace of which thou hast need at every successive moment in order to persevere in virtue. Thus perseverance is a gratuitous gift of God, not only with reference to the end of life, but to each moment of it : it is a gift He can refuse without inflicting any wrong on thee, since He is not bound to thee by any benefits thou hast conferred on Him ; on the contrary, it is He that has conferred numberless favours on thee, for which thou hast made no other return than ingratitude. Oh, how humble and fearful these truths ought to keep thee !

III. Consider that, in the midst of such great danger, thy safety lies in a constant fear ; and just as one who has a weak head, and has to pass over a very narrow bridge, beneath which rushes a roaring torrent, holds the hand of his guide tight, and keeps close to him, so also must thou cling fast to the fear of Almighty God by keeping constantly before thy eyes the need thou hast of His assistance, and thou must be ever earnestly begging Him for it, because although perseverance is a gratuitous gift of God, it is a gift that every one will of a surety obtain, if he only asks for it as he ought. The prayers of some are granted soon, those of others not till later—according to His own good Will ; and as thou dost not know how long it will be before He will grant thy petition, for this very reason thou canst not be certain of obtaining perseverance, however much thou hast prayed for it hitherto. However, cease not to beg for it earnestly : if once thou leavest off asking for it, it will be a bad sign for thee.

FRIDAY IN THE FOURTEENTH WEEK AFTER PENTECOST.

Quos prescivit et prædestinavit conformes fieri imaginis Filii sui.—Rom. viii. 29.

Whom He foreknew, He also predestinated to be made conformable to the image of His Son.

I. CONSIDER that the eternal Father sent His own divine Son to clothe Himself here on earth with our flesh, chiefly for this purpose—that He might serve as a model for us to recopy in our own lives; because all our perfection consists in reproducing in ourselves the holiness of the Son of God, in making ourselves living images of Jesus Christ. Every Christian is bound to model his conduct on this divine pattern, if he would find himself in the number of the elect; but with far greater reason is every religious so bound, because in his freedom from the entanglements of the world and its crooked maxims, he makes open profession of being a nearer and closer follower of Jesus. How far hast thou striven hitherto to form thy conduct on the example of Jesus? Canst thou truly say, with holy Job, *Vestigia ejus secutus est pes meus*—Job xxiii. 11—*My foot hath followed his steps?* God forbid that thou shouldst be of the number of those that deliberately turn their backs upon Him!

II. Consider in what thou hast to imitate Jesus most especially: it is in all that Jesus constantly professed from His birth to His death—poverty, suffering, contempt. During the thirty-three years He dwelt on earth He did not make it His constant practice either to teach or preach or cure the sick or work miracles; but He did continuously live in poverty, suffering and scorn. *Pauper sum ego et in laboribus a juventute mea*

—Ps. lxxxvii. 16—*I am poor and in labour from my youth.* To what extent art thou attached to these three inseparable companions of Jesus Christ ? How far dost thou go in search of them ? or in what spirit dost thou receive them when thou comest across them on occasion of feeling some practical effect of holy poverty, or hast to suffer some malady, or hast received some injury or affront ? These are the lines, these the colours best adapted for reproducing in thyself a true picture of Jesus—*conformes fieri imaginis Filii sui—to be made conformable to the image of His Son.*

III. Consider in what this imitation of Christ consists. It may perchance appear to thee to be an undertaking above thy strength to copy in thyself the virtues of Christ; but be not alarmed, because thou art not expected to equal Him, but to resemble Him, by following Him at least from afar; so that of thee it may be said as it was of Ezechias : *Adhæsit Domino, et non recessit a vestigiis ejus*—4 Reg. xviii. 6— *He stuck to the Lord, and departed not from His steps.* Neither art thou expected to imitate Him in everything, but only in so far as thy state of life demands it. All the faithful are members of the mystical body of Christ : *Unum corpus sumus in Christo*—Rom. xii. 5 —*We are one body in Christ.* Now just as each member of our body has different functions to fulfil—the eyes one function, the hands another, and the feet another —*omnia membra non eumdem actum habent—all the members have not the same office*—so also thou hast to emulate Jesus only in those works which are in accordance with the requirements of thy own religious order, in the observance of thy rule and in obedience, in poverty and mortification, in the diligent discharge of thy particular office or employment, endeavouring thus to liken thyself to thy divine model : *conformes fieri imaginis Filii sui—to be made conformable to the image of His Son.*

SATURDAY IN THE FOURTEENTH WEEK AFTER PENTECOST.

Sedebit populus meus in pulchritudine pacis, et in tabernaculis fiduciæ, et in requie opulenta.—Isa. xxxii. 18.

My people shall sit in the beauty of peace, and in the tabernacles of confidence and in wealthy rest.

I. CONSIDER that the favoured souls of whom Isaias here speaks, are those that by dint of constantly fighting against, and mastering their own wills, have at length arrived at the enjoyment of self-command without there being further need of conflict : *sedebit in pulchritudine pacis*—*My people shall sit in the beauty of peace.* Peace is defined, *tranquillitas ordinis*—*the calm of good order;* and it is He only that has obtained the mastery over his passions who is in possession of this well-ordered state of soul, because he is well-ordered with regard to his neighbour, whom he envies not, with whom he quarrels not, over whom he has no pretensions, and with whom he is able to live in peace. He is well-ordered in his own regard, because his appetites are subservient to right reason. Lastly, he is well-ordered with regard to God, because he submits himself wholly and entirely to His will. Oh, thrice happy wilt thou be, if thou canst ever attain this lovely peace, by the mastery over thy passions.

II. Consider that by means of this command over thyself thou wilt be enabled not only to live in peace, but thou wilt find thyself at the hour of death *in tabernaculis fiduciæ*—*in the tabernacles of confidence;* that is to say, in the wounds of thy Saviour, experiencing in thy soul a degree of confidence which will be proportionate to the reverential fear thou hast cultivated in life. Thou wilt then realise how impossible it will be for so good a Father to abandon thee in that hour of need, and how He will lovingly screen thee from the assaults of thy foes in the safe recesses of His sacred wounds, just as a dove in the holes of the rocks is safe from the aim of the huntsman—*columba in foraminibus petræ*—Cant. ii. 14. Thus, although thou be not entirely safe so long as thou hast the breath of life in thee, thou wilt at the last hour be full of confidence in the merits of Jesus.

III. Consider that as a sequel to the peace enjoyed in life and the confidence experienced in death, thou wilt then take up thy abode *in the wealthy rest* of Paradise—*in requie opulenta*. Then will thy desires be fully realised, and thou wilt be satiated with that same abundance which is in God Himself. For just as Almighty God has no need of anything outside Himself, so also thou wilt not stand in want of aught outside thyself, because thou wilt possess God Himself, with the certainty of never losing Him. But if thou wouldst attain this state of rest, so truly full of wealth and enjoyment, thou must beware of sitting down by the wayside before the proper time. If thou desirest peace, war must needs be waged beforehand, by bringing thy passions into subjection, and by mortifying thy whims and inclinations. If thou desirest confidence at the hour of death, it must necessarily be preceded now by a wholesome fear; and this fear has to consist in a lifelong and earnest avoidance of all that is displeasing to Him on Whom thou wilt then call to defend thee, and in oft-repeated commendations of thyself to His mercy. If thou desirest rest after death, toil and labour must needs prepare the way now, by devoting thyself wholly and entirely to the service of God, until such time as thou wilt be summoned *to rest from thy labours* : *ut requiescas a laboribus tuis*—Apoc. xiv. 13.

FIFTEENTH SUNDAY AFTER PENTECOST.

Defunctus efferebatur filius unicus matris suæ.—Luc. vii. 12.
A dead man was carried out, the only son of his mother.

I. CONSIDER that it is not without some mysterious meaning that the Gospel history contains the narrative of Christ's raising to life three dead people all in different stages of life : one a child, the daughter of the ruler of the synagogue, another a youth, the son of the widow of Naim, the third a grown-up man, the brother of Mary and Martha. By this thou art given to understand that death has no regard to age and makes no exception of rank, but it stalks along armed with a sword and a bow and arrows : with the sword it strikes down manhood, which is nearer to its reach, and with the bow and arrows it lays low youth that believes itself out of its reach. *Gladium suum vibrabit, et arcum suum tetendit*, says David, Ps. vii. 13—*He will brandish his sword, he hath bent his bow.* Therefore be ready for death whatever be thy age, and inasmuch as young and old are daily dying on every side of thee, when they least expectedst it, do be persuaded of the fact, that the same thing will happen to thee. Hast thou never heeded the warning thy Lord gives thee in the Gospel ? *Estote parati, quia qua hora non putatis, Filius hominis veniet*—Luc. xii. 40—*Be you then also ready, for at what hour you think not, the Son of Man will come.*

II. Consider how by these three dead bodies raised to life by Christ are represented three classes of souls all dead to grace by sin, yet raised again to life by Christ. By the dead child those souls are shadowed forth that sin through ignorance and natural frailty ; the dead body of the young man represents the fall of those who sin through the impulse of violent passion ;

whilst Lazarus is a figure of those who fall into sin through the malice of their own wills. Which of these three do thy own falls and sins resemble? For although it is to be believed that thy religious state is a sufficient safeguard against thy falling into mortal sins, yet is it but too probable that thou fallest daily into venial faults. Ponder therefore a while and see whether these daily falls of thine be the effect of natural frailty, or of the impetuosity of thy passions, or whether they be not rather committed with full deliberation and proceed from the perversity of thy own will; because, although all these faults be venial, they are not all equally hurtful. Even the saints fall at times through frailty; the violence of passions not thoroughly subdued will frequently cause the imperfect to slip, but in the case of those whom Our Lord allows to fall even into mortal sin, it is due to their own malice and perversity of will.

III. Consider that Christ would not allow any weeping on the occasion of the child's death, nor on the occasion of the young man's death either. His words to the widowed mother were: *Noli flere—Weep not*; whereas at the death of Lazarus, not only did He allow the two sisters, Martha and Magdalene, to weep, but He wept Himself: *Lacrymatus est Jesus—* Joan. xi. 35—*And Jesus wept.* The reason is to be found, as already stated, in the fact that in the person of Lazarus those are denoted who fall into sin through malice and with their eyes wide open. For one that lives amidst the dangers of the world, without the especial lights and helps of grace, and who falls into grievous sin, it will be much easier to find mercy and forgiveness; but it will not be so easy a matter in the case of a religious that sins grievously, fortified as he is by so many interior lights and external helps; the fall of such a one is most deplorable and execrable to the whole court of heaven.

MONDAY IN THE FIFTEENTH WEEK AFTER PENTECOST.

Si præstes animæ tuæ concupiscentias ejus, faciet te in gaudium inimicis tuis.—Eccl. xviii. 31.

If thou give to thy soul her desires, she will make thee a joy to thy enemies.

I. CONSIDER that thy mortal enemies, the evil spirits, are never better pleased than when they see that thou art prone to gratify thy own natural inclinations, and to yield to the vicious impulses of thy own will; because they well know that thou wilt be led on, as by an unbridled horse, to the brink of the precipice, and therefore they are filled with malicious glee when they see thee letting go the reins, and taking no heed of where thou art going. It behoves thee therefore, to accustom thyself to deny thy own will even in what is lawful, otherwise thou wilt very soon be gratifying it in what is unlawful.

II. Consider that this duty of self-denial is imposed on thee without limitation. Fasting, discipline, and prayer have each their own proper times assigned to them; but the denial of thy own will has no fixed time, it must be practised at all times and in everything. Thy will is like a vicious horse, that cannot be trusted without a curb. Thou must constantly hold it in, lest it should start off from the right path and throw thee over some precipice.

III. Consider that thou must not lose courage, as though this duty of self-denial were too much for thee, because by accustoming thyself to it, it will daily become easier and easier. It is like breaking in a restive horse. At first it is difficult to approach or manage, or guide, especially if it has been allowed its liberty for any length of time : *Equus indomitus evadet durus*—Eccl. xxx. 8—*A horse not broken becomes stubborn.* But so soon as it has become accustomed to the bridle it is no longer any trouble to manage or guide it. Thou wilt experience the same thing with thy will, if only thou acquire the habit of contradicting it at all times, and on every occasion that presents itself, whether in regard to thy superiors, equals, or inferiors. As soon as thy will perceives that it cannot get what it wants, it will demand of thee only what it knows it has a right to seek for.

TUESDAY IN THE FIFTEENTH WEEK AFTER PENTECOST.

Abundantius opportet observare nos ea quæ audivimus, ne forte perfluamus.—Hebr. ii. 1.
We ought more diligently to observe the things which we have heard, lest perhaps we should let them slip.

I. CONSIDER that these words apply to all Christians, who all lie under the obligation of observing the law of the Gospel with greater perfection than the Jews were bound to observe the law of Moses. The Mosaic law aimed at the attainment of earthly goods, and was extremely burdensome both by reason of the hard precepts it contained and the little help it was capable of conferring. The law of the Gospel, on the contrary, is directed to the attainment of heavenly goods : it is a yoke that is far easier to bear, and confers far greater aids by the grace it imparts. Since, therefore, thou enjoyest the happy lot of having been born in a Christian country, and findest thyself in the enjoyment of so grand a law, and of such abundance of grace, reflect awhile on the stricter obligtion thou art under of observing it, and how far more grievous thy condemnation will be, if thou failest to observe it.

II. Consider that this sentence of the Apostle has a still closer application in the case of those chosen Christians who have sequestered themselves from the world, and whose sole business is the practice of virtue and the fulfilment of the evangelical counsels. Consequently it behoves thee to observe perfectly all that thy Divine Lord demands of thee by the interior lights and the holy inspirations which He accompanies with so many consolations and devout desires, in order to enable thee to become perfect. Wherefore if thou neglectest these gifts and lights of His, He will abandon thee. *Erudire Jerusalem, ne forte recedat anima mea a te*—Jerem. vi. 8—*Be thou instructed, O Jerusalem, lest my soul depart from me.* Bear in mind that ordinary holiness is not enough for a religious: thou art studying in the school of perfection, and, therefore, thou art bound to avail thyself of the opportunity, otherwise thou wilt be lost.

III. Consider that these words have a still more immediate application in the case of those who are earnestly engaged in labouring for the good of their neighbour; because, of all others, these have most need of being particular in the perfect observance of all that Our Lord demands at their hands—otherwise they run the risk of losing themselves whilst they go in search of others. If thou shouldst happen to be of the number of these, take care to disburse the gifts of thy Lord on behalf of thy neighbour in such a manner that thou keep back a goodly proportion for thy own benefit. See that from time to time thou withdraw thyself into thy own heart, and think about thy own business, because it will avail thee simply nothing to gain the whole world, if by this gain thou shouldst lose thy own soul: *Quid prodest homini, si mundum universum lucretur, animæ vero suæ detrimentum patiatur*—Matth. xvi. 26—*What doth it profit a man, if he gain the whole world, and suffer the loss of his own soul?*

WEDNESDAY IN THE FIFTEENTH WEEK AFTER PENTECOST.

Dicebat ad omnes: Qui vult venire post me, abneget semetipsum, tollat crucem suam quotidie et sequatur me.—Luc. ix. 23.

*He said to all: If any man will come after Me, let him deny himself, and take up his cross **daily and follow Me**.*

I. CONSIDER that if Christ has universally promulgated and called the attention of all Christians to this great sentence of His Gospel, which thou hast just heard, about self-denial and mortification—*dicebat ad omnes*, etc—in a far more especial manner are these words addressed to every religious, because every religious professes to attend to perfection, and to be the intimate disciple and faithful follower of Christ. Now the fact of being a true disciple and companion of Our Lord does not consist in merely listening to His teaching and wearing His livery, but it consists, as thou hast just heard, in denying oneself, in carrying the cross, and in following Him step by step on the blood-stained track of Calvary. This truth is well worthy of thy serious attention. Take notice, moreover, that Christ says, *Qui vult*—*If any man wish*—because He expects that thou shouldst follow Him with a good will and of thy own accord, as, indeed, the invitation of so good a Lord deserves to be received, Who for love of thee has gone so far as to die on the gibbet of the Cross. Doubtless in thy religious state thou hast much to suffer, and thou must needs mortify thyself in various ways; but take heed if, and how far, thou bearest up under these crosses with a good will and for love of the Crucified One, because this it is that pleases thy Saviour. Remark also that He does not say *ferat crucem—let him bear his cross*—but *tollat crucem—let him take up his cross*—to denote that if thou wouldst be a true religious—a real follower of His, thou must embrace thy cross with cheerfulness and readiness, and not wait until it is forced on thy shoulders—as Simon of Cyrene did—nor drag it after thee like a dead weight. Oh, truly happy art thou, if thou carriest thy cross cheerfully: thou wilt merit more and suffer less!

II. Consider that this duty of embracing and carrying the cross with alacrity, is not to be for thee the occupation of merely a few days, or on certain occasions, but of every day and on all occasions. *Tollat crucem suam quotidie.* By the cross is to be understood any contrariety, suffering or trial whatsoever; and in the same way as crosses of this sort lie thick in the way of seculars living in the world, so also they are not wanting for religious, in the shape either of obedience, observance of rule, disappointments, or interior trials of mind and external ailments of body. In these and such like trials does thy cross more particularly consist, and thou must embrace it of thy own accord on all occasions: not like the hair-shirt, and discipline, and other instruments of mortification which sometimes thou puttest into requisition and at other times layest by. *Tollat crucem suam quotidie.* If thou actest in this manner thou wilt heap up for thyself great treasures of merit and of glory!

III. Consider that there is no greater obstacle to the cheerful and willing carrying of one's cross at all times, than self-love. The first thing, consequently, that Christ demands of thee, is the entire abnegation of thyself: *abneget semetipsum—let him deny himself.* And what, pray, is the meaning of denying one's self? It means that thou hast to contradict thy own inclinations, and go against the unruly cravings of nature, looking at and treating them as enemies, because thou hast but too often had occasion to find them out to be treacherous. Thou wilt never succeed in entirely uprooting these vicious inclinations, and therefore does Christ enjoin on thee to keep them under—*abneget semetipsum*—which is as much as to say, never to allow them to get the upper hand of thee, or as S. Paul says—*Non regnet peccatum in vestro mortali corpore, ut obediatis concupiscentiis ejus*—Rom. vi. 12—*Let not sin*—that is to say, concupiscence—*reign in your mortal body, so as to obey the lusts thereof.* If thou dost this, thy cross will prove to be a light one, and thou wilt embrace it cheerfully, and follow in Jesus' footsteps.

THURSDAY IN THE FIFTEENTH WEEK AFTER PENTECOST.

Cum consummaverit homo, tunc incipiet.—Eccl. xvii. 6.
When a man hath done, then shall he begin.

I. CONSIDER the first meaning of these words which is, that in the religious life thou hast always to look upon thyself as a beginner, and keep alive that fervour with which thou didst begin to serve God, by keeping fresh in thy mind those eternal truths which were the foundation of thy spiritual edifice. Thus, although thou wilt from day to day make progress in perfection, it will always be by the same road as that on which thou madest thy starting. Do not imagine, as some have done, that thou wilt ever arrive at a state of impeccability, or that thou hast already got far enough on the road to perfection : but it behoves thee to be ever on thy guard against sin, with a holy fear of God, and to be given to works of penance. If such be not thy line of conduct, thou wilt begin when advanced in years to fall into faults from which thou wert free in thy youth.

II. Consider a second meaning of this text, which is, that no sooner hast thou completed one undertaking in the service of Almighty God, than thou must at once set to work on another without losing a moment in idleness. Art thou desirous of enjoying vigour and health of spirit ?—be always occupied, because idleness is the origin of all evil. Thinkest thou, forsooth, that thou wilt not have to render to Almighty God a strict account of all the time thou wastest and hast wasted ? Thou wilt thoroughly grasp this truth on thy death-bed, because when time begins to fail thee, thou wilt then see how much good thou mightest have done during life. Wherefore, as the Wise man says, *Fili conserva tempus*—make most of thy time, passing from one good work to another; from prayer to active employment; from mental labour to manual labour, without losing time in idle gossip and useless laughter.

III. Consider the third meaning of these words—*Cum consummaverit homo, tunc incipiet*—Eccl. xvii. 6—*When a man hath done, then shall he begin*. It is this : when thou hast made great progress in the spiritual life, then thou wilt begin to perceive that thou art only beginning. Thou mayest perchance have a sort of half idea that thou art very perfect indeed, because thou art but a beginner. When thou art really making progress thou wilt see and know that thou art not at all what thou at present imaginest thyself to be. The higher a traveller climbs the mountain side, the further does he behold the real summit recede behind the far distant hills, whereas at first starting he believed that a few steps would find him there. So also in thy own case, the greater the progress thou makest in perfection, the further wilt thou acknowledge thyself to be from the true spirit of mortification and self-denial, from real humility and obedience, from thorough resignation and conformity to the will of God: then wilt thou also exclaim, as David did—*Nunc cœpi*—Ps. lxxvi. 11—*Now I have begun*—and this will be the best possible sign that thou hast made some way in the spiritual life.

FRIDAY IN THE FIFTEENTH WEEK AFTER PENTECOST.

An nescitis . . . quoniam non estis vestri? empti enim estis pretio magno.—1 Cor. vi. 19.
Know you not . . . that you are not your own, for you are bought with a great price.

I. CONSIDER how true it is that thou art not thy own, inasmuch as thy Saviour has purchased thee at the cost of His own blood. Reflect, then, what a wrong thou doest Him when thou wouldst dispose of thyself as best pleases thee. Thy eyes are not thy own, thy ears are not thine, thy tongue is not thine, and so on with thy whole person, because thou belongest entirely to that loving Lord Who bought thee. What shadow of a doubt is there, then, but that it is thy plain duty never to employ any part of thy being except on His behalf to Whom thou belongest?

II. Consider the great benefit thy Saviour has done thee in purchasing thee. Had He, perchance, any need of thee? Was He, perhaps, not equally happy without thee? Ah, it was for thy benefit alone that He ransomed thee from the slavery of Satan; and whereas it was sufficient, to effect this, to have given one single drop of His blood, He has chosen to give it all, and to offer up His very life in sacrifice, in the midst of frightful torture. If thou wert to see a person purchase a jewel for ten thousand pieces of gold, although he might have had it for one thousand, wouldst thou not at once exclaim: "What a determined will that man has to be possessed of the jewel!" Yet greater far was the yearning that Jesus had to set thee at liberty for thy own good, from the power of Lucifer; and wilt thou refuse to be His after He has ransomed thee with so much love, and at so great a cost?

III. Consider that if thou wouldst correspond with this refinement of thy Saviour's love, thou must employ and devote thy whole self to His honour, without looking to thy own individual interests. When thou hast to move about, for love of God, say to thy wearied feet, To whom do you belong? So also with thy eyes and ears, when thou art required to mortify them for love of God: repeat the same question to thy tongue and all thy other faculties, internal and external, reminding them that they are not their own masters: *Non estis vestri; empti enim estis pretio magno*—*You are not your own, for you are bought with a great price.* For this same reason must thou jealously guard thy soul from all danger, because it belongs to Jesus. Thou art, generally speaking, told to be in earnest about saving thy soul, because it is a question of the future of an immortal soul, which is thy own; but on the present occasion I would fain say the contrary, and that thou oughtest to think seriously about thy soul's salvation, because it is not thine, but belongs to Jesus, Who purchased it for Himself. This is the highest of all motives for striving to avoid hell.

SATURDAY IN THE FIFTEENTH WEEK AFTER PENTECOST.

Nolite gloriari et mendaces esse adversus veritatem. Non est enim ista sapientia desursum descendens, sed terrena, animalis, diabolica.—Jac. iii. 15.

Glory not, and be not liars against the truth; for this is not wisdom descending from above, but earthly, sensual, devilish.

I. CONSIDER that the teaching of worldlings who place their happiness in riches, pleasures, and honours, is the teaching of a lying wisdom styled by S. James earthly, sensual, and devilish. The wisdom that places happiness in riches is earthly, because it has for its object the goods of this earth. That which makes happiness consist in sensual pleasures, is animal-like and sensual, because it has for its end the comfort of the body; whilst that which constitutes happiness in honour is diabolical, because it aims at the same end as Lucifer had in view. None of these, therefore, can be true wisdom, since that only is real wisdom which recognises Almighty God as its ultimate end, and orders all things to the attainment of God, in conformity with the laws laid down by Himself.

II. Consider why each of these three sorts of wisdom is false and unworthy of the name. Earthly wisdom makes a rash and lying promise to render the heart happy by means of riches, which are by no means good in themselves as an ultimate end, but merely as a means—and an uncertain means too—for oftentimes *Conservantar divitiæ in malum domini sui*—Eccl. v. 12—*Riches are kept to the hurt of the owner.* Sensual wisdom promises to render its clients happy by means of the gratification of the senses, and not by means of intellectual and spiritual pursuits, whereas the soul is the nobler part of man, and this sort of wisdom would please the servant rather than the master. Lastly, that wisdom, which S. James calls devilish, promises to render its devotees happy by means of honours, whereas honour does not constitute a man's excellence, but is only a sign of its previous existence; and therefore honours are mere tokens—oftentimes fallacious and senseless—and very unlike the honour that is conferred by Almighty God, Who distributes His favours only in proportion to sterling merit.

III. Consider that the only true wisdom is that of Christ, which leads man to the attainment of his end, which is real happiness—the bliss of heaven. The more a soul is detached from riches, pleasures, and honours, the more is it disengaged from all that hampers it from freely tending to its end, to which at the same time it draws nigher by means of merit in this life and of reward in the next. Indeed, not unfrequently the saints begin to reap their reward even in this life, as a presage of the bliss that awaits them. But this real and sublime wisdom is to be learnt only in the school of Christ, Who brought it down with Him from heaven, and taught it with His Divine lips, when, amongst other axioms, He laid down *Beati pauperes spiritu*—Matth. v. 3—*Blessed are the poor in spirit.*

What, then, must thou do to acquire this wisdom? Thou must generously turn a deaf ear to the wisdom of the world, and make all the progress thou canst in the school of Christ, entreating Him perseveringly to make thee learned with His own divine wisdom, since through His mercy He has numbered thee amongst His chosen disciples.

SIXTEENTH SUNDAY AFTER PENTECOST.

Recumbe in novissimo loco . . . quia omnis qui se exaltat, humiliabitur, et qui se humiliat exaltabitur.— Luc. xiv. 11.

Sit down in the lowest place . . . because every one that exalteth himself shall be humbled, and he that humbleth himself shall be exalted.

I. CONSIDER this maxim of real humility which Christ here teaches thee: *Recumbe in novissimo loco—Sit down in the lowest place.* Thou oughtest to put thyself in the lowest place in thy own heart and in thy own estimation, looking upon every one else as superior to thyself. And in order that this practice may not prove too difficult for thy pride, reflect attentively on thy many shortcomings, both of nature and disposition, on thy ingratitude after so many benefits received from Almighty God, and on thy sins, on account of which thou hast deserved to be trampled under foot by the demons. With how good reason mayest not thou exclaim, as David did: *Ero humilis in oculis meis—* 2 Reg. vi.—*I will be little in my own eyes.* Yet hitherto thou hast always done just the reverse, closing thy eyes to thy own defects, sins, and pride, and keeping them open only to the faults of others. It is no wonder, therefore, that instead of placing thyself in the lowest grade in thy own opinion, thou shouldst be so apt to prefer thyself to others. Ah, how many there are amongst thy brethren whom thou thinkest, perhaps, inferior to thyself, and yet, before God, are at this present time superior to thee by far, and will be still more so in the next world ?

II. Consider that thou must place thyself *in novissimo loco—in the lowest place*, also as regards the exterior, seeking the lowest place in everything, so far as obedience will allow it, and feeling rejoiced when thou findest thyself there by the arrangements of thy superiors. When at times circumstances place thee in a more honourable post, thy exterior behaviour must by its humility betoken the low opinion thou hast of thyself, and the sincerity with which thou believest thyself to be inferior in talent and merit to others. This low opinion of thyself ought to manifest itself also in thy words, by remaining silent on all that might redound to thy glory, and by praising thy neighbour when there is an opportunity; by liking to be reproved for thy faults, and by passing over the shortcomings of thy brethren. If thou wilt attentively reflect on thy past conduct in this respect, thou wilt discover abundant matter to put thy pride to shame !

III. Consider a further motive to encourage thee to put down thy own pride and to like to be last, which is the difference that exists between the standard of weights and measures as used by Jesus Christ and by the world. The world looks up to, and holds most in esteem, the man that raises himself up the highest; but with Jesus Christ it is he that lowers himself the most whom He honours the most, because it is by humility that we become like unto Christ, Who humbled Himself, *humiliavit semetipsun*—Philip. ii. 8; and in proportion as we are like unto Him in this world by humility, shall we be also like unto Him in the next, in glory: *Qui se humiliat exaltabitur*—Luc. xviii. 14—*He that humbleth himself shall be exalted.* The deeper a spring is, the higher will its waters rise. Then again, who are the religious that, as a matter of fact, are most esteemed and revered, even by worldlings themselves? Certainly not the haughty, nor the ambitious, nor the proud, but the humble; such men as a *Franciscus Minor*, or a *Franciscus Minimus*, and so many others who, through their desire of following in the footsteps of their Master, have espoused poverty, and placed themselves at the beck of all, shunning to the utmost of their power all pre-eminence and honour. What greater anomaly can one conceive than to see a religious who makes profession of imitating the humility of Christ in his cloister—to see such a one, I say, egged on by ambition, going in search of distinction, standing on ceremonies, pushing himself before others, loud in his own praises, and busy about his own preferment? If it be true in the case of all Christians that *qui se exaltat humiliabitur—he that exalteth himself shall be humbled*, how exactly will not this be verified in the case of a proud and haughty religious, both in this world and in the next!

MONDAY IN THE SIXTEENTH WEEK AFTER PENTECOST.

Quid vides festucam in oculo fratris tui, trabem autem quæ in tuo est non consideras?—Luc. vi. 41.
Why seest thou the mote in thy brother's eye, but the beam that is in thy own eye thou considerest not?

I. CONSIDER how unreasonable it is that thou shouldst remark, criticise, and condemn the little failings of thy brethren, whilst thou hast greater ones thyself which call for thy attention, and yet thou heedest not. Before busying thyself in passing judgment on the defects of others, give an eye to thy own shortcomings : *Ante judicium interroga te ipsum*—Eccl. xviii. 20—*Before judgment, examine thyself.* Take not on thyself the part of a zealot, because he who acts in this ungracious manner is styled by Christ by the disgraceful epithet of hypocrite : *Hypocrita, ejice primum trabem de oculo tuo*—*Hypocrite, cast first the beam out of thy own eye.* And with good reason, because such a one would fain appear to be better than others—as all hypocrites seek to do—and that not at the expense of good works, such as alms-deeds, prayer, and the like, but, as the Pharisee did in the temple, by haughtily running down his neighbour, whom he ought to think better than himself. What, then, shall we say if thou shouldst be deserving of so disreputable a name, by seeking to extol thyself by abusing those who are thy betters ?

II. Consider that by condemning the trivial faults of thy brethren, even though thou shouldst do so from a motive of real zeal, and not from superciliousness—thou derivest no benefit thyself. Even supposing thou didst succeed in extracting every little mote from thy neighbour's eye, what good in the world will it do thee if all the while thou remainest with a much greater obstruction in thy own, that endangers thy safety ? *Qui alium doces, te non doces*—Rom. ii. 21— *Thou that teachest another, teachest not thyself.* What good wilt thou ever derive from this ? Neither dost thou confer any benefit on thy neighbour, because whilst thou showest thyself so zealous about the little shortcomings of others without being in the least anxious about thy own, not only will they laugh at thee, but they will be shocked at seeing thee assuming the office of superior and judge in a matter in which thou art more guilty than they, and reproving inobservance of rule in others, whilst thou thyself art guilty of a still more glaring breach. If, however, thou art desirous of correcting the faults of thy companions with profit to thyself, do so by good example, because by reflecting on thy own shortcomings, and amending them, each one will learn to correct his own.

III. Consider that when thou art tempted to reprove the faults of others, without first of all correcting thy own, thou not only dost what is useless and wrong, but what is highly prejudicial to thyself, because *wherein thou judgest another, thou condemnest thyself—in quo enim alterum judicas, te ipsum condemnas—*Rom. ii. 1. Thou usurpest an authority which does not belong to thee, who hast not the charge of others, and thou excitest the anger of God, Who does not wish thee to constitute thyself judge of thy neighbour. Turn thy thoughts, therefore, first of all, as to how thou mayest get rid of thy own faults, and then thou mayest lawfully warn thy brethren, in a spirit of charity, of those faults of which they themselves are not aware, and against which they cannot, therefore, be on their guard.

TUESDAY IN THE SIXTEENTH WEEK AFTER PENTECOST.

Fili, in mansuetudine serva animam tuam et da illi honorem secundum meritum suum—Eccl. x. 31.

My son, keep thy soul in meekness, and give it honour according to its desert.

I. CONSIDER what is this honour thou owest to thy soul. It is, in the first place, to see that it commands and is not made to obey, because it was created to command like a queen the desires of the body, and not obey them like a servant. *Sub te erit appetitus tuus, et tu dominaberis illius*—Gen. iv. 7—*The lust thereof shall be under thee, and thou shall have dominion over it.* Reflect therefore, what a great wrong thou inflictest on thy soul by obliging it, all the day long, to wait on the flesh in all its most humiliating requirements, such as eating and drinking, and sleeping, and to take part in its amusements, and even in its lusts. Act not in this manner, but give to thy soul its proper position, which is that of command.

II. Consider the second way in which thou oughtest to give honour to thy soul, by preferring it, as it deserves, to all that is of less worth, that is to say, to all that is perishable and endures only for a time; because all that is temporal will come to an end, whilst the soul is eternal. Hence, thou oughtest to value thy soul above the empty friendship of man, above the esteem of others, above riches, and above life itself, which is so dear to thee: this is what the soul deserves: *Cuncta que habet homo dabit pro anima sua*—Job ii. 4—*All that a man hath he will give for his life.* How lamentable then, it is, to behold so many in the world that are so ready to sell their souls to the infernal enemy for a mere nothing. Beware of imitating such as these; too bitterly wouldst thou repent it in eternity!

III. Consider the third way in which thou must do honour to thy soul, which is that thou shouldst not only treat it as queen, and give it the preference before all earthly goods, as is thy duty, but that thou shouldst enable it to enjoy God, Who is the end for which it was created, and that in thy quality of religious thou shouldst not put off its enjoyment of God to the next world, but give it every facility for reposing in Him in this life as well: *Anima mea illi vivet* Ps. xxi. 3—*To Him my soul shall live,* by earnest application and prayer, by thinking on God, by speaking about God, by conversing with God and keeping in His divine presence: *Vivemus in conspectu ejus—* Oseæ vii. 3—*We shall live in His sight.* If thou actest thus, thou dost indeed render great honour to thy soul. It will make it also much easier to give it the two-fold honour which is due to it, because, whoever converses much with God makes little account of the pleasures of the senses, and is not likely to subject the soul to the body as its slave; still less does he value all that the world can offer, nor would he sacrifice the one desire of his soul for its possession. If thou givest thy soul up to the exercise of interior recollection it will not go wandering like a commoner through every street and by-way, but will remain seated on its throne like a queen.

WEDNESDAY IN THE SIXTEENTH WEEK AFTER PENTECOST.

*Terra sæpe venientem super bibens imbrem et germinans herbam ... accipiet benedictionem a Deo: proferens autem spinas et tribulos, reproba est et maledicto proxima, cujus consummatio in combustionem—*Hebr. vi. 7.

The earth that drinketh in the rain which cometh often upon it, and bringeth forth herbs . . . receiveth blessing from God; but that which bringeth forth thorns and briars is reprobate and very near unto a curse, whose end is to be burnt.

I. CONSIDER, that just as no soil can produce a single blade of grass without the aid of rain, so also no soul can produce of itself the smallest fruit of virtue without the assistance of Divine grace. Endeavour to master this truth thoroughly, and then thou wilt succeed in obtaining an entire distrust of thyself, and say to Almighty God from thy heart: *Anima mea sicut terra sine aqua tibi*—*My soul is as earth without water before Thee.* But grace is not enough without thy correspondence, and thus there is the same difference between two souls equally favoured by Heaven—but not both equally faithful—as obtains between two plots of ground, both watered alike, but not both equally fertile; and thus it happens that the one is blessed by God and the other is cursed. To which class dost thou belong? There is no alternative here!

II. Consider awhile how far more frequently and more abundantly the rain of divine grace has fallen on thy soul than on so many others who are left in the world where there is a much greater scarcity of spiritual aids. And now examine how thou hast corresponded? What fruits hast thou borne with the abundance of help thou receivest from Our Lord in thy religious state? If thou hast produced good fruits, console thyself at thy Saviour's having blessed thee and prepared a reward for thee in heaven. But if instead of good works thou hast brought forth only *spinas et tribulos*—*thorns and briars*—that is, smaller sins signified by thorns, and more grievous sins signified by briars—oh, thou art to be pitied! What a dreadful punishment awaits thee!

III. Consider the three curses pronounced against the sterile soil. The first is reprobation, because one of the surest signs that a soul will be lost, is when it receives frequent assistance to act virtuously, and, nevertheless, does not avail itself of the opportunity afforded it. The second curse is its proximity to having the sentence of damnation passed on it, because Almighty God does not, as a rule, bear with such ingratitude for any length of time. The third curse is the punishment of the flames of hell, because fire is a torture commensurate with the heinousness of fruitless sterility. Strive, therefore, to correspond with the numberless graces Our Lord is continually showering down upon thee, and thus thy soul will become a fertile soil, watered daily with an increasing abundance of beneficial inspirations and favours—*et accipiet benedictionem a Deo*—and it will receive a blessing from God.

THURSDAY IN THE SIXTEENTH WEEK AFTER PENTECOST.

Etsi quis erit consummatus inter filios hominum, si ab illo abfuerit sapientia tua Domine in nihilum computabitur—Sap. ix. 6.

For if one be perfect among the children of men, yet if Thy wisdom be not with him, he shall be nothing regarded.

I. CONSIDER how many there are that toil and labour for every possible object except the one that alone is of any importance. How many schools are opened, and how many frequent them, one to acquire a knowledge of literature or of the sciences, another to acquire skill in riding or the use of arms, another to become expert in music or painting. But how few there are that frequent the school of salvation, and apply themselves to learn the holy fear of God. And yet, after all, this alone is true wisdom—to know how to direct our occupations to the attainment of our last end, which is a happy eternity ; because the man that possesses not this, let him be as skilled as possible in all the arts and sciences, possesses nothing: *ad nihilum computabitur—he shall be nothing regarded.* Thou hast been called to holy religion, which is the school of true wisdom, but hast thou yet learnt to esteem this holy fear of God above every other acquirement?

II. Consider that the wise man does not say absolutely that the possession of the accomplishments of literature, science, and art, is worthless, but the possession of them unaccompanied by the holy fear of God; because these accomplishments can very well be acquired with merit, and be directed to the increase of the fear of God in our hearts, and to His own service. Strive, therefore, to acquire that amount of learning and skill which will enable thee to fulfil thy charge and employment, and thus help thee as a religious to obtain the holy fear of God, which ought to be thy chief study. As for other accomplishments which will not help thee, but rather prove a hindrance to its acquisition, leave them alone. Examine thyself, and resolve accordingly.

III. Consider that the soul that is destitute of this divine wisdom of the fear of God is pronounced absolutely to be worthless: *in nihilum computabitur—he shall be nothing regarded*—and hence thou mayest learn what sort of money has currency in heaven. What, thinkest thou, is the value that is set in heaven on the valour of an Alexander, or the learning of an Aristotle, or the eloquence of a Cicero, or on the master-pieces of the greatest artists the world has produced? Simply nothing: *In nihilum computabitur—He shall be nothing regarded;* whereas, the poorest beggar, all covered with sores, but who lives in the holy fear of God, is thought more of in heaven than all these great men put together. Dost thou believe these truths? How comes it, then, that thou dost not put them into practice? And yet the washing of a dish done for the love of God, any mortification or hardship thou endurest, the smallest act of humility, obedience, or charity, renders thee far more estimable in the sight of Heaven than if thou wert a Plato or a Demosthenes.

FRIDAY IN THE SIXTEENTH WEEK AFTER PENTECOST.

Nemo nostrum sibi vivit, et nemo nostrum moritur; sive enim vivimus, Domino vivimus; sive morimur Domino morimur. Sive ergo vivimus, sive morimur, Domini sumus.—Rom. xiv. 8.

For whether we live, we live unto the Lord; or whether we die, we die unto the Lord. Therefore, whether we live or whether we die, we are the Lord's.

I. CONSIDER that not uncommonly the monarchs of the earth have amongst the soldiers of their armies a body that is styled by some such name as the king's body-guard; the soldiers of which are so devoted to their king that they hardly look upon their lives as their own, but will at all risks, for his safety, engage in the most desperate encounter. We see a soldier of this sort in the army of Jesus Christ, in the person of S. Paul, the sole aim of whose life was the service of his Lord, and whose only object in death was the glory of Christ. Now this is just what thou oughtest to aspire to in the religious state, by virtue of which thou hast dedicated thyself wholly and entirely to the service of God—to live and die for Him. Yet what is thy conduct? Thou hast not the courage to live entirely for God, by detaching thyself from those conveniences which make thee live for thyself, and will not suffer thee to run the remotest risk of dying for love of Him.

II. Consider who are they that live for themselves, and die likewise for themselves? They are those that live according to their own fancy and after their own fashion, and whose death is a consequence of the great disorders and excessive fatigue to which they have exposed themselves for the sake of ambition and the gratification of their own desires. On the contrary, they that live for God are those who live fully resigned to the dispositions of God and are wholly employed in promoting His glory, availing themselves of their tongues, of their hands, and of all their senses and faculties in Christ's honour; ready even for His sake to lay down their lives, which one day or other they must lose. Happy art thou if thou wilt but make up thy mind to live and die for God, and so avoid being of the number of those who live and die for themselves.

III. Consider that what most of all encourages a sovereign's body-guard to be heedless of their own safety is the thought that they are not fighting for themselves, but for their king whose standard they defend. So also ought this thought to give thee courage. Remember whose thou art and under how many titles thy divine Lord lays claim to thee: *empti enim estis pretio magno*—1 Cor. vi. 20—*for you are bought with a great price*. After all, what great thing is it that a vile slave like thee should live and die for Christ, when thou rememberest that Christ has deigned to spend His whole life and die for thee? Therefore devote thy life to the honour of God with a good will, and be not afraid of losing it for His sake, because thou wilt find thyself transported to an eternal life, the excellence of which will be in proportion to the earnestness with which thou wilt have employed and spent thyself for God during this fleeting and mortal life.

SATURDAY IN THE SIXTEENTH WEEK AFTER PENTECOST.

Homo sanctus in sapientia sua manet, sicut sol; nam stultus sicut luna mutatur.—Eccl. xxvii. 12.

A holy man continueth in wisdom as the sun; but a fool is changed as the moon.

I. CONSIDER that a wise and holy man is as different from a bad and foolish man as the sun is from the moon. The sun is a fixed orb, not that it has no motion, but because it is always the same and never wanes or loses its power. The moon, on the contrary, performs its revolutions, wanes and changes every moment; at one time full and resplendent, at another darksome and deprived of light. So also the holy man moves about and remains still at one and the same time. He moves by his continual growth in virtue, and he remains still by not losing any of the excellence of the virtue he has already acquired. The fool does just the reverse; he is always changing; because what he may gain one day he will lose on another. If he begins to do some little good, he changes his mind and undoes the good he may have done. How fares it with thy own firmness of purpose?

II. Consider how the good and prudent man remains constant in the practice of virtue; he never swerves from the end he has once proposed to himself, of always seeking God. He is occupied at one time with prayer, at another with study; now in serving his neighbour, and now in the fulfilment of the duties entrusted to him by obedience. Yet he is always steady in his wise principle of having the good pleasure of God for his aim in all he does. He neither loses courage nor stops half way by reason of the difficulties he encounters; but he goes on perseveringly with his undertaking, namely, the attainment of his end. Thou wilt indeed be a favoured soul if thou succeedest in remaining staunch and constant in this only true wisdom of seeking thy end and of directing all thy actions to the good pleasure of Almighty God. Thou wilt thus soon arrive at holiness.

III. Consider the reason why the foolish man so easily changes his mind, and is therefore likened to the moon that is ever changing its phases. It is because he has no fixed rule of life, and his eyes are not fixed on his last end; but he regulates his conduct by the principles of the age and the bad example of others: the object he proposes to himself is not to please God, but to be like other people; and thus modelling his conduct on the principles and examples he comes across, he never remains in the same state—*numquam in eodem statu permanet.* Another still stronger reason is because he is scared by every little difficulty that crosses his path in any good pursuit, whether in the shape of human respect or natural repugnance, and he at once draws back from his undertaking. Oh! how important it is that thou shouldst have a clear knowledge of thy duty and thus not be led astray so easily by bad example, and that thou shouldst courageously overcome the obstacles that come in thy way and go straight to the goal, as true wisdom demands of thee.

SEVENTEENTH SUNDAY AFTER PENTECOST.

Diliges Dominum Deum tuum ex toto corde tuo, et in tota anima tua, et in tota mente tua—Matth. xxii. 37.

Thou shalt love the Lord thy God with thy whole heart, and with thy whole soul, and with thy whole mind.

I. CONSIDER that in order to fulfil this first and greatest precept of loving Almighty God, thou must attentively weigh these three considerations: how lovable God is in Himself, how much He loves thee, and how desirous He is of thy love. There is nothing better calculated to win over thy heart and urge thee to love any one than the fact of his proving himself anxious to gain thy affection by the benefits he confers on thee. Now this is just what Almighty God has done in thy regard. As the Author of nature, He has created thee from nothing and given the preference to thee over numberless other possible beings; he preserves thee every instant of thy existence, and exerts His omnipotence in preserving so many other creatures also in this world for thy benefit. As the Author of grace, He has redeemed thee with His blood; He has caused thee to be born of Christian parents; He has privileged thee with the gift of faith in holy baptism—a gift denied to so many others; he has called thee by His especial inspiration to the religious life. Lastly, as the Author of glory, He is fitting thee for His kingdom, and has promised to make thee happy with the possession of Himself. Are not such great and innumerable benefits an ample claim on thy heart? are they not capable of moving thee to love Him? But bear in mind that true love is known by deeds; it resembles fire, which cannot remain inactive: therefore, as St. John says: *Non diligamus verbo, neque lingua, sed opere et veritate*—1 Joan. iii. 18— *Let us not love in word nor in tongue, but in deed and in truth.*

II. Consider how fondly Almighty God loves thee. Love is above every gift—it is the soul of a gift—and God has loved thee, and loves thee now without limit—without any need of thee and without any correspondence on thy part. He loves thee without limit because His love for thee is coeval with His own eternal existence; and, as far as He is concerned, He desires to love thee for ever. He loves thee without having any need of thee; and pray how could He need thee, since He had always been most fully happy in Himself? He loves thee without meeting with any return; for in exchange for His love He meets with nothing at thy hands day after day, but numberless slights and acts of ingratitude: in spite of which He persists in loving thee. Where could a human heart be found that on beholding such an ill return from the object of its love, would not cool in its affection or cease loving altogether? Learn hence, once for all, to serve Almighty God from a motive of pure love and for His own glory's sake, without regard to thy own interest.

III. Consider how lovable Almighty God is in Himself by reason of His intrinsic excellence and infinite attributes. We are at once carried away by our admiration of any one whom we know to be possessed of extraordinary worth and merit, and we feel ourselves constrained to love him; how much more should we be love-smitten if we beheld any one person possessed of all the most amiable virtues and estimable qualities which we generally see divided amongst a variety of individuals! Now Almighty God contains in Himself all that goodness and beauty which He has shadowed forth here and there amongst His creatures, but enhanced to an infinite degree; and indeed He is possessed of numberless attributes that infinitely surpass all idea. How then canst thou refrain from loving Almighty God for His own sake ? All else that is good and beautiful in His creatures thou must love in Him, Who is the origin and source of all good.

MONDAY IN THE SEVENTEENTH WEEK AFTER PENTECOST.

Esto fidelis usque ad mortem, et dabo tibi coronam vitæ.—Apoc. ii. 10.
Be thou faithful unto death, and I will give thee the crown of life.

I. CONSIDER that in a servant fidelity is of all virtues the most estimable. *Si est tibi servus fidelis, sit tibi quasi anima tua*—Eccl. xxxiii. 31—*If thou have a faithful servant, let him be to thee as thy own soul.* Thou art God's servant—a servant in the strictest sense—and therefore it is no wonder if He incites thee to ever-increasing fidelity by so great promises. But what is meant by being a faithful servant? It means that thou shouldst regard God's interests as thy own; that when it is a question of pleasing thy Divine Master, thou shouldst give no heed to any consideration of either health, reputation, or life itself. A faithful servant thinks more about his master than himself. What sayest thou? art thou possessed of this fidelity? Without it thou wilt never win thy crown.

II. Consider that it is not enough to practise this fidelity for a short time only; it must be persevered in

—*usque ad mortem*—*unto death*—because it is perseverance that is the proof of real fidelity. Thou art anxious only about dying well, but art not so eager to live well. Act not in this fashion, but be desirous of being faithful to thy Lord all thy life long—*usque ad mortem*—to such a degree that if He sends thee sickness, or disgrace, or persecution—even till the day of thy death—thou remain steadfast all through these trials. Fidelity is especially proved in time of adversity, and therefore when it has been fully tested it receives its reward. Reflect for a while on the manner in which thou facest the little trials that cross thy path in the religious life : if thou receivest them courageously thou mayest hope to bear up against heavier trials also.

III. Consider that the thought of having to be faithful under affliction—*usque ad mortem*—*unto death*—is a source of alarm to thee, because thou imaginest that thou hast to live the years of Adam ; death follows much closer on thy heels, perhaps, than thou thinkest : but even though thy lifetime should be as long as thou supposest, it will certainly appear very short indeed, if thou keepest present to thy mind the eternal reward held out to thee ;—*Dabo tibi coronam vitæ*—*I will give thee a crown of life*—a life that will continually repeat itself and never come to an end—a life of bliss, where enjoyment will be everlasting. Is not this thought sufficient to lessen thy dread of that little amount of suffering which thou must undergo to prove thy fidelity to God in this world ? Indeed, thou oughtest rather to be concerned at the shortness of the time allotted thee for suffering, considering that thy joy will be eternal.

TUESDAY IN THE SEVENTEENTH WEEK AFTER PENTECOST.

Omnis qui me confessus fuerit coram hominibus, et Filius hominis confitebitur illum coram angelis Dei.—Luc. xii. 8.

Whosoever shall confess Me before men, him shall the Son of man also confess before the angels of God.

I. CONSIDER what a very great honour Our Lord promises thee; He promises to confess thee before all the angels who on the day of judgment will encircle His throne, in the same way as thou shalt have faithfully confessed Him before men. He declares that He will show Himself proud of thee in the presence of so many most exalted spirits, and that He will recognise thee as worthy of having a seat amidst their gorgeous thrones, as His own true subject and brave soldier. What honour is there on earth that thou canst compare with this? If thou esteemest it such a great matter that some exalted personage should patronise thee and speak favourably of thee in the presence of his own equals, how much more oughtest thou to look up to the honour of being patronised and commended by Almighty God Himself, in the presence of all the choirs of angels! Think often on this most desirable expression of esteem and its consequent honour, and thou wilt not care much about the esteem and praise of men in this world.

II. Consider that, to deserve this great honour, thou must confess Jesus Christ in this present life, and this confession has to be made, not only with thy heart, but by word of mouth and by deed: *Corde, ore, et opere.* It stands to reason that if thou confessest Him only in thy heart—by holding fast to His faith, and by acknowledging Him to be thy Master, Leader, and King, but in no other way—thou givest Him but a scanty meed of honour. Hence He designedly adds *coram hominibus—before men*, to give thee to understand that thou hast to lay aside all human respect, and make it thy glory to confess and honour Jesus, not only within the walls of thy cell, but, if the occasion presents itself, in the streets and in the houses of the great ; not only in choir, but in every place, how public soever it be. Jesus will then own thee in the presence of all His angels—*coram angelis suis ;* and it is therefore thy duty to own Him and preach Him just as He is, and, as His infinite excellence deserves, in the presence of all men. This duty has to be fulfilled, not only from the pulpit, if thou be in a position to do as much, but still more in a humbler and easier way, in thy conversation, by praising His teaching, His maxims, and His virtues, and so inciting others to honour Him ; by freely condemning the crooked principles of the world, so utterly at variance with those of the gospel, and by reproving the injurious and blasphemous language that not unfrequently is to be heard in the mouths of seculars. Would it not, indeed, be a lamentable thing that no other language should be heard in the mouth of a religious who has consecrated himself to promote the glory of Jesus, but the language of the world, by constantly making a great ado about its magnificence and greatness, and making but little account of the things of heaven ?

III. Consider that in order to render this confession complete which Our Lord demands of thee, it is not enough to employ the heart and the tongue : deeds are also required, so that thou mayest give open and public testimony by thy line of conduct that thy life is that of a true religious and faithful follower of Jesus. What honour, pray, canst thou give Him if thou art ashamed to make open profession in the sight of the world of that humility and patience, of that meekness and modesty, which He has taught thee by His own example, and which is so proper to the religious state? Thou art rather an occasion of shame to Him; for it is a matter of greater confusion to Jesus to be refused this public homage of works and words by thee who art of His own household, than by a stranger; and so much the greater, therefore, will thy shame be at the day of judgment.

WEDNESDAY IN THE SEVENTEENTH WEEK AFTER PENTECOST.

Omnia possum in eo qui me confortat.—Philip. iv. 13.
I can do all things in Him Who strengtheneth me.

I. CONSIDER the great courage that the apostle shows in these words. He would appear to have believed himself almost omnipotent: *Omnia possum—I can do all things*—not by his own strength, but in virtue of Almighty God, Who alone could render him capable of so much. Now this frame of mind did not bespeak pride in S. Paul, but courage; because humility does not consist in thinking that one can do nothing good for God, but in realising that we can do nothing good as of ourselves. At times it seems an impossibility to thee to overcome this or that failing, to perform some particular penitential work, to live in that place or in that particular office, imposed on thee by obedience, because thou lookest to thyself only. Raise thy eyes and fix them on God, believing and realising that thy power has to come from that divine Master Who chooses to avail Himself of a weak and unfitted subject like thee to show that He is the Author and First Beginning of the works He imposes on thee. Acting in this way, thou wilt be both humble and courageous.

II. Consider that when the apostle said: *Omnia possum in eo qui me confortat—I can do all things in Him Who strengtheneth me,* he wished to show that he really could do anything, not in virtue of his own natural strength, but in virtue of Him that infused into his soul a strength and vigour above nature. What, therefore, ought to encourage thee also to great undertakings, is the thought that thou hast to accomplish them by the grace of Almighty God. Imagine thyself to be in the position of a dwarf to whom a giant imparts his own strength to move a huge mass by their joint efforts: *Dominus astitit mihi, et confortavit me—* 2 Tim. iv. 17—*The Lord stood by me and strengthened me.* Thus did S. Paul write to Timothy, clearly indicating that the strengthening aid of grace is given to us in order that we may co-operate of our own freewill, and so, through His infinite goodness, have the merit of the work attributed to us.

III. Consider to what sort of things S. Paul referred when he said *omnia possum—I can do all things.* He meant such things as the endurance of the discomforts of poverty, and bearing up against torments which were unbearable, by the strength of unaided nature, but which he declares himself ready to endure with the assistance of divine grace. It is certain that his readiness to undergo sufferings did not cause him to lose all sense of pain and discomfort, but he suffered courageously. Do thou also put thy trust in God, and be careful to put no hindrance to an unreserved acceptance of grace, in which thou wilt find the strength thou needest, and then thou wilt not lose heart in the midst of even the heaviest trials, but thou wilt say, as the apostle did: *Omnia possum in eo qui me confortat—I can do all things in Him that strengtheneth me.*

THURSDAY IN THE SEVENTEENTH WEEK AFTER PENTECOST.

Fideles in dilectione acquiescent illi.—Sap. iii. 9.
They that are faithful in love shall rest in Him.

I. CONSIDER that a sure sign by which thou mayest know if thou lovest thy Saviour faithfully, is if thou conformest thyself in everything to His holy Will. It is easy enough to love Him when He grants thee everything to thy liking—*acquiescit tibi*—by giving thee peace of mind, and health of body, and spiritual sweetness. The difficulty is to love Him when it is thy turn to act as He likes—*acquiescere illi*—in ailments, and disgrace, and in spiritual aridity and desolation. Now it certainly is His Will that suffering of some sort should never be wanting to thee. Thou makest this request in so many words each time thou sayest *Fiat voluntas tua*—*Thy will be done*, because the will of Our Lord is that thou shouldst sanctify thyself: *Hæc est voluntas Dei sanctificatio vestra*—Thess. iv. 3—*This is the Will of God, your sanctification;* and it is certain that no one will ever attain sanctity by any other means than by suffering: *Omnes qui placuerunt Deo, per multas tribulationes transierunt fideles*—Jud. viii. 23—*All that have pleased God passed through many tribulations, remaining faithful.*

II. Consider that for this conformity to be perfect, it must be a complete acquiescence in all that God ordains; not in the sense that thy inferior nature has to remain undisturbed in the midst of trials, but in the sense that thy superior faculties have to maintain a peaceful submission. Thy will must acquiesce, thy intellect must acquiesce. It often happens, with spiritual persons, that it is easier to calm the will than the intellect; it will appear strange that Our Lord should treat them in such a manner, and they cannot get themselves to believe that the illness from which they are suffering, or the persecution they are undergoing at the hands of wicked men, or that the particular arrangement a superior has made in their regard, and which hinders them from doing many good works, and effecting much good on behalf of their neighbours —they cannot believe, I say, that this is really the best thing for them. Shouldst thou be of this number, thou dost not conform thyself fully to the Will of God, nor art thou *fidelis in dilectione—faithful in love.*

III. Consider that it is this perfect conformity to the Will of God which will, more than anything else, give rest and calm to thy soul; and hence the act of conforming oneself to the will of another, is called an act of acquiescence. So long as thou seekest to draw over the Will of Our Lord, or of thy superior, who stands in His place, to thy own, thou wilt never be at peace, but wilt always be restless, disturbed by fears, anxiety, and remorse of conscience. Then only wilt thou calm down when thou allowest Our Lord, or His representative, to draw over thy will to His, with the full and entire submission of thy intellect. Put thyself therefore, once for all, without reserve at His entire disposition, according to the advice of Job : *Acquiesce igitur et habeto pacem*—Job xxii. 21—*Submit thyself then to Him, and be at peace.*

FRIDAY IN THE SEVENTEENTH WEEK AFTER PENTECOST.*

Quos præscivit, et prædestinavit conformes fieri imaginis Filii sui; ut sit ipse primogenitus in multis fratribus.—Rom. viii. 29.

Whom He foreknew He also predestinated to be made conformable to the image of His Son; that they might be the firstborn amongst many brethren.

I. CONSIDER that the surest sign of thy predestination is if thou resemblest Jesus, as a copy resembles its original. Jesus was chosen by the Eternal Father as His own and first-begotten Son, and was predestined to win for Himself the glorious title of Redeemer by the exercise of most laborious virtues. So also has He chosen others to be His adopted children in the likeness of Jesus, Who is their model; and as He intends these adopted ones to resemble their eldest brother in His glory in paradise, so also must they become like unto Him in His sufferings and humiliation on earth : *Sicut portavimus imaginem terreni, portemus imaginem cœlestis*—1 Cor. xv. 49—*As we have borne the image of the earthly, let us bear also the image of the heavenly.* So true is this, that our resemblance to Christ in heaven will correspond to the degree in which we have resembled Him on earth. Examine, therefore, awhile how far thou art a true copy of this divine model; if thou seest no resemblance, fear and tremble lest thou art not included in the number of the elect.

* The following Meditation is that assigned by the author for the Friday after the Octave of Corpus Christi; this day's Meditation having been transposed to that Friday as being especially adapted for the Feast of the Sacred Heart, which is kept on that day.—THE TRANSLATOR.

II. Consider that as Almighty God willed that Christ should be *primogenitus in multis fratribus—the firstborn amongst many brethren*, He could not allow us adopted children to share the glory of paradise except on the condition that we should imitate His firstborn, and win it at the cost of much suffering. Hence it is quite certain that thorns and crosses are to be found on all sides, and every one has his share of them. Besides, it is much more within every one's reach to be poor, as Christ was, than to abound in riches, to humble oneself than to lord it over others, to obey than to command, and so on. All that is necessary is a determined will; and it is this precisely of which thou standest most in need in order to effect a resemblance to thy divine model.

III. Consider that if thou wouldst be really in earnest about effecting this resemblance in thyself, thy favourite subject of prayer must be the consideration of the examples which Jesus has left thee of poverty, humility, obedience, meekness, and the great actual dissimilarity that exists between the pattern and the copy. Gaze thoughtfully on the image of the crucified One, and say to thyself: Christ is naked, I am well clothed; Christ is in the midst of tortures, and I am in the lap of comfort; Christ is forsaken, I seek amusements; Christ is despised, I am made much of. If after this comparison thou hast not courage to make up thy mind to court suffering, beg thy Saviour to be pleased to make thee suffer by force, so that thou mayest in one way or another bear some resemblance to thy model: *Conformes fieri imaginis Filii sui—To be made conformable to the image of His Son.*

SATURDAY IN THE SEVENTEENTH WEEK AFTER PENTECOST.

Qui timet Deum, nihil negligit.—Eccl. vii. 19.
He that feareth God, neglecteth nothing.

I. CONSIDER the first meaning of these words by which the Wise man affirms that he who fears God *nihil negligit—neglecteth nothing*. He means that the soul that possesses the fear of God does not allow any occasion for doing good to pass by unheeded. Even the saints will from time to time leave undone some good deed through frailty or weakness; but to neglect doing some good work which might easily be done, through recklessness, and to be satisfied with doing only just what is requisite to avoid mortal sin, this is the negligence so hateful to God, and so characteristic of the soul that has but little of His holy fear, because this is a positive surrendering of all claim to those abundant helps which Almighty God generally grants to the soul that is anxious to please Him, and without which so many are continually being lost. Even where a negligence of this sort does not amount to a grievous sin, it disposes the soul to incur it. Entertain, therefore, a lively horror of this danger.

II. Consider the second meaning of these words: *Qui timet Deum, nihil negligit—He that feareth God, neglecteth nothing*. It is that the soul that fears God never despises any sin or fault as trivial and unimportant. The saints themselves occasionally commit at least some venial sin. *In multis offendimus omnes* —Jac. iii. 2—*In many things we all offend*: but they never make little of their faults, especially if they are deliberate; on the contrary, they exceedingly grieve over them. It is only the remiss and foolhardy soul that despises venial sin, and thinks that is of no consequence because it is "only a venial sin." Shouldst thou be blinded by such a foolish delusion thou art indeed worthy of compassion! One single venial sin is a greater evil than all the other evils that exist in the world, with the sole exception of mortal sin: so that the being guilty of any one venial sin is in reality a greater evil for thee than if thou wert attacked by every sort of fever or by all the devils in hell. Hence, thou couldst not with a good conscience commit a single venial sin in order to escape the greatest calamity. Not even couldst thou lawfully commit a venial sin if by so doing thou hadst it in thy power to bring back to the faith of Christ all the Jews, Turks, and heretics in the world; and if thou didst so, Almighty God would punish thee most severely with the dreadful pains of purgatory, because by that venial sin thou dishonourest and offendest Him. Such being the case, wilt thou be so foolish as to make little account of venial sin?

III. Consider that the habit of not overlooking any virtuous action as superfluous, and of not underrating any venial fault as of no consequence, is not a habit that is peculiar to the saints alone, but it is a positive duty incumbent on all who have the fear of God and have their salvation at heart. It is certain that Almighty God in many an instance withdraws that abundance of spiritual aid without which an individual soul will not be saved, on account of venial sins of omission and commission. Reflect, therefore, with how far greater reason is this frame of mind expected of thee who art a religious, and as such art bound to tend to perfection. If in thy holy state thou makest no account of venial sins, and art negligent in the performance of good works because thou art not bound to perform them under mortal sin, thou mayest well fear and tremble lest Almighty God should abandon thee, and that the words of the Psalmist, which have been verified in the case of so many others, should become true in thy regard also: *Declinantes autem in obligationes adducet Dominus cum operantibus iniquitatem*—Ps. cxxiv. 5.

EIGHTEENTH SUNDAY AFTER PENTECOST.

Confide, fili, remittuntur tibi peccata tua . . . Surge, tolle lectum tuum.—Matth. ix. 26.
Be of good heart, son, thy sins are forgiven thee . . . . Arise, take up thy bed.

I. CONSIDER how Our Lord was moved to compassion by the faith of these good men, who being hindered from bringing the paralysed cripple into His presence on account of the throng of people, let him down through the roof, in the hope that the sight of his helplessness would induce Our Divine Lord to heal him. At this strange sight Jesus began to exhort the sick man most lovingly to hope and trust in the help of God: *Confide, fili*—*Be of good heart, son.* He thus gives thee to understand that though the help thou obtainest, through the prayers of others, is good and useful, it is absolutely necessary that thou thyself shouldst dispose thy soul to receive grace from heaven, by thy own personal acts of petition and confidence. Our Lord has pledged Himself to grant our prayer only in so far as we ask for ourselves, and not when we ask for others, although in His goodness He often does grant the requests we make in behalf of others as well: *Petite, et dabitur vobis*—Matth. vii. 7—*Ask, and it shall be given you.* Why, then, art thou so anxious in time of need that others should pray for thee, and at the same time so negligent in having recourse to Almighty God thyself, and in putting forth thy own prayers to Him? It is right enough that others should pray for thee, and that thou shouldst pray for others, but the important thing is that thou shouldst appeal to thy Saviour on thy own behalf with trusting and earnest prayer.

II. Consider how the paralytic desired and asked for the restoration of his bodily health only; but Jesus, Who is always desirous of giving us more than we ask for, gave him at one and the same moment the health of both body and soul, freeing his soul from the guilt of sin, and his limbs from paralysis. It is exactly the same in thy own case when thou hast recourse to Our Lord in thy necessities and trials. For instance, thou beggest Him in prayer to free thee from some troublesome temptation or some anxiety of mind or bodily ailment; if thy request be made as it ought to be made, and is beneficial to thy salvation, He will grant thee more even than thou askest, because not only will He grant thy particular request, but He will enrich thy soul with merit and with various habits of virtue, in consequence of the acts of reverence, humility and confidence thou hast elicited in the course of thy prayer itself. Besides, even when thou failest to obtain the special object of thy petition, thou gainest all this extra amount of spiritual riches, and is not this a sufficient motive to incite thee to make speedy recourse to thy Lord in all thy needs?

III. Consider that Jesus gave the paralytic first of all health of soul and then health of body, to give us to understand that very frequently temporal afflictions and bodily ailments owe their origin to the spiritual ailings of the soul; and also to show of how much greater moment it is that we should be cured of the spiritual paralysis and weaknesses of our souls. If, perchance, by reason of thy lukewarmness thou shouldst be weighed down by spiritual sickness, hasten to make heartfelt recourse to Jesus in order that thou mayest hear Him speak to thy heart with those efficacious words: *Surge, tolle lectum tuum—Arise, take up thy bed.* He will then enable thee to rise generously from thy evil habits and to recover thy vigour of soul to such an extent that thou wilt carry the bed of thy own flesh and sensuality, on which thou hast for so long a time been laid low, and wilt set about doing what the interests of thy soul and right reason demand of thee.

MONDAY IN THE EIGHTEENTH WEEK AFTER PENTECOST.

Habe fiduciam in Domino ex toto corde tuo, ne innitaris prudentiæ tuæ. In omnibus viis tuis cogita illum, et ipse diriget gressus tuos.—Prov. iii. 5.

Have confidence in the Lord with all thy heart, and lean not upon thy own prudence. In all thy ways think on Him, and He will direct thy steps.

I. CONSIDER that whilst thou art told in these words to trust in God, it does not mean that thou art not at the same time to avail thyself of that amount of prudence which God has given thee. The meaning is that thou shouldst not rely and lean upon thy own prudence. S. Peter tells us: *Estote prudentes, et vigi-*

lantes in orationibus—1 Pet. iv. 7—*Be prudent and watch in prayers;* because these two things, namely, prudence and recourse to God in prayer, ought to accompany thy every action. If thou wouldst guide thyself by thy own prudence, thou wouldst seem to believe thyself able to dispense with the help and light of God. If, on the other hand, thou callest on God and dost not make use of the means which prudence dictates, thou aspirest to oblige Almighty God to work miracles. Remember, therefore, that Almighty God is equally displeased with rash presumption and an overweening reliance on thy own prudence.

II. Consider the reason why thou must not lean on thy own prudence, but trust in God. It is because with all thy prudence thou art apt to be deceived, and canst not have a foreknowledge of future eventualities, nor provide against them. However, it is thy duty to make up thy mind according as prudence and right reason advise; but when this is done thou must have recourse to God by prayer and look to Him for success, trusting only in Him and not in thy own judgment. *Habe fiduciam in Domino—Have confidence in the Lord.* This confidence which the Wise man demands of thee, must be a firm and ardent hope that leaves no room in thy heart for any fear of the contrary, and that drives from thee that overgreat anxiety into which excessive prudence but too often degenerates. If thou hast confidence in the Lord *ex toto corde—with all thy heart*—He will always be ready to protect thee.

III. Consider that if thou desirest Almighty God to protect thee, thou must keep Him in thy thoughts —*in omnibus viis tuis cogita illum—in all thy ways think on Him*—that is, use diligence in renewing as far as possible, in every action, the upright intention of pleasing Him alone; so that by keeping thy eyes fixed on Him, He only may be the end and aim of thy actions. If thou actest thus, fear nothing, because He will direct thy every step, thy every undertaking, in such a way that He will lead thee on towards heaven, and keep thee away from every precipice. Neither wilt thou experience any difficulty in keeping thy eyes earnestly turned towards Him if once thou masterest the great truth that of thyself thou art capable of nothing, and that however clever thou thinkest thyself, thou art a lost man unless Almighty God help thee and direct thee. Hast thou ever had occasion to walk along a mountain path on a dark night, in danger of taking a false step at any moment? if so, thou certainly hadst no difficulty in giving thy continued attention to the guide that accompanied thee. Such also will be thy attitude towards Almighty God so soon as thou understandest the great need thou hast of His aid in every action, in order not to go astray and be lost. Whatever good thou hast been able to effect, whatever virtuous habits thou hast acquired, thou standest in equally great need of the help and protection of Almighty God. Thou art in the position of a little child, who is none the less dependent on its mother's support to enable it to walk, because she has supported him so far as he has reached.

TUESDAY IN THE EIGHTEENTH WEEK AFTER PENTECOST.

Gaudium erit coram angelis Dei super uno peccatore pœnitentiam agente, quam super nonaginta novem justis qui non indigent pœnitentia.—Luc. xv. 7.

There shall be joy in heaven upon one sinner that doth penance, more than upon ninety-nine just who need not penance.

I. CONSIDER that Our Lord asserts in these words, that there is greater festivity and joy in heaven on occasion of the conversion of one sinner than over the virtue of ninety-nine just; and the reason is, because although the just enjoy a normal state of greater esteem in the eyes of heaven, yet a penitent is the occasion of greater joy on account of the fresh acquisition of an immortal soul, and this joy is great in proportion to the previous difficulty and hopelessness of its conversion. Thus we read of the kind-hearted father who made the return of his prodigal son the occasion of unwonted rejoicing, because he had him with him again after so many years, and beheld him, as it were, raised from death to life. Hence thou mayest learn the yearning love thy Saviour has for thee, since He has made thy conversion from a state of sin to grace the occasion of great rejoicing, and His heart has been gladdened at having recovered thee. What other motive could He have for rejoicing, unless it were the earnestness with which He has thy interests at heart, and the ardour with which He loves thee? He is equally happy in Himself without thee. How comes it, then, that thou on thy side art not inflamed with an ardent love for thy Saviour? Thou oughtest, therefore, to strive earnestly after thy own salvation;

not only for thy own sake, but still more for sake of the pleasure thou thus givest thy Redeemer in so doing.

II. Consider how the angels also rejoice with Christ over the conversion of a sinner, and this for three reasons. First of all, on Almighty God's account, because they see the glory that is thus given to Him. Secondly, on man's account, because as they earnestly desire to share the eternal joys of heaven with us children of Eve, so also are they gladdened at beholding any one sinner regain that right to the bliss of heaven which he had lost by sin. Thirdly, on their own account, because as the angels also are employed in working out man's salvation, they are well pleased when they exercise their friendly office with success, and are victorious over those fallen spirits that are ever so active in thwarting their labours. Learn a lesson from the angels, and always rejoice and be glad from all three of these motives, whenever thou witnessest or hearest of the conversion of a sinner. It is a truer motive for joy than any worldly prosperity—and thou knowest what matter for congratulation this is held to be.

III. Consider that thou oughtest to derive from this consideration still stronger motives for procuring the conversion of guilty souls, according as thy state and strength permit. Sinners are not converted by sermons and missions only: many an interior conversion has been brought about by wholesome advice, by a private conversation, by good example, and, above all, by fervent prayer, accompanied by various acts of penance offered up to Almighty God for this especial end. Hence it comes to pass, that many a sinner whose conversion is attributed to some sermon he has heard, has in reality been more benefited by the secret prayer of some humble religious than by all the toil and labour of the public preacher. Take, therefore, the advice of the Holy Ghost, and *recupera proximum tuum secundum virtutem tuam*—Eccl. xxix. 26—*recover thy neighbour according to thy power:* thou wilt thus have greater merit, and less occasion for vainglory.

WEDNESDAY IN THE EIGHTEENTH WEEK AFTER PENTECOST.

Adjutor meus et protector meus es tu.—Ps. xxxix. 18.
Thou art my helper and protector.

I. CONSIDER what thou hast to do when thou art entrusted with any arduous office, or perhaps appointed to go elsewhere. On such occasions a host of difficulties and imaginations of dangers, or of possible failing of health, will assault thee, and in consequence thou art troubled in spirit and thy heart fails thee, in the belief that thou hast not strength of mind or body to overcome them. But thou must not, under these circumstances, concentrate thy thoughts on the real or imaginary dangers thou apprehendest; because thou wilt only but too easily succeed in alarming thyself: and should the tempter try to bring them more distinctly before thy mind, for the purpose of making thee lose courage, thou must get rid of them, saying to thy Saviour: *Adjutor meus et protector meus es tu—Thou art my helper and protector.* By this means all the greatest difficulties that would otherwise terrify thee will depart from thy mind, and vanish like clouds that momentarily darken the bright sky.

II. Consider that in the same way as the diffidence thou experiencest arises from an intimate and true knowledge of thy own weakness and misery, and justly causes thee to fear thyself; so also thy confidence in God must take its rise in a lively realisation of the loving-kindness of Almighty God, and of the certainty of His divine assistance, which will be great in proportion to the diffidence thou hast in thy own strength. This distrust of self is a better means by far for obtaining help from God than the assurance of remaining firm and of being quite safe, because Our Lord delights in confounding the presumptuous. Thus it comes to pass that many a soul that had a great amount of self-reliance has made an ugly fall, when it found itself face to face with the occasion; whilst others that were all in a tremble beforehand, remained steadfast: because, on account of the lively feeling they had of their own frailty, they were careful to fortify themselves with the help of God by humility and earnest prayer. Knowing, as thou dost, thy own weakness, put thy trust in the help of God, and strive to do what is required of thee, in order to deserve His help. This will not be presumption, but prudent confidence.

III. Consider that thou must never cease to confide in Almighty God, merely because at the present moment thou dost not feel in thyself the strength of mind that is necessary to overcome the particular difficulty that frightens thy weakness. Even though Almighty God does not grant thee this moral courage at the present moment, He will bestow it on thee soon enough to enable thee to come out of the struggle victorious. Our Lord is styled, *Adjutor in opportunitatibus*—Ps. ix. 10—*A helper in due time*, because He gives His especial help when there is need for it, and not otherwise, and when there is no need for it. When the critical moment arrives, He will give thee that energy which thou lackest now: *Insiliet in te Spiritus Domini . . . et mutaberis in virum alterum*—1 Reg. x. 6—*The Spirit of the Lord shall come upon thee*

... *and thou shalt be changed into another man.* It is said of the saints who confided in God, that *fortis facti sunt in bello*—Heb. xi. 34—*they became valiant in battle,* because they were endowed with supernatural strength at the very moment they were called upon to put out their strength for the honour of God.

THURSDAY IN THE EIGHTEENTH WEEK AFTER PENTECOST.

Ducam te per semitis æquitatis, quas cum ingressus fueris, non arctabuntur gressus tui, et currens non habetis offendientum.—Prov. iv. 11.

I will lead thee by the paths of equity, which when thou shalt have entered, thy steps shall not be straightened, and when thou runnest thou shalt not meet a stumbling-block.

I. CONSIDER that in the same way that the commandments are called the road or way to heaven, *viam mandatorum tuorum cucurre*—Ps. cxviii. 32—*I have run the road of Thy commandments,* so also the evangelical counsels are called paths: *et semitas tuas edoce me*—Ps. xxiv. 4—*teach me Thy paths.* The counsels are called paths for three reasons: firstly, because they constitute a narrower road than the highway of the commandments; but be not alarmed if the path is narrow at first, thou wilt afterwards go forward with ease: *cum ingressus fueris, non arctabuntur gressus tui—when thou shalt have entered, thy steps shall not be straightened.* The affections of the will are, as it were, the strides by which the soul betakes itself to God; but spiritual progress is not like the progress made in walking, in which the pace slackens after long continuance. In our spiritual progress the pace becomes swifter and more vigorous by continued running; because this running is simply an ardent love of Our Lord, and a soul that loves finds neither difficulty nor hindrance in the observance of the counsels: it runs forward securely in an ever-increasing love of purity, poverty, and obedience. On the contrary, how easy it is for a soul to stumble and fall that goes slowly and leisurely in the service of God!

II. Consider the second reason why the counsels are called paths. It is because they are trodden by the few. But remember that paradise belongs to the few, and not to the many. Dost thou not perceive that for the very reason that these paths are less frequented, thou art the better able to make way, without being obliged to run counter to nearly as many of those obstacles which hinder thy going straight ahead, as thou wouldst have encountered on the highway with the crowd—I mean, such obstacles as human respect, distracting amusements, and bad example. Although monks and nuns are the few, when compared with the world at large, they are nevertheless the many relatively to the number of those who go to heaven, and even relatively to the number of those that are canonised as saints. Thank thy Saviour, therefore, with all thy heart for having chosen thee to tread these paths of the evangelical counsels.

III. Consider, in the third place, that the counsels are called paths, because they are like short-cuts from the high-road that take thee more speedily to heaven: not in the sense that they cause thee to die sooner—for it is not mortification that hastens death, but surfeit, sensuality, and other excesses—*stimulis mortis peccatum*—1 Cor. xv. 56; but the evangelical counsels are short-cuts to heaven, because they are a straighter road, and cause thee to lead a life of greater perfection, and consequently are the cause of thy remaining a shorter time in purgatory, especially if seconded by penances, indulgences, and suffrages. Hence thou mayest perceive that for many reasons *non arctabuntur gressus tui, et currens non habetis offendientum—thy steps shall not be straightened, and when thou runnest thou shalt not meet a stumbling-block*, if only thou keepest to these paths that are narrower, more direct, and shorter than the rest. But there is one condition to be fulfilled, if thou wouldst succeed on this road: never grow tired of running, never stop, and never turn back; because shouldst thou fail in this condition, thou wouldst encounter numberless difficulties and hindrances: and then, instead of the evangelical counsels serving thee as a guide to heaven, they would prove to be little else than a short-cut to a most disastrous and grievous downfall into the bottomless abyss.

FRIDAY IN THE EIGHTEENTH WEEK AFTER PENTECOST.

Quis nos separabit a charitate Christi ? tribulatio ? an augustia ? an fames ? . . . Sed in hic omnibus superamus, propter eum qui dilexit nos.—Rom. viii. 35.

Who shall separate us from the love of Christ ? shall tribulation ? or distress ? or famine ? . . . But in all these things we overcome, because of Him that hath loved us.

I. CONSIDER how great was the union of love that linked the Apostle S. Paul so inseparably with his divine Master. He declared that no accumulation of misfortunes would ever make him cease to love Him. He even counted himself happy if in His service he should encounter either tribulation, or distress, or hunger, or nakedness, or persecution, or death itself. Now, if any one of these misfortunes singly is enough to separate thee from the love of Jesus, gather thence how great must S. Paul's love have been, who defied their united force to tear him away from Jesus.

II. Consider that when at times thou picturest thyself, in prayer, as condemned to be cast into chains by persecution, or about to be executed in the presence of an infuriated mob, thou mayest perhaps imagine that thou hast the courage to undergo similar hardships for Jesus' sake: but these are dangers that are a long way off, and not at all probable. Perhaps even thou mayest, in time of prayer, believe thyself ready to undergo other trials, and which may actually befall thee, as for instance having to put up with scanty and poor living and clothing, or the privation of the conveniences to which thou art accustomed: but unfortunately when the time arrives to put thy courage to the test, thou at once becomest down-hearted, or if thou overcomest thyself in one matter, thou yieldest in others; or, again, if thou art firm in thy purpose so far as bodily discomforts are concerned, thou allowest thyself to be conquered by interior trials of the soul. See, therefore, how strong and deeply rooted was S. Paul's love for our divine Master; he was not only prepared to bid defiance to all the trials he enumerates, but he even went forward of his own accord to meet them, and he actually overcame them all: *in hic omnibus superamus—in all these things we overcome.*

III. Consider that if thou really desirest, in imitation of S. Paul, to overcome generously all the difficulties that assail thee throughout the course of the day, thou hast within thy reach the means of succeeding, according to the requirements of thy particular state of life. All that is necessary, is, that thou also shouldst become an ardent lover of thy Jesus: it was love—and love alone—that inspired the apostle with so great a courage, to face and overcome every kind of trial. *In hic omnibus superamus, propter eum qui dilexit nos.—In all these things we overcame, because of Him that hath loved us.* Now, the words *propter eum —because of Him*, denote the agency of two causes, namely, the love that he bore for Christ, and the help that he received from Christ; and both of these causes are available in thy own case also. Wherefore, if thou sincerely desirest to experience this ardent love and efficacious assistance, set thyself to weigh well how deeply thy Saviour has deigned to love thee and how bitterly He has suffered for thee. Remember how many trials and cares He has undergone for thy sake, what hunger and scanty clothing, what great persecution He endured, and what an accumulation of deadly wounds He received from the thorns, nails and spear, on the altar of the cross. If, therefore, He has loved thee to such a pitch, wilt not thou likewise consecrate to Him thy undivided love, and thus have an assurance of receiving from Him all the assistance thou needest, and be thus able in all thy trials to exclaim, as the apostle did: *In hic omnibus superamus, propter eum qui dilexit nos—In all things we overcome, because of Him that hath loved us.*

SATURDAY IN THE EIGHTEENTH WEEK AFTER PENTECOST.

Nescit homo, utrum amore an odio dignis sit; sed omnia in futurum servantur incerta.—Eccles. ix. 1.

Man knoweth not whether he be worthy of love or hatred, but all things are kept uncertain for the time to come.

I. CONSIDER that although the soul that is aware of being in a state of sin is in a position to know full well that it is the object of God's hatred, no one, on the other hand, though he be never so holy, can know for a certainty that he is worthy of God's love. We know, of course, that the sanctifying grace conferred in baptism cancels the blot of original sin, as does that conferred by the sacrament of penance wipe away the stains of actual sin; but we cannot know for certain if the necessary previous dispositions exist, either on the part of the minister, or on the part of the recipient. Neither can any one have a certain knowledge as to whether he be worthy of that love that Almighty God bears towards His elect on account of their future state of perfect grace, or worthy of that hatred of final reprobation which may be his lot on account of the state of sin in which he is capable of dying, and therein receiving his warrant for eternal damnation. Until we shall be summoned to appear at the tribunal of our Judge, we must necessarily live in this uncertainty of our salvation. If thou feelest no apprehension or dread on account of this uncertainty of thy present and future state, it is but too clear that thou art in lamentable darkness.

II. Consider that this uncertainty about thy present and future state may be made very useful to thee for thy present requirements. If thou wert certain of being actually quite safe, and in a state of grace, thou wouldst very easily grow proud; and if thou wert sure of a blissful future, thou wouldst easily be induced to neglect the present. Oh, what great benefit have not the saints derived from this state of uncertainty! it has been the cause of their keeping themselves humble in the sight of God, in Whose hands they saw that their future must necessarily depend; and humble also before men, by esteeming others as better than themselves on account of the present and future uncertainty attending their own lot. How then canst thou presume to put thyself down so frankly as better than so many others, who are haply in the actual possession of a higher state of grace than thou hast, and who will also perhaps be possessed of a higher degree of glory? Be humble, therefore: thou canst not afford to judge others, whilst everything is so uncertain regarding thyself.

III. Consider that this uncertainty is so advantageous for thee, that even though it lay in thy choice to have a warranty for thy future salvation, it is almost beyond doubt that thou wouldst do better to leave it alone. Oh, if thou didst but know how meritorious it is to rely with great confidence for everything on the mercy of thy Saviour—saying to Him: *Ecce, Deus salvator meus; fiducialiter agam, et non timebo*—Isa. xii. 2—*Behold, God is my Saviour; I will deal confidently, and will not fear.* Didst thou but realise the merit of this act of confidence, thou also wouldst imitate a great servant of God, who protested that had he in his very hands a bond assuring him of his eternal predestination, he would at once tear it to pieces, and depend entirely on the goodness of his God. Be content, therefore, with the testimony of a good conscience that does not lay to thy charge the present guilt of mortal sin; and never cease recommending thyself to Almighty God, and praying Him never to allow thee to lose His grace. Thus thou mayest reasonably hope to secure thy salvation.

NINETEENTH SUNDAY AFTER PENTECOST.

Amice, quomodo hoc intrasti, non habens vestem nuptialem ? . . . . Multi sunt vocati, pauci vero electi.— Matth. xxii. 12.

Friend, how camest thou in hither, not having a wedding garment ? . . . . Many are called, but few are chosen.

I. CONSIDER that Our Lord invites all to partake of the supper, prepared on occasion of the nuptials of the Eternal Word with His sacred Humanity; but those who are in an especial manner invited to assist at this supper are religious. These are the privileged souls, who, unhampered by the cares of business and other worldly ties, sit down at this table and partake more plentifully of the repast afforded them in the sacraments of the Church, the lights and inspirations of heaven, and the examples of virtue that surround them. This call to a religious life has been a sheer mercy of Almighty God in thy regard, without any connection with thy previous inclinations and merits. How many has not Almighty God left in the world, who were far better and more deserving than thou! Acknowledge the greatness of the benefit conferred upon thee, and never let a day pass without heartily thanking the goodness of Almighty God in thy regard.

II. Consider that in proportion as thou art more highly favoured by Our Lord, in being called to religion, so much the less can He tolerate seeing thee without the nuptial garment—that is to say, without those virtuous habits that are peculiar to thy state of life. Reflect seriously on thy general behaviour and manner of living. If they are not such as are becoming to a true religious, fear and tremble that these words be not addressed to thee: *Amice, quomodo hoc intrasti, non habens vestem nuptialem?—Friend, how camest thou in hither, not having a wedding garment?* And although thou be not actually driven out of the cloister, thou wilt be driven from the presence of God, *in tenebras exteriores—into the exterior darkness,* by being deprived of His heavenly light, and becoming spiritually blind—*legatis manibus ac pedibus*—with thy hands and feet bound, so as to be hardly able to rid thyself of thy vicious habits, or take a single step forward on the path to heaven. Notice, too, in this day's Gospel how much more severely the man was punished that presumed to come to the supper without the wedding garment than those who refused the invitation altogether, and that, too, uncouthly. So also will thou be punished with great severity, if thou livest in religion merely as seculars do in the world.

III. Consider that many are called to religion, but few are they that attain religious perfection: *Multi sunt vocati, pauci vero electi*—*Many are called, but few are chosen.* Think, not, therefore, that thou hast done a great deal in abandoning the world and embracing the religious life. All this has been the bounty of Almighty God. It is thy turn now to co-operate with the grace of Almighty God by acquiring habits of virtue and uprooting the vices of the old man. Yet this, which is the most important duty of a religious man, is overlooked by many. Do not, therefore, follow the example of those who lead a lax tenor of life, but imitate those who are fervent. Remember that it will be no excuse for thee at the judgment-seat of God that thou hast allowed thyself to be guided by the example of the many, whilst thou hast those words ringing in thy ears: *Multi sunt vocati, pauci vero electi!—Many are called, but few are chosen!*

MONDAY IN THE NINETEENTH WEEK AFTER PENTECOST.

Beati mortui qui in Domino moriuntur. Amodo jam, dicit Spiritus, ut requiescant a laboribus suis.—Apoc. xiv. 13.

Blessed are the dead who die in the Lord. From henceforth now, saith the Spirit, that they may rest from their labours.

I. CONSIDER who are those happy ones that *in Domino moriuntur—die in the Lord.* They are those who die, if not for Our Lord as martyrs die, die at least in the Lord, as Confessors and Virgins, because they breathe forth their last in a spirit of entire abandonment of themselves to the loving mercy of Our Lord; they die, as it were, in His bosom, in the wound of His sacred side, in His Sacred Heart, and in the peace-giving embrace of His loving arms: *In Osculo Domini.** What a beautiful death is this! How much to be envied and sought after! but remember that it is not enough to desire it; thou must deserve it also.

II. Consider that this especially privileged death does not fall to the lot of all who die in a state of

---

* This teaching is beautifully illustrated by the following passage of the holy Abbot Blosius, taken from the *Appendix* to his Treatise entitled *Institutio Spiritualis*, cap. iii:—"There is no exercise so profitable, at the hour of death, as an entire abandonment and resignation of oneself to the Will of God, desiring simply and solely the accomplishment of His holy will in time and in eternity, to the exclusion of any wish or desire of one's own. It is impossible that a soul that quits this world in dispositions of such real and perfect resignation should not forthwith wing its flight to heaven; because, just as Almighty God cannot Himself be liable to any sort of penalty, or be subjected to any kind of purgation in the flames of purgatory, so neither can the soul that is thus intimately united to Him by conformity of will and ardent love."

grace ; it is reserved for those only who have already died to themselves, to live entirely for God. Now, what is meant by dying to oneself ? It means a previously acquired habit of detachment from everything that the unsparing hand of death will in its own time snatch away from us, whether property, country, relations, amusements, and, above all, that domestic idol, self-love; but, in addition to this actual detachment, there must be the aim and endeavour to live, as far as may be, in the body, without a body. By becoming a religious, thou hast made open profession to aspire after this life-giving death by the fulfilment of thy religious vows ; but bear in mind that it is not enough to have begun the enterprise, thou must carry it through perseveringly to the end. What will it avail thee to have been, once upon a time, dead to thyself, and living, as it were, in Our Lord, if afterwards thou beginnest to live again to thyself, by seeking thy own comfort, by allowing inordinate affection to relatives and country to regain possession of thy heart, and by seconding continually the vicious whims of self-love ? If thou wouldst *die in the Lord*, thou must needs be content to remain dead to thyself until thou art called away.

III. Consider that if the thought of this previous death to self scares thee, thou mayest well console thyself by the thought of the sweetness of the second death that follows it, because this second death will bring with it eternal rest : *Amodo jam, dicit Spiritus, ut requiescant a laboribus suis—From henceforth now, saith the Spirit, that they may rest from their labours*. Take notice, too, that the Spirit which now urges thee on to suffer much for God's sake, to toil and to mortify thyself, and which will at the hour of death bid thee take thy rest, is the Spirit of God. Whereas the spirit which would induce thee to give over working for God and mortifying thyself on this side of the grave, is not the Spirit of God; it is thy own spirit, or the spirit of the world, or the evil spirit. The bidding of the Spirit of God is that those only who have toiled enough already should cease from their labours on the arrival of death. How, then, canst thou lay claim to this desirable repose without having undergone the previous task of toil? See how hard the saints have worked to obtain this blissful repose, and what bitter toil Our Lord underwent to put thee in the way of gaining it also; but remember that all that Our Lord underwent, with all its infinite merit, is not enough to put thee in possession of it without thy own individual labour. Mark the words: *Ut requiescant a laboribus*—" *suis* "—*that they may rest from their own personal labours.*

TUESDAY IN THE NINETEENTH WEEK AFTER PENTECOST.

Ecce, sto ad ostium, et pulso. Si quis audierit vocem meam, et aperuerit, januam, intrabo ad illum et cœnabo cum illo, et ipse mecum.—Apoc. iii. 20.

Behold, I stand at the gate, and knock. If any man shall hear My voice, and open to Me the door, I will come in to him, and will sup with him, and he with Me.

I. CONSIDER that Our Lord comes and calls thee, and knocks at the wicket of thy heart, in order that thou shouldst open to Him and give Him admittance each time that He favours thee with His holy inspiration, and awakens remorse of conscience in thy heart. It is His rule never to force admittance; He leaves thee the full control of thy liberty, to enable thee to have the merit of receiving Him of thy own free will.

When, over and over again, thou hearest Him call, and knowest full well that He is knocking at thy heart, what degree of readiness dost thou manifest to hearken to His voice, and open the doors of thy heart to this divine Guest? If thou losest time in drawing near to the wicket of thy heart, at the first summons of thy Lord, to listen to what He has to say, by means of retirement and recollection, or if, instead of doing so, thou seekest to turn away thy attention in order not to hear Him, what wonder is it that thy divine Guest should, in the end, withdraw, and refrain from seeking admittance?

II. Consider that when Our Lord does call thee, it is not enough merely to listen to what He has to say, to hearken to His inspiration, but thou must open the door if thou desirest Him to enter thy house. This opening of the door of thy heart consists in promptly making an offering of thy will to perform the good work Our Lord demands at thy hands, and in asking Him for the help of His grace to do it well, saying with St. Augustine: *Da quod jubes, et jube quod vis—Enable me to fulfil what Thou biddest, and then bid whatever Thou listest.* How sadly at variance is thy conduct with this line of duty! No sooner hast thou heard the voice of thy Saviour than, instead of offering Him thy services, thou allowest thyself to be frightened by the difficulties which thy own self-love puts in the way, and thou givest no heed at all to the great advantages thy Lord holds out to thee. Reflect seriously Who it is that thus deigns to come to thee, and why He comes to thee, and then thou wilt no longer hesitate a moment to open to Him.

III. Consider that no sooner does our Lord enter thy heart than a twofold repast is in readiness there, one prepared by thee for thy Lord, the other by thy Lord for thee: *Cœnabo cum illo, et ille mecum—I will sup with him, and he with Me.* The supper that thou spreadest for thy Lord, and with which thou refreshest Him, consists in the good works thou performest in obedience to His inspirations. The supper He lays for thee consists in spiritual consolation, and in His strengthening grace, which He bestows on thee in proportion to the diligence which thou hast thyself manifested in receiving Him. But, besides this sort of repast He is preparing, meanwhile, another—a final banquet, which will be given in the light, not of faith, but of glory. Happy wilt thou be if it shall fall to thy lot some day to seat thyself at so royal a feast! First of all, however, thou must needs provide the repast which Our Lord expects of thee, by obeying His call and admitting Him into thy heart. If thou turnest a deaf ear to His invitations, it will, alas! but too easily come to pass that thou wilt find thyself refused admittance to the supper of eternal glory.

WEDNESDAY IN THE NINETEENTH WEEK AFTER PENTECOST.

Quod hominibus altum est abominatio est ante Deum.— Luc. xvi. 15.
That which is high to men is an abomination before God.

I. CONSIDER the import of this great sentence pronounced by the Incarnate Wisdom of God. He declares that whatever is held in the general estimation of men of the world to constitute rank, and greatness, and glory, is all an abomination in the sight of Almighty God. In the estimation of the world, rank and position mean, as a rule, a great display and haughty assumption of superiority; greatness implies profusion and extravagance, coupled, generally speaking, with vanity and pride; and glory is thought to be found in thwarting a rival or crushing an enemy. Yet all this *quod hominibus altum est—which is high to men*—is, without exception *abominatio apud Deum—an abomination before God.* What are thy sentiments on this matter? what view dost thou take, who frequentest the school of the Gospel? Dost thou lean to the teaching of the world, or to that of Jesus Christ? Which dost thou value more, talent or virtue? Examine carefully thy notions and ideas, and see if, perchance, thou hast a leaning towards the wrong side.

II. Consider who they are on each side that hold such widely differing views about worldly greatness, and what claims they have to thy practical estimation of the same. It is esteemed by men, yet not by all men; not by men who are possessed of a greater amount of holiness, of reason, and of real common sense, but only by such as are most likely to be deceived themselves, and to deceive others; by those who are more swayed by their passions, and are more animal-like in their manner of living, and who will shortly be the food of worms. On the other hand, reflect on the excellence of that great Being in Whose sight all that such men consider as worthy of being sought after is simply an abomination; it is no other than God Almighty—*ante Deum.* What comparison, therefore, wouldst thou institute between a vile heap of corruption, such as man is, and a God of infinite majesty? Art thou capable of such a crying wrong as to value the esteem of man more highly than that of God and of so many millions of angels and saints —in a word of the whole court of paradise? If thou takest pleasure in what Almighty God detests, it is a clear sign that thou frequentest the school of the world more than that of Christ.

III. Consider that in order to render worldly greatness despicable in the eyes of men, who, as a rule, make so much of it, Christ Our Lord came down from heaven to earth; He was born in a miserable outhouse in poverty and neglect; in order to screen Himself from Herod's fury, He was obliged to fly by night into Egypt and lead there a life of obscurity, working in St. Joseph's poor and unpretending carpenter's shop; he had to put up with affronts, persecution and ill-treatment of all sorts from his own people; and, finally, he was condemned to the most shameful and infamous sort of death—to the death of the cross. Is not the example of Christ enough to induce thee to correct thy ideas, and make thee detest worldly ostentation and love humility, that amiable virtue of which thy Saviour gave thee so many practical lessons during the whole course of His lifetime.

THURSDAY IN THE NINETEENTH WEEK AFTER PENTECOST.

Habeo adversum te, quod charitatem primam reliquisti.
—Apoc. ii. 4.
I have somewhat against thee, because thou hast left thy first charity.

I. CONSIDER that this complaint, made by Almighty God, strikes home with great truth in the case of any soul that has at one time begun to serve God fervently, and has afterwards given itself up to a tepid life, by continually going in search of comfort and shunning the practice of mortification, or by neglecting regular observance and its wonted exercises of piety, or, lastly, by making little of deliberate venial faults. This state of tepidity is most hurtful from three points of view. First of all, as concerns the tepid soul itself; it makes the soul resemble a tree on which great pains have been bestowed, and which has been planted out in excellent soil and yet yields no fruit in the shape of good works. Where, pray, is the result, the fruit, of so many communions, of so many daily spiritual exercises, of so much good example on the part of fervent companions. Then, again, tepidity causes all its fruitfulness to consist only in a tangled mass of briars, fit only for the fire; that is to say, in numberless acts of inobservance, in a heap of vices and faults, so numerous that they are beyond reckoning. Lastly, tepidity is the reason of its leading a most unhappy life, because, on the one hand, it feels great repugnance and disrelish for every sort of spiritual exercise and all the occupations of a religious life, whilst, on the other hand, it is deprived of the many worldly consolations in which it would fain indulge. Oh, if thou couldst but behold the interior state of mind of two religious, the one mortified and fervent, the other lax and tepid, how thou wouldst envy the peace of the one that is fervent and pity the misery of the other that is tepid!

II. Consider from a second point of view the great harm tepidity occasions, namely, with regard to one's neighbour. A religious who leads a community life has a bounden duty to be of some help to his neighbour, and this is done by prayer, by good example and edifying conversation and good advice. Now a tepid religious gives no assistance by prayer, for he either leaves it alone or gets through it as quickly as he can; his example is only an occasion of harm to the weak, and his conversation and advice is still worse. In a word, a tepid religious is like a tree that is not only sterile, but is poisonous as well; he is like a two-edged sword that wounds both himself and his neighbour. Alas, how many accusers he will have to meet at the tribunal of God, who will demand vengeance on his head!

III. Consider the third standpoint from which tepidity may be seen to be so injurious—and that is in its bearings to Almighty God. The tepid soul robs Him of that glory, of that especial tribute of homage, which He looked for at its hands, from the fact of having called it to religion, and thus signally favoured it. By its ingratitude it keeps back the flow of His infinite bounty, and hinders Him from pouring into the soul those especial gifts He would otherwise bestow upon it; and, lastly, the tepidity of such a soul provokes and incites the justice of God to abandon it and deprive it of those especial aids which are needful to enable a religious to last out, as it were, in religion, and to obtain the gift of final perseverance. How many instances there are of religious that, from growing lax and tepid little by little, have at last fallen into frightful excesses, and died a most pitiable death! The worst of it is, too, that although there are many instances recorded in which souls have been raised to great holiness and virtue, from the icy chill of a positively bad life, there are hardly any instances in which a tepid soul has been known to return to its first fervour. Such a soul renders itself positively undeserving of experiencing the merciful kindness of Almighty God, by its black ingratitude. Entertain, therefore, a great horror and dread lest such an evil should befall thee.

FRIDAY IN THE NINETEENTH WEEK AFTER PENTECOST.

Nunc judicium est mundi; nunc princeps hujus mundi ejicietur foras; et ego si exaltatus fuero a terra, omnia traham ad meipsum.—Joan. xii. 31.

Now is the judgment of the world; now shall the prince of this world be cast out; and I, if I be lifted up from the earth, will draw all things to Myself.

I. CONSIDER how in these words Our Lord meant to indicate two most desirable achievements that would result from His death. Firstly, that He would deprive the devil of the power he held over mankind; and, in the second place, that He would Himself assume the right to our fealty by cancelling with the merits of His own death on the cross, the debt incurred by our sins, which had themselves been the cause of our thraldom under Satan's tyranny. Hence it follows that in the case of all those who still remain under the devil's power, this is not due to any right the devil actually has, though he would have had a right if Christ had not died for them, but merely because they themselves foolishly choose to remain under his rule and act as those meanest and most despicable of slaves, who remain such of their own free choice. Bewail the disastrous and wide-spread folly of so many infidels and bad Catholics. But stay! before lamenting the folly of others, examine whether perhaps thou thyself do not help to swell their number by thy own misconduct.

II. Consider that since the power formerly held by Satan over all mankind, has been vested in Jesus by the fact of His having ransomed them at the cost of

His own life, He has good reason to say that He has drawn all men to Himself—*Omnia traham ad meipsum*—*I will draw all things to Myself*—because all belong to Him and are His subjects. Mark, too, that all are His without distinction, devout and indevout, good and bad—*Ad te omnis caro veniet*—Ps. lxiv. 3—*All flesh shall come to Thee*—and therefore on the day of judgment, *Omnes stabimus ante tribunal Christi*—Rom. xiv. 10—*We shall all stand before the judgment-seat of Christ.* The good and the devout will then become the sharers of His kingdom; the indevout and the bad will be condemned for their faithlessness and sentenced to eternal punishments. Enter seriously into thyself and bethink thee that sooner or later thou must necessarily surrender thyself at Jesus' feet, either now as a faithful follower and future sharer of His glory, or, later on, as a faithless renegade and guilty victim of His justice: make thy choice now of that alternative which is more to thy advantage.

III. Consider how and by what means our crucified Jesus draws us to Himself, to make us His faithful followers, and then share His kingdom with us. He draws us by persuasion, by lovingkindness, by sympathy. In the first place, then, He persuades us by His heavenly teaching, and still more by His example; for He went so far as to die, naked and forsaken, on a cross between two thieves, yet so peacefully and humbly, that His very executioners were touched with awe and love: *Vere, hic erat Filius Dei*—Matth. xxvii. 54—*Indeed, this was the Son of God.* He draws us by His lovingkindness in having, at the cost of His own life, freed us from eternal death, and opened to us the gates of paradise. He draws us, lastly, by sympathy, proving Himself to be true man by undergoing death on the cross, and true God by triumphing over death. As man He draws us by that sympathetic love which results from His having become one of ourselves, and as God He draws us still more vehemently as our true centre and last end. Is it possible that not one of these three powerful modes of drawing thee to Him should succeed in thy regard, but that all fail to make thee a devoted and faithful companion of the Crucified One!

SATURDAY IN THE NINETEENTH WEEK AFTER PENTECOST.

Filioli mei, non diligamus verbo et lingua, sed opere et veritate.—1 Joan. iii. 18.
My little children, let us not love in word nor in tongue, but in deed and in truth.

I. CONSIDER that our love for Jesus must not be love in appearance only, consisting in a great display of words, or even in sensible sweetness and tears of tenderness; it must not resemble the unproductive tree that makes a great show of only leaves and flowers. It must be a love ennobled by these three qualities: it must be a practical love, a patient love, a triumphant love. In the first place, therefore, it must be a practical love. Just as a person's state of health may be known from the beating of the pulse, so may the quality of our love be known from our works. For the three-and-thirty years of his mortal life, the Son of God was continually working in thy behalf, offering up His toil and sweat for thy salvation. Now, if thou pretendest at all to love Jesus, see with what degree of earnestness thou spendest thyself in His service and for His glory. Fire that does not burn is no fire at all—it is but a sham; so also with love: *si non operatur, amor non est*—says a holy writer—*if it does not manifest itself in deeds, it is not love at all;* and thus practice is the sure sign by which thou mayest ascertain if thou lovest Jesus in real earnest.

II. Consider that the love of Jesus must be not only practical, but patient also; because long-suffering is the surest and safest token of true love. So long as thou art not prepared to endure and even embrace the cross for God's sake, thou canst never be certain that thou lovest Him; because what perhaps seems to thee to be an inspiration of grace or an effect of zeal and charity, may prove to be simply a natural impulse and the offspring of self-love. The cross only is the touchstone by which thou canst distinguish real love from counterfeit love, earthly love from heavenly love. The reason is, because in the act of suffering thou must necessarily contradict thy self-love and the inclinations of corrupt nature. Gold that will not stand the fire test, is alloyed and is of little value.

III. Consider that our love of Jesus must be, moreover, a triumphant love. Fire overcomes every obstacle, because it envelops and over-reaches everything it comes across; it transforms fertile plains into arid wastes with its devouring flames, and changes everything into its own fiery nature. So also the love of Jesus ought to reign supreme in thy heart, and be the master of all thy other affections, so that when any sort of competition arises between the love of God and the love of any creature whatsoever, the love of God may prevail, and always retain the first place in thy heart. But more than this, the love of God ought to have not only the first place, but to have sole possession of thy heart, by destroying in it every other love, just as the flame envelops and destroys all else than itself; because Jesus is thy only good, Who is true to thee in life, will not fail thee in death, and after death will constitute thy complete and never-failing joy. Cast a glance over the whole of creation, and thou wilt find nought that is worthy of thy love besides Jesus, or what is loved in reference to Jesus. If the love Jesus bears for thee has triumphed in His own sacred Heart over every other consideration, why not allow thy love for Him to do as much in thy heart?

TWENTIETH SUNDAY AFTER PENTECOST.

Domine, descende, priusquam moriatur filius meus.—Joan. iv. 49.
Lord, come down, before that my son die.

I. CONSIDER what was the reason why Jesus, Who showed Himself so ready to go to the Centurion's house to cure his servant that lay dangerously ill, now refuses the earnest entreaties of a person of great distinction to betake Himself to his palace and restore health to his dying son. The reason, says S. Gregory, is because He wishes to humble our pride, which makes us ready enough to tender our services to the great ones of the world at the first intimation, but will not allow us to bestir ourselves to help the poor and neglected ones of Christ, though, as a rule, they are dearer to Him. It is quite contrary to true charity to make such distinctions as these: true charity looks at the handiwork and the image of God in our neighbour, not at his dignity and wealth—these are merely outward appendages of no intrinsic worth. *Non est acceptio personarum apud Deum*—Coloss. iii. 25—*There is no respect of persons with God;* and this ought to be equally true in the case of one who, in serving his neighbour, professes to serve him in God and for God.

II. Consider the second reason why Our Lord did

not choose to go to the house of the ruler: it was to correct the imperfection of his faith. He looked upon Jesus as a great prophet, Who was beloved of God and able to work miracles; but he did not believe that He was at one and the same time both man and God, and therefore present everywhere. Hence he thought that His bodily presence was quite necessary to enable Him to restore health to his dying son. See here one of the chief hindrances that prevent thy prayers from being heard—it is the imperfection and weakness of thy faith. Faith is the first step that man takes towards God, as it is also the first requisite which is of absolute necessity to obtain His holy grace. Strive, therefore, in time of prayer to quicken and enliven thy faith, so that it be changed into a firm trust and confidence in God: to this end beg Our Lord with these words: *Credo, Domine; adjuva incredulitatem meam*—Marc. ix. 23—*I do believe, Lord; help my unbelief.*

III. Consider that at first Jesus rejected the entreaty of the ruler, to the end that by persevering to his own great benefit in asking for the favour he desired, he might dispose himself to become worthy of it. Constancy in asking for grace is so pleasing in the sight of Almighty God, that He makes good our shortcomings in our manner of asking, and enables us to obtain what is far beyond our deserts. He cannot reject the petition of any one that assiduously waits upon Him, as He Himself declares in these words: *Si perseveraverit, pulsans . . . si non dabit illi, eo quod amicus ejus sit; propter importunitatem . . . dabit*—Luc. xi. 8—*If he shall continue knocking . . . although he will not give him, because he is his friend; yet because of his importunity . . . he will give.*

MONDAY IN THE TWENTIETH WEEK AFTER PENTECOST.

Quasi peccatum ariolandi est repugnare ; et quasi scelus idololatriæ noli acquiescere.—1 Reg. xv. 23.
It is like the sin of witchcraft to rebel ; and like the crime of idolatry to refuse to obey.

I. CONSIDER that in order to be truly obedient it is not enough merely to execute thy superior's behest, either because it happens to fall in with thy own humour, or because thou fearest the consequences of neglecting it, or because thou hopest to be the gainer by fulfilling it. What thou must do is to fulfil his wish precisely because he wishes it, conforming thyself to the will of thy superior not only in the material execution of the thing enjoined, but also with thy will. True obedience consists in the settling down of one's own will to that of a superior. However, to accomplish this, thou must be fully persuaded, first of all, that thy superior is right in commanding what he does. Thou art not forbidden to represent the difficulties thou seest in the way ; but when once thou hast represented them, thou art forbidden to contradict or make difficulties with a view to drawing the will of thy superior over to thy own.

II. Consider why it is said that to rebel against the judgment of a superior is like the sin of witchcraft : *quasi peccatum ariolandi ;* it is because by so doing thy rule of action becomes mere guess-work, and thou canst only guess what is right and what is wrong. When thou conformest thyself to the judgment of thy superiors in anything that is not clearly sinful, thou art certain of pleasing God and of doing what is best ; because every action done from a motive of obedience is, as it were, grafted on to the parent-stem of the good pleasure of Almighty God, and so becomes the joint offspring of the Will of God and of thy own. But when thou followest thy own judgment, thou art not so sure of pleasing God, even in the performance of works otherwise good and praiseworthy, as, for instance, works of penance and private devotion; and God forbid that when thou comest to die, it be not said to thee, as it was to the Hebrews: *Quis quæsivit hæc de manibus vestris?* —Isa. i. 12—*Who required these things at your hands?* Now, when thou forsakest a certain good which obedience demands of thee, to undertake works of uncertain merit at thy own caprice, is not this mere guesswork, a sort of divination? Why, then, wouldst thou so often act in this way by withstanding the arrangements of thy superior as to thy residence, employment, or particular undertakings?

III. Consider on what grounds the refusal to obey is said to be like the crime of idolatry. The reason is because when a disobedient religious is bent on acting as he himself thinks best, he practically recognises his own will as his primary rule of action, and this belongs of right to Almighty God, and to those whom He has delegated to hold His place in thy regard: *Qui vos audit, me audit*—Luc. x. 16—*He that heareth you, heareth Me.* When, therefore, thou attemptest to deprive Our Lord's delegate of this right, and transfer it to thy own will, thou comest to idolise thyself, as it were, and to raise altar against altar, by giving the preference to thy own will against that of Almighty God, in the very fact of making it thy rule of action. See, therefore, what a grievous fault it is to rebel against and oppose the judgment of thy superiors to maintain thy own! and how still more blameworthy it is to aim at obliging those who hold the place of God in thy regard, to yield to thy stubbornness, thus upsetting and reversing the relative positions of superior and inferior!

TUESDAY IN THE TWENTIETH WEEK AFTER PENTECOST.

Qui fidelis est in minimo, et in majori fidelis est ; et qui in modico iniquus est, et in majori iniquus est.—Luc. xvi. 10.

He that is faithful in that which is least, is faithful also in that which is greater ; and he that is unjust in that which is little, is unjust also in that which is greater.

I. CONSIDER that one of the greatest mistakes in the spiritual life is to launch forth in mighty desires of undertaking great projects for God, which will probably never be realised, and at the same time neglecting the nice and punctual discharge of the actual duties Our Lord has entrusted to thee. These longings after great enterprises, however fervent they may be, may easily prove highly prejudicial, because they turn away thy heart and mind from thy daily duties, and oftentimes make thy self-conceit increase, by making thee believe thyself endowed with great virtue. Before thou aspirest to great undertakings, as, for instance, distant and laborious missionary labours in India or elsewhere, or again, the bright crown of martyrdom, and so on, accustom thyself first of all to the exact performance of little duties, and then thou mayest aspire to something more difficult. If thou art faithful to the best of thy power in the midst of lesser dangers, it may then be hoped that thou wilt be faithful in greater ones also.

II. Consider how important and how meritorious is this fidelity in doing little things well, precisely because they are of such frequent and continual recurrence, and are therefore more troublesome to nature and contradictory to self-love ; and because, again, there is in such little things as these no food for vanity, and consequently thou gainest great merit by them, and acquirest that excellent habit of overcoming natural repugnances. On the other hand, occasions for the exercise of heroic virtue are seldom met with, and the fewness of such acts is unable to induce an habitual exercise of them, especially since, besides their scarcity, it is so easy for vainglory to creep in and taint them. Make it thy study, therefore, to learn to put up with cutting remarks, to pay no heed to acts of rudeness on the part of thy neighbour, to perform punctually and carefully all the seemingly trivial actions thy state of life demands of thee, and thou wilt make great progress : *Qui fidelis est in minimo, et in majori fidelis est*—*He that is faithful in that which is least, is faithful also in that which is greater.* If thou art not exact in little things, depend upon it, neither wilt thou be faithful in great things.

III. Consider that in the same way as the tradesman who scorns little gains may look in vain to meet with success in large transactions, so also may the religious who has no fear of lesser sins, with good reason fear a fall into grievous sin : *Qui in modico iniquus est, et in majori iniquus est*—*He that is unjust in that which is little, is unjust also in that which is greater.* The danger of falling into grievous sin does not equally threaten a soul that occasionally slips almost involuntarily into lesser faults, through inadvertence, or the frailty of fallen nature, but it especially affects the soul that has no scruple about frequently and wilfully falling into lesser faults without the slightest fear or remorse, because the force of bad habit, added to the tendency of nature, will make it very easy to slip so as to fall into mortal sin. Wherefore, if thou art careless in allowing thyself to be misled, with thy eyes wide open, and to commit lesser faults in the shape of ambition, immortification, sensuality, and avarice, thou wilt but too easily be hoodwinked, and before long go from lesser to great, from venial sin to mortal sin. Mark also the words, *iniquus est—is unjust;* where it is declared not that such a one *will be* grievously guilty —*erit*, but that *he is—est*, because although the evil is actually to come, it is so close at hand that Our Lord speaks of it as though it were present; and when once thou hast fallen into mortal sin, God grant that thy fall be not fatal and irreparable.

WEDNESDAY IN THE TWENTIETH WEEK AFTER PENTECOST.

Peccavi et vere deliqui, et ut eram dignus non recepi.—Job xxxiii. 27.

I have sinned, and indeed I have offended, and I have not received what I have deserved.

I. CONSIDER with how great reason thou oughtest to have ever on thy lips these words of holy Job. Thou oftentimes complainest because Almighty God allows thee to be tried and harassed, and it would almost seem to thee that His hand lies too heavily on thee. Oh, what unseemly language is this! By all means change thy tone, and say rather that these trials that God Almighty sends thee, this ill health, this disgrace, which seems to thy self-love so hard to endure—say that all these are but a fractional part of the debt thou owest to the justice of God for thy sins of commission and omission. Exclaim: *Peccavi et vere deliqui, et ut eram dignus, non recepi*—*I have sinned, and indeed I have offended, and I have not received what I have deserved.*

II. Consider that if thou wouldst *utter* these words

with an intimate sense of their truth in thy own regard, thou must first of all *believe* them to be true in thy own regard, and this thou wilt not succeed in doing unless thou endeavourest to realise the extent of thy ingratitude towards thy Saviour. Reflect, therefore, how faithless and unjust was thy conduct whilst thou wast still living in the world, and how ungrateful thou hast shown thyself for the great benefit He has conferred on thee in rescuing thee from the dangers of the world; how careless thou hast been in acting up to the obligations of thy vows and of thy rule, and how backward thou art in the acquisition of the virtues demanded of thee by thy holy state of life. Reflect on all this, and then, indeed, thou wilt say, from the depths of thy heart: *Peccavi et vere deliqui, et ut eram dignus non recepi—I have sinned, and indeed I have offended, and I have not received what I have deserved.* Thou wilt recognise that there is no proportion at all between the trials Our Lord sends thee and the torments that would be thy due in hell.

III. Consider that all the damned souls in hell itself may truly say these same words, although, as a matter of fact, they do not say them, because truth will never be admitted where blind rage reigns supreme. Yet however much Almighty God were to torture a damned soul, its torments would be always less than it has deserved for even one single sin. Reckon up, then, and see if the trials Almighty God sends thee in this life are more or less than thou hast deserved for thy many sins. What, pray, are all the pains of this world in comparison with those of the next, and which Our Lord has spared thee? They are no more than what painted fire is to real fire. If, therefore, thou hast to undergo great humiliation here below for a short time, think it not too much for thee, who hast deserved to be for ever trampled under foot by Lucifer. If thou findest it irksome and painful to be confined to a bed of aching and pain, remember that thou hast deserved to be bound down for never-ending ages amidst the frightful flames of hell. If at times life seems wearisome, with so little comfort and such a dearth of worldly amusements, bear in mind that, like the rich man of the gospel, thou wouldst not find one drop of water in the bottomless abyss of hell wherewith to moisten thy lips. Think earnestly on all this, and thou wilt feel the truth of those words: *Peccavi, et vere deliqui*—*I have sinned, and indeed have offended ;* and thou wilt subjoin : *Et ut eram dignus non recepi*—*and I have not received what I have deserved.*

THURSDAY IN THE TWENTIETH WEEK AFTER PENTECOST.

Oculi mei semper ad Dominum; quoniam ipse evellet de laqueo pedes meos.—Ps. xxiv. 15.
My eyes are ever towards the Lord ; for He shall pluck my feet out of the snare.

I. CONSIDER that the world is full of snares laid by the devil, and if thou wouldst escape being entrapped by them, instead of keeping thy eyes turned to the ground thou must raise them above and keep them fixed on thy Saviour, as slaves were wont to work, with their faces towards their master. Slaves work in this way for three reasons : in order the better to execute the orders of their master, to be ready to follow him everywhere, and to seek either assistance when needed, or pardon when careless or guilty. In like manner oughtest thou also to keep thy eyes turned to Almighty God ; firstly, to be ready at the first indication to obey His wishes, whether made known to thee by Himself or through His ministers. If thou obeyest with great punctuality, there will be no danger, not only of falling, but not even of tripping up amidst the many snares laid for thee by the devil. It is the especial privilege of the obedient to proceed with safety where others would be lost. Why, then, dost thou make so little account of so great a privilege? *Qui custodit præceptum, non experietur quidquam mali*—Eccl. viii. 5—*He that keepeth the commandment, shall find no evil.*

II. Consider that a second reason why a servant keeps his eyes fixed on his master, is to enable him to follow and keep up with him. So also must thou act towards thy divine Saviour if thou wouldst tread in His footsteps, under all circumstances. But how canst thou possibly do this effectually unless thou keepest thy eyes turned towards Him, by reflecting, as occasion demands, [how He acted under similar circumstances whilst He sojourned on earth? If in all thy actions and occupations thou lookest to the example left thee by Our Lord for thy imitation, thou wilt be sure never to make a false step: *Quicumque hanc regulam secuti fuerint, pax super illos*—Gal. vi. 16—*Whosoever shall follow this rule, peace on them.* Why, then, dost thou not set thyself to meditate seriously on the actions of Jesus as described in the gospels? They will serve as a guide and safe escort, just as at sea the pilot makes use of his chart to bring the ship safely to port.

III. Consider that another reason why a slave is wont to keep his eyes fixed on his master, is to beg either for pardon, or for assistance, or for protection; and this is just how thou hast to act towards thy Saviour, because thy greatest safeguard against the snares of thy spiritual enemies must consist, beyond everything else, in continually begging pardon for thy offences, and seeking for aid in thy many needs. So soon as thou leavest off asking for His assistance, thou wilt begin to disobey His holy Will and fail to imitate His example. Hence thou must always continue asking, even when thou hast obtained what thou hadst desired, because it is unfortunately but too easy to lose the gifts of God, unless He be at hand to help thee. Thou art guilty, thou art poverty-stricken, thou art in danger, but still it lies in thy power to acquire a right to paradise. Why, then, wouldst thou grow weary of keeping thy gaze fixed on that Almighty Master on Whom thy every hope depends? Say, rather: *Oculi mei semper ad Dominum*—Ps. xxiv. 15—*My eyes are ever towards the Lord.*

FRIDAY IN THE TWENTIETH WEEK AFTER PENTECOST.

In fide vivo Filii Dei, qui dilexit me, et tradidit semetipsum pro me.—Gal. ii. 20.
I live in the faith of the Son of God, Who loved me and delivered Himself for me.

I. CONSIDER what is the meaning of *vivere in fide—living in faith*. It means that thou must place entire confidence in Jesus Christ, being certain that so long as thou leavest thyself in His hands, all will go well with thee. Whether He send thee desolation of spirit, or sickness of body, or humiliations, thou must cast thyself unreservedly into the arms of that Saviour Who has ever loved thee so tenderly, and will make everything turn out to thy own greater good. Say therefore, with all the fervour of thy heart: *In fide vivo Filii Dei*—*I live in the faith of the Son of God.*

II. Consider to what a pitch He has loved thee: *Tradidit semetipsum pro te*—*He has delivered Himself for thee.* He has fixed upon Himself in person to be the priceless victim that was to be slain for thy salvation; and thus He suffered Himself to be betrayed by Judas and handed over to the power of His enemies, because *tradidit semetipsum*—*He delivered Himself.* Moreover, He underwent all this for thee individually—*dilexit me, et tradidit semetipsum pro me*—*He loved me, and delivered Himself for me;* and thus He died as much for thee alone as for all together, and in the very act of dying He thought of thee, He prayed for thee, He offered that great sacrifice of the cross to His Eternal Father for thee. Had it been necessary, He would have come down from heaven for thy sake alone, just as He has actually become man and died for all mankind. See, therefore, whether He loves thee in real earnest or not, and whether thou hast not good reason to put thy whole trust in Him, and submit thyself entirely, in every circumstance, to His fatherly dispositions.

III. Consider what wrong thou dost thy Saviour, if, when He has given His whole self up for thy sake to the death of the cross, thou art unwilling to give thyself up wholly to Him by living in the arms of His loving Providence. Now, the way to give thyself up wholly to Him, is to place thyself unreservedly at the disposition of His holy Will, the victim, as it were, of obedience, and leave Him to dispose of thee in whatever way He thinks fit, whether through His own direct agency, or by means of His representatives, whom He has appointed to be thy superiors. Busy not thyself to find out how thy affairs and interests are progressing, but live *in fide*—*in faith*, just like the infant that lives on its mother's bosom, where it rests and takes its nourishment with the utmost peace and security.

SATURDAY IN THE TWENTIETH WEEK AFTER PENTECOST.

Confige timore tuo carnes meas; a judiciis enim tuis timui.—Ps. cxviii. 120.

Pierce thou my flesh with Thy fear; for I am afraid of Thy judgments.

I. CONSIDER that although David was conscious of having feared God in his past life, and, indeed, of fearing Him at the very time he was speaking, he nevertheless begged Almighty God to fill Him with His holy fear anew, because he was desirous that the fear which reigned in his soul should also hold its sway in his flesh, and that thus he might be enabled to subdue the rebellion of his inferior and animal nature in the same way as he held his superior faculties in subjection. Happy wouldst thou be if thou wert able to effect this! At least be ever praying Almighty God to possess with His holy fear thy eyes, and tongue, and ears, and all thy senses and thy whole self, so that thou mayest not have to suffer much from the insolence of thy flesh. When the body is pierced materially, the weapon passes through the body to the heart; when the soul is pierced spiritually, the fear of God passes from the heart to the body. Thus when the saints are crucified spiritually, by making their souls obedient to Almighty God, they succeed in course of time in crucifying their flesh also, and in bringing it into subjection to the spirit. Marvel not, therefore, if thy own flesh is always growing more and more insolent; and why? Because thou hast not the fear of God, not even in thy spiritual faculties; thou hast a lax conscience, and therefore it is useless to expect to find the fear of God reigning supreme in thy flesh, which is always the last to surrender.

II. Consider that David's motive in asking for this holy fear, was because he dreaded the judgments of Almighty God: *A judiciis enim tuis timui—For I am afraid of Thy judgments.* By these judgments may be understood the commandments of God according to that of the Psalmist: *Sprevisti omnes discedentes a judiciis tuis*—Ps. cxviii. 118—*Thou hast despised all them that fall off from Thy judgments.* So also it may mean the unsearchable judgments of God's decrees, as it is said: *Judicia tua abyssus multa*—Ps. xxxv.—*Thy judgments are a great deep.* And, lastly, they may be taken for the rigorous judgment to which Almighty God will subject each one of us on our departure from this world. David, therefore, begged of Almighty God to quench the lust of his flesh, because he feared it might be the cause of his falling into grievous sin, and that on that account he might be allowed, by the hidden judgments of Almighty God, to go to perdition. Another reason was, because he well knew how rigorously every thought and word and most trivial action will be judged, and he feared lest the waywardness of concupiscence should make him commit some excess in action or in thought, or consent to some half-repressed desire which might afterwards be brought against him at the tribunal of God's justice. What hast thou to say to all this? thou who hast so little fear of losing the grace of God, who so easily promisest thyself the gift of final perseverance, and who thinkest so lightly of the evil suggestions that assail thee? Security is not the fruit of presumption, but of the holy fear of God.

III. Consider that thy duty is not restricted merely

to asking Almighty God very earnestly to be enabled to keep thy flesh in subjection, *Confige timore tuo carnes meas—Pierce Thou my flesh with Thy fear;* but thou must also co-operate on thy side in thy endeavours to do so; thou must imitate David, who punished his body by night-watching, by haircloth and ashes, and by fasting and other austerities. If thou art a stranger to all this, thy flesh will never be crucified, but will always be in rebellion against the spirit.

TWENTY-FIRST SUNDAY AFTER PENTECOST.

Oblatus est ei unus, qui debebat ei decem millia talenta.
—Matth. xviii. 24.

One was brought to him that owed him ten thousand talents.

I. CONSIDER that thou art this servant that owest Almighty God ten thousand talents, by reason of the numberless occasions and ways in which thou hast broken His law. Thy debt is so excessive, both as regards guilt and penalty, that thou canst not properly understand it, inasmuch as the debt thou incurrest for thy smallest fault is so great, that all the saints together could not of themselves atone for it, with all their acts of homage, because the hatred Almighty God bears to the slightest venial sin is greater than the pleasure he derives from the homage of all His creatures together; the debt of punishment also is so great, that it cannot be understood except by the guilty soul that is actually cancelling it to the last farthing, either in purgatory or in hell. Why, then, dost not thou, who art a debtor to Almighty God to so serious an extent, hasten to humble thyself sincerely in His sight and entreat His forgiveness, as the servant in the gospel begged his master's forgiveness: *Procidens orabat dicens: patientiam habe in me—Falling down, he besought him, saying: Have patience with me.*

II. Consider how very ready and easy Almighty God is to condone these thy heavy debts of guilt and punishment, provided only thou turn away from the evil done, by sincere contrition, and accuse thyself of it in the sacrament of confession, and perform the penance enjoined thee by the priest. By means of this great sacrament, Jesus Christ Himself satisfies the claims of divine justice in thy regard by the infinite worth of His own expiation. Thank Jesus, therefore, with all thy heart, for having gained so complete a pardon for thee; a pardon, indeed, which, though it costs thee little to obtain, has cost thy Redeemer a very great deal.

III. Consider that in proportion as Our Lord is ready to forgive thee the offences thou hast committed against Him, so also He wishes thee to forgive thy brethren the little grievances thou hast against them; and He protests that He will never condone the enormous debt of thy sins unless thou from thy heart forgivest the offence,—it may be an especial one—of thy brother: *Sic Pater vester cœlestis faciet vobis, si non remiseritis unusquisque fratri suo de cordibus vestris.* Almighty God loves each one of us so tenderly that nothing gives Him greater pleasure than to behold us living in peace with one another like good and fond brothers. Wherefore it is no wonder that he is especially beloved of God who forgets and forgives grievances the remembrance of which would only disturb him, as on the other hand it is no matter for astonishment that he is most displeasing in His sight who keeps bitterness rankling in his heart, ready at any moment to foment dissension and ill-will. Hence, we read of more instances than one in which a single generous act of forgiveness of injuries has sufficed to make a great saint, as in the case of S. John Gualbert; whereas, on the other hand, a refusal of forgiveness has been known to be the occasion of forfeiting the palm of a martyr's death, as witness the unfortunate Sapricius.*

* The historical fact here referred to is narrated by Surius and others in the life of S. Nicephoras (Feb. 9th). Sapricius was a priest of Antioch who had formed an intimate friendship with a layman of the same city, named Nicephoras. Sapricius, however, took grave offence at some act of Nicephoras, and, notwithstanding, all the humble apologies of the latter refused obstinately to forgive him or to be reconciled with him. Meanwhile the persecution of the Christians under Valerian and Gallien made itself felt at Antioch, and Sapricius, amongst others, was apprehended as a priest, and condemned to lose his life for preaching the faith of Jesus Christ. On his way to the scene of martyrdom, he was met by Nicephoras, who, forgetful of all the animosity shown him by his former friend, was only anxious to effect a reconciliation with one whom shortly he expected to revere as a martyr of Christ. Casting himself therefore on his knees, he implored Sapricius for the love of Jesus Christ to give him the kiss of peace. The only reply vouchsafed him was a haughty refusal, and Sapricius pursued his way to the arena. And now with his hands bound fast and the admiring eyes of the Christians who were present fixed upon him, he seemed to be on the point of gaining the martyr's palm, when suddenly his pallid features betoken the throes of violent terror, and turning to the judge, he appeals for mercy and for life. Who could have believed it? Sapricius lacks the love of the Christian, and he therefore fails to obtain the constancy of the martyr. With the promise of his life he consents to deny Christ and to offer incense to Jupiter. Nicephoras, who had followed with a sorrowing heart, on beholding the perfidy of the priest was fired with zeal for the honour of Jesus Christ, and boldly proclaiming himself a Christian, demanded that he might satisfy with his own blood the injury offered to the true God by the apostasy of Sapricius. The prayer of the confessor was heard: he was condemned there and then, and bore off the palm and the crown that had been prepared for Sapricius, but of which he had rendered himself unworthy by the unchristian hatred that rankled in his bosom. S. Nicephoras suffered martyrdom A.D. 260.

MONDAY IN THE TWENTY-FIRST WEEK AFTER PENTECOST.

Hoc est præceptum meum, ut diligatis invicem.—Joan. xv. 12.
This is My commandment, that you love one another.

I. CONSIDER how cheerfully thou oughtest to fulfil this precept of brotherly love, considering that it alone amongst so many other precepts is called by Our Lord His own commandment; *præceptum meum—My commandment.* But that this love should be what it ought to be, it must fulfil three conditions; thou must love thy neighbour properly, efficaciously and gratuitously. First of all, then, thy love must be proper, and well-ordered, by giving the preference to his spiritual rather than his temporal welfare; by loving the beauty of the nature he has received from God, and which is modelled after God's own likeness, and at the same time hating the evil of sin which is his own creation, by loving all in general and each one in particular, from the highest of motives: namely, the express wish of Almighty God, which ought to urge thee to love all without distinction. How far dost thou realise this uprightness of intention, this standard of true love? Which dost thou take most to heart, the spiritual or the temporal welfare of thy neighbour? Dost thou love him on the grounds on which thou oughtest to love him, or rather perhaps from congeniality of disposition, or ties of relationship, or because of his individual good qualities and attractions.

II. Consider that thy love for thy neighbour ought

to be efficacious—not confined to thy goodwill, but extending itself to thy actions. Christ Our Lord might, if He had chosen, have wrought our salvation by a single sorrow, a single sigh, and yet He willed to purchase it at the cost of His blood. How far art thou able to pride thyself on the practical activity of thy love for thy neighbour? Where canst thou show any expenditure of toil and sweat for thy neighbour's weal either in soul or body—in so far as thy actual employments give thee occasion for doing so? Let us hope that thou art not one of those who make a show of love in words, but not in deeds, or what would be worse—one of those who pretend to love their neighbour, but in reality hate him. The first is a sham, the second the mock feint of a traitor. Real love of one's neighbour is *dilectio sine simulatione*—Rom. xii. 9 —*love without dissimulation.*

III. Consider the third and most excellent quality, which ought to crown thy love of thy neighbour. It ought to be gratuitous; that is to say, not on account of favours that thou lookest for at his hands, nor on account of past benefits already received, but simply with a view to doing something that is most pleasing to God, and from a motive of obedience to the commandment of thy Saviour Who has called thy especial attention to it. If thou lovest thy neighbour on account of the favour thou lookest for at his hands, thou thyself art the object of thy love—not thy neighbour. If thou lovest him for past benefits already received, thou dischargest a debt of gratitude which is praiseworthy in itself, but meanwhile thou failest to comply with the divine precept in its entirety, because this precept requires that thou shouldst love thy neighbour not only when he is friendly to thee but even when he is unfriendly. See how Christ Our Lord, hanging on the cross, prays to His heavenly Father on behalf of those very ruffians who had fastened Him to that infamous gibbet. Yet He prays for them without any regard to His own interests. He could have obtained just as well under the title of His Divine Sonship, all that glory which, as a matter of fact, He acquired through becoming our Redeemer.

TUESDAY IN THE TWENTY-FIRST WEEK AFTER PENTECOST.

Oportet semper orare, et non deficere.—Luc. xviii. 1.
We ought always to pray, and not to faint.

I. CONSIDER what Our Lord demands of thee when he says: *Oportet semper orare, et non deficere—We ought always to pray, and not to faint.* Does He perhaps mean thou shouldst be always on thy knees in prayer? Certainly not. What He does mean is, in the first place, that thou shouldst not fail to pray at the proper times appointed by thy rule, just as thou dost not let go by the fixed hours for thy meals without refreshing thy body. Secondly, that thou shouldst be given to prayer, in so far as thou art able to do so, even out of the appointed times. A student that devotes as much time as he can to study, is said to be always studying, because of the fondness he has for study; and this ought to be true of thee with reference to prayer. Thirdly, these words signify that in the event of thy not being heard, thou shouldst not give up in despair, nor leave off asking, but shouldst persevere faithfully; and this is the real meaning of the words, *Oportet semper orare, et non deficere—We ought always to pray, and not to faint.* Examine thyself awhile and see whether thou prayest at the proper times, and whether out of such times thou fallest to thy prayers as much as thou canst, and, lastly, whether thou perseverest in asking even when it appears to thee that thy Saviour pays no heed to thy affairs. When thou discoverest that thou art faithful in carrying out all this, thou mayest rest assured that thou prayest always, and wilt work out thy salvation.

II. Consider the reason why Our Lord desires us to be always beseeching Him, because it might seem unbecoming that He Who is naturally so inclined to be bountiful and liberal, should take pleasure in being incessantly besieged with our petitions. But no—it is not unbecoming—He likes to be sought after precisely because He loves us so earnestly. Petitioning Almighty God is not like petitioning an earthly prince; in the case of the latter it is not only not a gain, but it is a loss to do so—at least in the event of failure—but in the case of Almighty God the mere fact of petitioning Him is a very great gain, because in so doing a number of meritorious acts are elicited, such as of religion, faith, trust in God, humility, patience and so on. Thus, no petition presented to Almighty God is ever fruitless: when it is granted, the favour directly asked for is the result; when it is not granted, there is at least the merit of having asked as an indirect result. Therefore, with reason does Our Lord say to thee: *Oportet semper orare, et non deficere—We must always pray, and not faint.*

III. Consider what great harm comes to thee from neglecting prayer, considering that all the time thou art praying thou art certain of gaining something, even though thou shouldst not obtain what thou askest; and so soon as thou givest over praying thou losest ground, by losing very great merit. Wherefore prayer is not only a means, it is also an end, and hence we are told: *Sine intermissione orate*—1 Thess. v. 17—*Pray without ceasing.* What matters it if thou obtainest not what thou askest for, since so long as thou prayest thou obtainest what is in reality still more desirable, namely, the being admitted to treat with Almighty God? See how a court-favourite esteems himself fortunate to get a chance of speaking to his prince, even though he does not obtain what he asks for; and wilt thou think thyself less fortunate to be able to speak to Almighty God?

WEDNESDAY IN THE TWENTY-FIRST WEEK AFTER PENTECOST.

Justus autem meus ex fide vivit.—Hebr. x. 38.
My just man liveth by faith.

I. CONSIDER who are they whom Our Lord calls His beloved just ones. They are those that lead a life of lively faith—that is to say, faith burning with love—because a torpid faith is a dead faith, incapable of imparting life or heat to the soul that possesses it. Now the just man is said to live by faith, because the life of the soul is God, and faith is that first of all virtues which brings the soul into contact with God. The body is said to derive its life from the heart, because it is by the beating of the heart that the soul is united with the body. It is the same with regard to faith: according to those words—*Accedentem ad Deum oportet credere*—Hebr. xi. 6—*He that cometh to God must believe.* See, then, how jealously thou oughtest to watch over this life-giving faith. It is a duty, of course, to watch over other virtues also, over charity, patience and the like; but in an especial manner we must keep guard over faith, which is to all other virtues what the heart is to the other members of the body. Be careful,

therefore, to drive away every temptation against it
by renewing thy protestations of fidelity and loyalty
to thy liege Lord, and bowing thy head *in obsequium
fidei*, with humble submission, without giving thyself
any concern about what thy thoughts suggest to the
contrary against thy will: *Omni custodia serva cor tuum,
quia ex ipso vita procedit*—Prov. iv. 23—*With all watchfulness keep thy heart, because life issueth out from it.*

II. Consider that the just man lives by faith, not
only because faith imparts life to the soul, but also
because it nourishes it and strengthens it: much in
the same way we are accustomed to say that the hawk
lives by rapine, and the chameleon on air. Hence, if
we observe carefully, we shall see that the source of
all the harm that is done to the soul is weakness of
faith. Whosoever has a firm, solid faith, and stands
fast with his intellect—*in verbo veritatis*—2 Cor. vi. 7
—*in the word of truth*—stands equally fast with his
will—*in virtute Dei—in the power of God.* Such a
one is as heedless to prosperity as he is unflinching in
adversity. And why? Because he always bears in
mind, and is thoroughly convinced, that nothing is
worth caring for but eternity. On the other hand, a
soul that is weak in faith keeps sinking away like a
poor, half-starved, sickly child. Strive, therefore, to
increase thy fund of faith by eliciting frequent acts of
faith, by reading books that will help to strengthen it,
and, above all, by often asking Almighty God to increase thy faith—*Domine adauge nobis fidem*—Luc.
xvii. 5—*Lord, increase our faith.*

III. Consider that the just man lives also on faith,
because this is his ordinary food. We never say that
a person lives on a food which forms his repast in
only one meal out of a hundred; but he is said to live
on that which forms the staple of his meals: and so
faith is that which constitutes the principal nourishment of the souls of the just; indeed, sometimes it is

their only food. This comes to pass when at times the soul seems to be bereft of all aid from Almighty God, to be left without light and deprived of all consolation, and in this state it is reduced to live by pure faith alone and to exclaim : *Scio cui credidi*—2 Tim. i. 12—*I know whom I have believed.* See, then, what a good store of faith thou must lay up, to be able to maintain life in thy soul during a season of such spiritual dearth and want. If on such an occasion thou art unprovided with a good supply of faith, thou wilt not last out long : *Si non credideritis, non permanebitis*—Isa. vii. 9—*If you will not believe, you shall not continue.*

THURSDAY IN THE TWENTY-FIRST WEEK AFTER PENTECOST.

In timore Domini esto tota die, quia habebis spem in novissimo die.—Prov. xxiii. 17.
Be thou in the fear of the Lord all the day long, because thou shalt have hope in the latter end.

I. CONSIDER what a great benefit the holy fear of God brings along with it, were it only the confidence it inspires at the hour of death. This is a universal rule. Very probably thou mayest have witnessed the death of several of the members of thy community, and thou wilt have remarked that those who during their lifetime were of a bolder frame of conscience, less precise and exact in carrying out their rule, and less scrupulous in the nice observance of their holy vows, gave at that dread hour signs of being harassed with diffidence and fear ; whereas, on the other hand, those who during their lifetime had been of a more delicate and timid conscience, showed themselves to be full of confidence and hope. Reflect for a little to which class thou belongest, and thus thou wilt be able to foresee with pretty great certainty what thy case will be—*in novissimo die—in thy latter end.*

II. Consider that if thou wouldst enjoy this confidence at the hour of death, it is not enough to have now an ordinary commonplace sort of fear; it must be a great fear that will make its influence felt at all times and in everything. It must be a fear, not, indeed, like that of certain scrupulous souls, who, in some particular matter, or on some particular occasion, are over apprehensive, but in all else have an uncommonly lax conscience; but it must be a sort of fear that from morning till night will put thee on thy guard against doing or saying anything that can displease or aggrieve Almighty God; a fear, in a word, which will surround thee on all sides, as the sea envelops a fish, and so hem thee in that it be impossible for thee to get beyond its reach. *In timore Domini esto tota die—Be thou in the fear of the Lord all the day long.* Thy lot is indeed enviable if thy life shall be spent not merely in frequent, but in continual fear.

III. Consider that he who is in possession of this holy fear is promised at his death the enjoyment of a lively confidence of being enabled to make that dark and narrow passage from this world to the next, that frightful plunge into the deep of eternity, successfully, and with the assurance of being saved: *Habebis spem in novissimo die—Thou shalt have hope in the latter end.* Notice that thou art not promised certainty, but a well-grounded hope, to impress on thee that no one can put his salvation entirely out of the reach of danger, even though his life be actually spent in the holy fear of God; because the eternal salvation of each individual, however holy, depends, up to the very last moment, on those especial aids of actual grace which Almighty God chooses in His bounty to bestow on him. If, then, the saints themselves can have no further security than hope at that all-important hour of death, what will thy condition be, who livest with so little fear of God and of His judgments? Set thyself therefore to think seriously how to acquire an habitual fear of doing aught, however small and insignificant, which is displeasing to Almighty God, and then when death comes thou also wilt enjoy the assurance of His assistance.

FRIDAY IN THE TWENTY-FIRST WEEK AFTER PENTECOST.

Ego sum via, et veritas et vita.—Joan. xiv. 6.
I am the way, and the truth and the life.

I. CONSIDER that Christ is the Way, and, as such, teaches thee the quickest path to paradise. And what may this path be which Christ Our Lord points out? It is the path of the evangelical counsels, which He not only pointed out, but which He followed also in His own daily life. There are three obstacles which hinder us from making way on the road to paradise, love of comfort, love of riches, and love of one's own will. Now by the fact of Our Lord's teaching thee by His own example to embrace the counsels of voluntary poverty, perpetual chastity and entire obedience, He teaches thee the straightest and the best way to heaven. These counsels are laws not imposed by authority, they are laws undertaken from love; hence they were never given to the Jewish people, because a law of love was not adapted to their condition of servile bondage. Reflect then awhile how earnestly thou oughtest to thank thy Saviour, for having enabled thee to enjoy this great privilege, and how necessary it is that thou shouldst observe these counsels from a spirit of love and not of constraint.

II. Consider that Christ is also the Truth, sent unto the world to teach men the truths of eternity by His preaching: *Evangelizare pauperibus misit me*—Luc. iv. 18—*To preach the gospel to the poor He hath sent me.* These great truths He still continues to impress on all those who desire to become His followers and disciples. The means He makes use of to teach these truths of eternity are the Holy Scriptures, which He bequeathed to His Church, and which He still continues to teach His disciples individually by the secret instructions He gives them interiorly, and by His silent whisperings to the heart of such as are eager to listen to Him, and who, like Magdalene, betake themselves in humility to His feet: *Secus pedes Domini, audiebat verbum illius*—Luc. x. 39—*Who sitting also at the Lord's feet, heard His word.* What is thy anxiety to make progress in this school, and to listen to so great a Master, Who alone has the power and the knowledge necessary to ground thee thoroughly in these important truths? What is thy love for the Holy Scriptures and spiritual reading generally? With what amount of willingness dost thou stay at the foot of the crucifix to hearken to the voice of Jesus? *Qui appropinquant pedibus ejus, accipient de doctrina illius*—Deut. xxxiii. 3—*They that approach to His feet, shall receive of His doctrine.*

III. Consider that Christ is not only the Way and the Truth, but He is also the Life. He is our Life now by grace, and hereafter by glory. As the life of glory constitutes the bliss of our heavenly country, so also the life of grace is the greatest happiness of our earthly exile; and whosoever fulfils the evangelical counsels in their entirety, and earnestly strives to give ear to the teaching of Christ, is in the enjoyment of this life of grace, and wants nothing else to lead a life of happiness and contentment. How many there are, who, at this present moment, find their hearts full of peace, in the seclusion of their cells, and of a happy solitude, occupied only in listening to their Saviour and in fulfilling His counsels. If, religious as thou art, thou failest to lead a life of happy contentment, the reason is because thou dost not observe the evangelical counsels as perfectly as thou oughtest, and because, instead of hearkening to the teaching of thy Lord, thou wanderest about in search of worldly news and worldly conversation. Oh, what a pity it is to lose the real charm of holy religion, which in itself is capable of ensuring a contented and happy life, by going in pursuit of vain and empty consolations!

SATURDAY IN THE TWENTY-FIRST WEEK AFTER PENTECOST.

Divitiæ salutis, sapientia et scientia. Timor Domini ipse est thesaurus ejus.—Isa. xxxiii. 6.

(The) riches of salvation (are) wisdom and knowledge. The fear of the Lord is His treasure.

I. CONSIDER the difference that obtains between temporal and spiritual riches. Earthly riches are the occasion of damnation to those who love them to excess, whereas the more we love spiritual riches the more do they help us on in the way of salvation. Earthly riches can avail us only in so far as good use is made of them; spiritual riches, on the contrary, are profitable in the mere fact of preserving them and taking care of them. Yet who is there, alas, that bestows one half of the amount of toil and anxiety that is commonly lavished in heaping up earthly riches for the benefit of the body, for the purpose of accumulating spiritual riches for the benefit of the soul? Bear in mind, also, that whereas one may unexpectedly acquire earthly riches by way of gift, or inheritance, spiritual riches, on the contrary, cannot be obtained but by working for them.

II. Consider that these spiritual riches of salvation here mentioned consist in wisdom and knowledge. Wisdom has for its object our last end, which is God. Knowledge has for its object the means which will lead us to the attainment of so great an end. If thou art desirous of possessing true wisdom, study well the end for which thou wert created; if thou wouldst possess true knowledge, learn to distinguish what means are best adapted for its attainment, because here are to be found the true riches of salvation. Search the depths of thy heart and see what end thou art wont to prefix to thyself in thy life and undertakings as a religious; is it Almighty God, or is it the idol of vainglory, of honour, or of thy own comfort? Beg Almighty God unceasingly to bestow on thee true wisdom, which will cause thee to labour for thy true end alone, and beg Him likewise to give thee true knowledge which will show thee how to set to work to attain thy end.

III. Consider that it is not enough to possess these riches unless thou hast some safe place where thou canst store them. Therefore, just as the miser has his treasure, that is to say, his coffer where he keeps his money under lock and key, so also must thou have thy treasury, thy safe, and this is the fear of God : *Timor Domini ipse est thesaurus ejus*—*The fear of the Lord is his treasure.* It is this that will keep thy treasures of true wisdom and knowledge safe from the thieves that would rob thee of them. It is this that will preserve them against human respect, because as thou wilt be more afraid of displeasing God than man, thou wilt not allow thyself to be led away by men to neglect thy end, or the means that conduce to its attainment. It is this fear of God that will defend thee from the assaults of the devils, because as thou wilt have a greater dread of the anger of God than of all their impotent rage, thou wilt shut thy ears at once to their evil suggestions. It is the fear of God, again, that wilt screen thee from the wily attacks of thy household enemies, thy own unruly passions, because as thou wilt be more apprehensive of losing God than any temporal advantage, thou wilt be slow to believe their crafty insinuations. Take, therefore, for thy keeper and watch the holy fear of God, otherwise these riches of salvation wilt be but too easily snatched away from thee.

TWENTY-SECOND SUNDAY AFTER PENTECOST.

Reddite quæ sunt Cæsaris, Cæsari, et quæ sunt Dei Deo.
—Matth. xxii. 21.
Render, therefore, to Cæsar the things that are Cæsar's, and to God the things that are God's.

I. CONSIDER the beautiful answer given by Our Lord to the malicious question of the Pharisees as to whether tribute ought to be paid to Cæsar, and by which they thought to get Him into disgrace, either with the Roman authorities if He said it could not be done, or with the Jews if He advocated its payment. *Reddite quæ sunt Cæsaris Cæsari, et quæ sunt Dei Deo—Give to Cæsar the things that are Cæsar's, and to God the things that are God's.* This is just what thou must do, leave to the world what belongs to the world. To the world belong honours, grandeur, comfort and riches, and all this thou must leave alone for those who live in the world. Thou hast abandoned all these things when thou turnedst thy back upon the world and didst embrace the religious state by means of thy holy vows; but examine if thou hast left all this in affection as well. Dost thou endeavour to live with thy heart estranged from these worldly allurements, or dost thou rather procure as much distinction and comfort as thou canst? Be ashamed of thy manner of living, which is so much at variance with what thou professest.

II. Consider that it is not enough to leave to the world what belongs to the world, but thou must also give to God what belongs to God. Thou belongest to Almighty God under several titles, by creation, redemption, and donation. In the first place, thou art His by title of creation, having drawn thee out of nothingness and given thee a body which is perfect in itself, and an immortal soul made after the likeness of God. Then thou art His by title of redemption, since He has ransomed thee from the slavery of sin and the bondage of the devil at the cost of His own blood and of His very life itself. Lastly, thou art His by title of donation, because thou hast given thyself of thy own accord, wholly and entirely to His service, in the offering thou madest of thyself by the holy vows of religion. Yet, nothwithstanding, how often hast thou not withdrawn thyself from the service of Almighty God to pander to thy own whims and fancies, and employed thy faculties and talents in pleasing creatures to the displeasure of thy Creator?

III. Consider in what this *rendering to God the things that are God's* consists. It consists in being practically persuaded that whatever thou hast and all that thou art, all belongs to Almighty God. Thy body, soul, senses, and faculties, they all belong to God Who gave them to thee, and to God must thou give them back by employing them for His glory and in His service. Talent, health, and other natural gifts, all come from God, as also all the good thou performest through their instrumentality; see, therefore, that thou givest them all back again to God by recognising them to be His gifts, and attributing to Him alone all the praise and glory without waxing proud thyself. So also to God belong all the gifts of grace thou hast received, because the only thing thou hast of thy own is sin. Learn, therefore, to realise that all grace is from God; to thank Him for it, and freely own that of thyself thou art not capable of aught else but evil. If thou provest thyself faithful in always giving unto God the things that are God's, and which thou hast received from Him, He will, on His side, be more liberal still in enriching thee with His gifts.

MONDAY IN THE TWENTY-SECOND WEEK AFTER PENTECOST.

Non intres in judicium cum servo tuo, quia non justificabitur in conspectu tuo omnis vivens—Ps. cxlii. 2.
Enter not into judgment with thy servant, for in thy sight no man living shall be justified.

I. CONSIDER how all the saints have dreaded the judgment of Almighty God. We see the Holy Abbot Hilarion horror-stricken and trembling at the thought, after persevering for seventy years faithfully in the service of God. If thou art not afraid of it there is all the greater reason why thou oughtest to fear it, because thou art so unlike the saints. The reason why thou oughtest to apprehend this judgment in thy own particular case is that if no one, even amongst the saints themselves, can pronounce himself free from sin—*Quis potest dicere: mundum est cor meum*—Prov. xx. 9.—*Who can say, My heart is clean?* How much less canst thou do so, who, by sinning over and over again, hast lost thy baptismal grace and innocence, and art not certain of having recovered it by fitting penance? And even though thou shouldst have recovered it, what assurance hast thou that thou wilt not again lose it? Listen to Job, who says—*Ecce inter sanctos ejus nemo immutabilis*—*—Job xv. 15—*Behold, among His saints none is unchangeable.* If, therefore, the most terrible falls are witnessed even amongst the saints, how much greater reason hast thou to fear for thyself, who, all thy life long, hast so ill corresponded with the lights, the invitations, and the inspirations of God; thou, who art so careless in doing good, so ungrateful for the grace of a religious vocation, and who day after day committest so many venial faults! See now whether thou hast not great reason to fear the judgment of God.

II. Consider that thou hast still greater reason to fear this judgment on account of the Judge, Who is holiness itself, and has the greatest abhorrence of even the slightest stain of sin, and searches it out with the keenest of eyes and punishes it with the utmost rigour : *Ego sum scrutans renes et corda*—Apoc. ii. 23—*I am He that searcheth the reins and hearts*, without overlooking the smallest speck or leaving it unpunished. Hence, David was right in exclaiming : *Non justificabitur in conspectu tuo omnis vivens*—Ps. cxlii. 2—*In Thy sight no man living shall be justified ;* because His piercing ken will discover blemishes in no matter what degree of sanctity.—*Cœli non sunt mundi in conspectu ejus*—Job xv. 15.—*The heavens are not pure in His sight.* Oh, it would be well for thee if thou couldst exempt thyself from such a judgment as this!

III. Consider that the only way of escaping from this terrible judgment of Almighty God is to proclaim thyself now convicted and disgraced, and to plead guilty beforehand. If thou dost this, Almighty God will not enter into judgment with thee, because thou wilt have already judged thyself. The great advantage that a soul gains by sincerely confessing from his heart that it is guilty, is that it is forthwith acquitted and absolved. *Si nosmetipsos judicaremus, non utique judicaremur*—1 Cor. xi. 31—*If we would judge ourselves, we should not be judged.* Endeavour, therefore, to be thoroughly alive to thy own misery, by frequently reminding Almighty God of it, and repeatedly avowing it, saying with a contrite heart : *Non intres in judicium cum servo tuo*—*Enter not into judgment with thy servant*, and thou wilt see the immense benefit thou wilt derive from so doing.

TUESDAY IN THE TWENTY-SECOND WEEK AFTER PENTECOST.

Vos estis qui permansistis mecum in tentationibus meis: et ego dispono vobis, sicut disposuit mihi Pater meus, regnum, ut edatis et bibatis super mensam meam— Luc. xxii. 28.

You are they who have continued with Me in My temptations; and I dispose to you, as My Father has disposed to Me, a kingdom, that you may eat and drink at My table.

I. CONSIDER that Christ promised to entertain His apostles at His table in paradise, not that there is any eating and drinking in heaven, for *regnum Dei non est esca et potus*—Rom. xiv. 17—*The kingdom of God is not meat and drink;* but to give them to understand under the metaphor of a feast, as their understandings were still unrefined, that they should enjoy in that bright kingdom an abundance of delights which would satisfy their cravings, and that they should have the honour of always sitting with Him at table—that is, they should be near Him in His kingdom. Akin to this promise is that other one, that at the universal judgment the apostles will be seated on thrones of power like unto His Own, in order to judge, together with Himself, the whole of mankind. He assures them that He will confer His kingdom on them just as His Own Divine Father had conferred it on Him, that is to say, with the same love and the same privilege of beholding God. What sayest thou to having such a dowry, and to such glory and kingly power as Christ has bestowed on His apostles? Yet, if only thou art faithful to Christ in thy religious state, thou wilt share these same privileges in proportion to thy fidelity.

II. Consider what was the reason that induced Our Redeemer to raise the apostles to so lofty a position. It was because they had been faithful to Him in His trials—*Vos estis qui permansistis mecum in tentationibus meis.* Admire in this the generosity of so generous a Master towards his servants: because the apostles had shown a little fidelity to Him during His sufferings, He makes them almost His equals in His kingdom. Dost not thou also burn with eager desire to accompany Him, to adhere to Him, and to be His faithful follower wherever He goes with His life-giving cross, and to strive to keep close to Him in imitation of the holy apostles?

III. Consider that the holy apostles were, it is true, faithful to Jesus in His hardships during the first three years, but afterwards, at the time of His passion, they forsook Him; and, nevertheless, Our Lord pronounced them faithful, because immediately after His resurrection they would have returned to His allegiance with greater fidelity than ever, like lost sheep to their shepherd's fold. It is Our Lord's wont not to pay any attention to faults that have been wept over with the burning tears of sincere contrition. If, unfortunately, thou shouldst have forsaken Christ by thy lax sort of life, so little in conformity with that of one who professes to follow Christ, make no delay in returning—*Non tardes converti ad Dominum*—Eccl. v. 8.—*Delay not to be converted to the Lord*, because, notwithstanding such a faithless departure, He will treat thee just as though thou hadst never forsaken Him, provided thou art truly contrite.

WEDNESDAY IN THE TWENTY-SECOND WEEK AFTER PENTECOST.

Melior est patiens viro forti : et qui dominatur animo suo expugnatore urbium.—Prov. xvi. 32.

The patient man is better than the valiant : and he that ruleth his spirit than he that taketh cities.

I. CONSIDER that by the valiant man is meant to be understood he that virtuously encounters any considerable evil, and by the patient man he that virtuously bears up against it and endures it with patience. Now, the Wise Man declares that he that patiently puts up with the evils that come across his path, and which are not of his own choice, is preferable to the man that goes of his own accord in search of them and confronts them ; because the virtue of the former is more solid and stable. Thou haply mayest be a lover of suffering, in the shape of self-imposed fasting, mortifications, and disciplines ; but if Almighty God sends thee any contrariety, if thou art mortified by thy superior, or taken up by any one, thou forthwith resentest the imaginary injury. Now, it would be well for thee to know that there is far greater virtue and merit in embracing the little occasions of suffering that present themselves during the course of the day with entire resignation to the Will of God, than in searching after them at thy own caprice ; because self-complacency may easily work its way into mortifications of thy choice or making, whereas thou practisest very great humility in patiently enduring mortifications that come to thee from others.

II. Consider that if thou wouldst attain to this practice of patience, thou must learn to gain a complete mastery over thyself : and if thou succeedest in this, thou wilt have no need to envy the valour and prowess of the most far-famed conquerors and stormers of cities, nor the brilliant success of the most fervent and popular preachers, whose name may happen to be in everybody's mouth, by reason of the sensation they create and the conversions they effect. In the sight of Almighty God a simple-minded, unlettered lay brother, who has succeeded in gaining the mastery over his passions, is more estimable by far than the zealous and learned preacher who has not yet learnt how to keep under the inordinate motions of vanity and the undue seeking of his own interests, and allows himself to be overcome by anger and jealousy and such-like failings, which hold their sway in his heart. See, therefore, how important it is that thou shouldst give thy earnest attention to subduing thy own passions, if thou wouldst obtain this mastery over thyself, and be possessed of that sterling patience which is more valuable than daring and courage.

III. Consider that the attainment of this mastery over self is a very glorious and, at the same time, very difficult achievement; because thou art not in a position to avail thyself of thy whole person in the undertaking of withstanding and overcoming thy passions: thou art at one and the same time fighting and fought against by thyself. Moreover, thy own self-love causes thee to sympathise with and to cherish thy own defects, and in the very act of resisting thy faults thou defendest and screenest them under numberless pretexts and excuses. If, therefore, thou really wishest to subdue thy evil inclinations, thou must treat them like rebels: and since it is impossible to subdue them thoroughly, thy business must be to weaken them by oft-repeated victories over them, without ever making peace or even a truce with them. This is the only means by which to overcome them. *Vince te ipsum*—says the Abbot Gersen—*Overcome thyself.*

THURSDAY IN THE TWENTY-SECOND WEEK AFTER PENTECOST.

Medius vestrum stetit, quem vos nescitis.—Joan. i. 26.
There hath stood one in the midst of you whom you know not.

I. CONSIDER that these words were addressed by S. John the Baptist to the Jews, because Our Lord was actually living in the midst of Judæa, and still the greater number of them knew Him not : and those who did know Him, heeded Him not. It would seem that this is precisely what happens in thy own case. Thou hast thy Lord constantly with thee, not only under the sacramental species, but also in the very midst of thy heart, and yet *nescis illum—thou knowest Him not*, because thou heedest Him not. Now, is it not a crying shame that Our Divine Lord should have been so long in the very midst of thee, and that thou shouldst pay no attention to Him, and not even get so far as to make His acquaintance, so to speak : *Tanto tempore vobiscum sum et non cognovistis me*—Joan. xiv. 9—may Our Lord truly say to thee—*So long a time have I been with you, and you have not known Me*. Wherefore, if thou desirest to arrive speedily at perfection, try and master the truth of this fact, that thou hast thy God intimately present to thee, and never lose sight of Him. How couldst thou possibly be induced to do anything displeasing to Him, if thou didst but realise that thou art in the presence of thy God ? *Ambula coram me, et esto perfectus*—Gen. xvii. 1—*Walk before Me, and be perfect*.

II. Consider that there are two things in which thou hast to exercise thyself, in order to acquire the practice of realising the presence of God : one regards the intellect, the other the will. Thou must seriously apply thy intellectual faculties to grasp the fact that Our Lord takes up His abode in thee by means of lively faith. Thou hast, therefore, to picture to thyself that Our Lord resides in thy heart, as a prince does in his kingdom, and that He is really with thee in several ways: first of all by His personal presence, and again from the intimate knowledge He has of all that goes on within thee, and by the power He exerts in thy whole being. Thus Our Lord resides in thee by being personally present to thy whole being, He resides in thee by that knowledge which enables Him to see whatever is going on in the most secret recesses of thy heart, and He resides in thee by that power in virtue of which He can do with thee just as He pleases. If thou givest serious attention to these three ways in which Our Lord is present to thee thou wilt not lose sight of Him so easily, but thou wilt reap the abundant fruits that follow from the practice of realising the presence of God.

III. Consider in what manner thou hast to exercise thy will. Thou must do so, first of all, by frequent and devout affections of love from time to time during the day, by acts of thanksgiving, of contrition and other such acts, so as not to leave Him alone in thy midst, like a king seated on his throne and abandoned by his attendants; and in the next place, by frequently calling upon Him to guide thee and to help thee in time of temptation, to strengthen thee in thy trials. Thus wilt thou give proof of thy entire dependence on Him. Our Lord is within thee all anxiety to bestow His graces on thee; His only desire is to heap benefits upon thee, but He will have thee ask Him. Ask Him, therefore, by keeping thyself in His presence in the manner just explained, and be diligent in this holy practice both from gratitude and from necessity; for if thou losest sight of thy God, thou becomest like a garden-plot shaded from the rays of the sun, and productive only of nettles, and without fruit.

FRIDAY IN THE TWENTY-SECOND WEEK AFTER PENTECOST.

Filii sanctorum sumus, et vitam illam expectamus quam Deus daturus est iis qui fidem suam numquam mutant ab eo.—Job ii. 18.

We are the children of saints, and look for that life which God will give to those that never change their faith from Him.

I. CONSIDER in what the life of all the saints has consisted whilst on earth: it has always been a life of constant expectation. Before the coming of Christ the saints of God did nothing but sigh after the fulfilment of the promise Almighty God had given of sending His Divine Son as the author of faith to redeem them from sin, and to enlighten them by His teaching and encourage them by His example. After the coming of Christ, the saints of God are constantly engaged in awaiting the return of their Lord, as of Him that will put the seal to their faith by their glorification. *Populus meus pendebit ad reditum meum*—Osee xi. 7—*My people shall long for My return.* Thou seest, therefore, that this life must necessarily consist in waiting: *et vos similes hominibus expectantibus Dominum suum*—Luc. xii. 36—*and you yourselves like to men who wait for their Lord.* It is perhaps hard and wearisome to be always on the look-out for thy Lord, and meanwhile to be always depriving thyself of thy own pleasure and amusement—but there is no help for it.

II. Consider that the saints have become such precisely because they lived, as it were, in seclusion from the rest of mankind; they looked upon themselves as having nothing to do with this world, only awaiting and yearning like pilgrims to arrive at their true fatherland—heaven. It behoves thee, therefore, not to degenerate in so base a manner from their example. It ought to be a matter of great confusion to thee that thou art so attached to the gewgaws of a country which is not thy own, and which thou hast formally abandoned on thy entrance into religion? Thou art the representative of men who were totally detached from the world, of men who were truly spiritual and holy; and such ought thou also to be. Where would be the good sense of praising the waters of a river on account of the purity of its fountain-head, if meanwhile the river-bed itself were all foul with mud?

III. Consider what a mistake it is to wish before the proper time to go in search of what is reserved for hereafter. All the pleasure and amusement which thou so eagerly endeavourest to procure, are only, as it were, the buds which will burst into a fulness of incomprehensible delight, if only thou wilt but wait, and then in the next world thou wilt reap their full benefit. Be content, therefore, to wait, and be not in a hurry. The present life is the time fixed for leading a life of simple faith, with faith for thy only consolation, thy only encouragement, and it behoves thee to cleave to it both in prosperity and adversity. Everything will not always turn out equally well in thy regard: at one time thou wilt find thyself downhearted, at another full of joyous buoyancy, now honoured, now despised, to-day in the enjoyment of good health, to-morrow ailing and sick. Learn, therefore, to be equally faithful to Almighty God under all circumstances, and to plod along by the light of faith to thy fatherland, where the glory promised thee by Our

Lord is called life—real life—far better and happier than this wearisome and painful life of ours on earth. This present life is one thou must not lay great store by, but despise it, and willingly employ it in the service of God, in order to arrive one day at the enjoyment of that true life, *quam daturus est Deus iis qui fidem suam numquam mutant ab eo—which God will give to those that never change their faith from Him.*

SATURDAY IN THE TWENTY-SECOND WEEK AFTER PENTECOST.

Militia est vita hominis super terram.—Job vii. 1.
The life of man upon earth is a warfare.

I. CONSIDER that this life is a battlefield where thou hast to fight against thy evil inclinations, which are backed up by the devil, and are indeed his allies. Hence, as a natural consequence, it is a time of toil, not of repose. Soldiers have no holidays, and even though the enemy does not give much to do, every soldier is obliged to be in readiness for action, must remain in the quarters assigned to him, must mount guard or be on the march, undergo the injuries of the seasons and the hardships of hunger and want of sleep. What sayest thou to all this? thou who wouldst fain lead a life of quiet rest and enjoy every comfort. This is not the frame of mind to be looked for in a soldier on the battlefield.

II. Consider that because this life is a time of warfare, it is not a season for enjoying reward but for winning merit—it is a period during which we must needs toil and struggle through hairbreadth escapes and extreme dangers. Thou must not forget that it is always the bravest soldiers who place themselves in the first ranks and face the enemy's fire. Why, then, wouldst thou find fault so easily with divine Providence? because it not unfrequently happens that the most virtuous are just those who suffer the most in this world. Wait awhile, on the last day thou wilt see how those who have fought and toiled more than others will also be recompensed more than the rest. Here below Our Lord gives them only their pay and rations, in the shape of grace proportioned to the fatigue He demands of them.

III. Consider that since this life is a time of warfare, it follows that it is a period of very great danger and not of security, owing to the manœuvres and attacks to which we are constantly liable. Oh, if thou couldst but see the sad falls of some of those miserable wretches who are now bewailing their irreparable losses in hell, perhaps thou wouldst be less self-confident, and not promise thyself such complete security! *In medio laqueorum ingrederis, et super dolentium arma ambulas—* Eccl. ix. 20—*Thou art going in the midst of snares, and walking upon the arms of them that are grieved.* The true way of escaping danger is not to act or live according to one's own whims and caprice, but to stand fast to obedience. Obedience is nowhere exacted so minutely as it is in military service in regard of the commander-in-chief: and a true soldier ought never in time of war to remain stationary, or go elsewhere, or take part in an engagement without the orders of his captain. Since, therefore, the present life is in thy regard a time of war, it is also a time in which thou must stand fast by obedience and be entirely dependent on the commands of Almighty God, and of those who stand in His stead. In like manner wilt thou be safe amidst perils, and come off victorious. *Vir obediens loquetur victorias*—Prov. xxi. 28—*An obedient man shall speak of victory.*

TWENTY-THIRD SUNDAY AFTER PENTECOST.

Cum ejecta esset turba intravit, et tenuit manum ejus, et surrexit puella.—Matth. ix. 25.

When the multitude was put forth, He went in and took her by the hand, and the maid arose.

I. CONSIDER how when Jesus was about to work for the first time the great miracle of raising the dead to life, in the person of the daughter of Jairus, the ruler of the synagogue, He gave directions that the room in which the corpse was lying should be cleared of all the people that were there, weeping and wailing over her loss. Why did Jesus act thus? It was because He did not wish to make any show in the performance of His wondrous work. In this He gives thee an example not to seek to perform thy good works in the presence of others, nor to perform them in order to be seen and praised. However, thou must distinguish between two sorts of good works; some are common to all, and are prescribed by the rules and customs of thy order; others are singular and out of the common. Good works of the first kind thou must of course perform in public, in order not to be wanting in regular observance; but those of the second kind, and which are out of the common, thou must perform, as far as possible, in secret to avoid vainglory. If at times circumstances demand the public performance of such actions, either for example-sake or otherwise, take care that thy motive in so doing be the honour of God or thy neighbour's good, and not self-conceit; otherwise it will be said to thee: *Recepisti mercedem tuam*—Matth. vi. 16—*Thou hast received thy reward.*

II. Consider that Our Lord turned all those people out of the room when about to raise the dead child to life, to teach thee that if thou wouldst rise to a new life from thy weaknesses and timidity, thou must get rid of that motley crowd of thoughts and inordinate affections, and hush that noisy hum of distraction and idle conversation which disturb thy heart and bewilder thy mind. Thou canst cultivate a greater spirit of retirement and interior recollection, and thereby dispose thyself to receive stronger light and more effectual help from heaven, according to the promise of Almighty God: *Ducam eam in solitudinem et loquar ad cor ejus*—Osee. ii. 14—*I will lead her into the wilderness, and I will speak to her heart.*

III. Consider that Our Lord wrought the miracle of raising the dead child to life in the act of stretching forth His arm and taking her by the hand: *Tenuit manum ejus, et surrexit puella*—*He took her by the hand, and the maid arose.* By that almighty touch He imbued her with vital power, and awoke her from the sleep of death. Oh almighty touch of the right hand of the Most High! But, alas! thou also standest in sore need of thy Saviour's outstretched hand to arouse thee from the lethargy of thy tepidity, and enable thee to arise to a new life of spiritual fervour. Unless He stretches forth His holy hand to raise thee up from thy misery, thou also wilt have but too great reason to exclaim: *Infixus sum in limo profundi, et non est substantia*—Ps. lxviii. 3—*I stick fast in the mire of the deep, and there is no sure standing;* and wilt remain, without the slightest hope of extricating thyself. However, since *non est abbreviata manus Domini*—Isa. lix. 1—*the hand of the Lord is not shortened*, beseech Him earnestly to stretch forth His merciful hand and touch thy heart; to raise thee up from the mire of thy faults, that thou mayest press forward in the path of perfection.

MONDAY IN THE TWENTY-THIRD WEEK AFTER PENTECOST.

Vigilate omni tempore orantes, ut digni habeamini fugere ista omnia, quæ futura sunt, et stare ante Filium hominis.—Luc. xxi. 36.

Watch ye therefore, praying at all times, that you may be accounted worthy to escape all these things that are to come, and to stand before the Son of man.

I. CONSIDER that by these words Our Lord gives thee to understand that thy eternal salvation is an undertaking which does not depend entirely either on Him alone or on thee alone. Thou hast to do on thy side what thou canst, and on this account He bids thee watch—*vigilate*—by great caution in not laying thyself open to temptation, and by assiduity in doing good; then, after all this, thou must pray and betake thyself to Almighty God just as though thou hadst done nothing at all—*orantes*—humbly begging Him to protect thee with His holy grace. This is the real way to save one's soul.

II. Consider that it is not enough to begin after this fashion, but it is necessary to continue until the end, without stopping, without growing weary: *Omni tempore.* It is not enough to watch and pray merely in time of temptation; thou must watch and pray at all times. Shepherds guard their flocks even when wolves and thieves are far away, to hinder their coming. So also must thou act on behalf of thy soul, thou must watch and pray lest temptations should surprise thee: *Vigilate et orate, ut non intretis in tentationem*—Luc. xxii. 46—*Watch and pray, lest you enter into temptation.* Because thou dost not keep an eye to thyself, but neglectest prayer, and failest to recommend thyself to God frequently during the day, it comes to pass, that instead of temptation coming to find thee, thou goest headlong into it of thy own accord, and by casting aside thy weapons, thou becomest unable to defend thyself. In the same way as there is no time in which thou dost not run evident risk of perishing, if left to thy own feeble resources, so also there is no time in which it is not most necessary for thee to watch and pray.

III. Consider that all the diligence in the world will never of itself suffice to make thee deserving of salvation. Therefore thou must entreat Almighty God with persevering prayer: *ut dignus habearis—to be accounted worthy;* that is to say, that in His mercy He would treat thee as though thou wert in reality worthy of escaping damnation and of inheriting salvation on the last day, and thus be able *to stand before the Son of man—stare ante Filium hominis.* It is only the just that will stand firm at that awful tribunal in virtue of a good conscience: *Stabunt justi in magna constantia—* Sap. v. 1—*The just shall stand with great constancy;* whereas the wicked will fall, without the faintest hope of ever rising again: *Non resurgent impii in judicio—* Ps. i. 5—*The wicked shall not rise again in judgment.* Oh, what a difference between the fate of each!

TUESDAY IN THE TWENTY-THIRD WEEK AFTER PENTECOST.

In patientia vestra possidebitis animas vestras.—Luc. xxi. 19.
In your patience you shall possess your souls.

I. CONSIDER how great are the evils to which an impatient man exposes himself. He is not his own master, because he is not master of his own mental faculties; he acts hastily and foolishly, without heeding the dictates of right reason. Neither is he master of his own will, because he is overpowered by his unruly whims and passions, whether of sadness, or of wearisomeness, or of intemperance, or of restlessness, which cause him to tack and turn about in all directions, like a small boat that is tossed about at the mercy of the winds and waves. Our Lord, therefore, says, with but too great truth: *In patientia vestra possidebitis animas vestras*—*In your patience you shall possess your souls.* This virtue of patience, which gives a man the mastery over himself, is especially necessary for every religious; there is hardly a sadder sight than to behold an impatient man carried away in his speech and conduct by impatience, and living like an irrational being. Reflect on thy own conduct, and strive to correct thyself in good earnest, shouldst thou be enslaved by this vice.

II. Consider that the impatient man has always this peculiarity about him, that he is unstable in the practice of virtue; because as soon as he begins to feel the irksomeness and fatigue of his undertaking, he at once grows sick and tired of it. Should he give himself to the study of prayer, or to the reading of spiritual books, in a very short time he lets it all go;

if he applies himself to the practice of penance and mortification, he very soon overlooks it; in a word, he never stands fast to his good resolutions. *Tamquam pulvis quem projicit ventus a facie terra*—Ps. i. 4—*Like the dust which the wind driveth from the face of the earth.* What good results, therefore, can the impatient man look for? because it is precisely perseverance in a life of virtue that disposes us, more than anything else, for the grace of final perseverance. Where the Vulgate version reads: *Qui perseveraverit usque in finem, hic salvus erit*, another version has *Qui tolleraverit usque in finem*, etc.—*he that shall endure until the end shall be saved*, because perseverance implies patience.

III. Consider that there are three means which thou must employ to acquire this so necessary virtue of patience. The first is to ask Almighty God for it often and with great earnestness. The second is to reflect on, and to foresee, the occasions that are capable of ruffling thy evenness of mind—such as wrongs, disgrace, sickness, or injunctions that are hard to execute. Then thou wilt be in readiness for them; even the strongest fortresses are in danger of being taken, if attacked by surprise. Remember that thou art in this world as on a battlefield, and that peace and the reward of valour have to follow, and that thy sins are deserving of a much heavier penalty than any toil that is demanded of thee. The third means is to exercise thyself in as many acts of patience as thou canst in the contradictions and annoyances that fall to thy lot, however frequent or trifling they may be in themselves; endeavour to bear up against the shortcomings of thy neighbour, the inconveniences of the seasons, thy own ailings of body and interior trials, which every now and then keep crossing thy path; and if thou feelest thy temper beginning to rise within thee, recollect thyself, and commend thyself to Our Lord, imagining that He says to thee, with His own divine lips: *In patientia tua possidebis animam tuam—In thy patience thou shalt possess thy soul.*

WEDNESDAY IN THE TWENTY-THIRD WEEK AFTER PENTECOST.

Quid necesse est homini majora se quærere, cum ignoret, quid conducit sibi in vita sua, numero dierum peregrinationis suæ, et tempore, quod velut umbra præterit.—Eccl. vii. 1.

What needeth a man to seek things that are above him, whereas he knoweth not what is profitable for him in his life, in all the days of his pilgrimage, and the time that passeth like a shadow?

I. CONSIDER that these words of the Wise Man are directed against all those who, through discontent with the actual condition in which Our Lord has placed them, are anxiously engaged in trying to advance themselves, without even knowing if the dignity, or the employment, or position they aspire after, will turn to their loss or gain. Hence it comes to pass that oftentimes they strive after what is quite above them —*majora se*, because they cannot see into the future. Almighty God alone knows which is the path thou must pursue to save thy soul, because it is He that has prearranged the whole series of events on which thy predestination depends. Wherefore, just as a pilgrim that is unacquainted with the road must allow himself to be directed towards his fatherland by the guides that are familiar with the road, so also it behoves thee to abandon thyself to the guidance of Almighty God, or of those who on earth hold His place in thy regard. What folly is it not, then, to be bent on looking out for thyself, and procuring at all costs—even against the will of God—this appointment or that employment! Entrust thyself to the sure guidance of obedience, and thou wilt find in the end that thou wilt never have done thyself any harm by having obeyed.

II. Consider that even though the attainment of that honour or charge thou so eagerly desirest, should not prove hurtful to thee, it is quite certain that thy going in quest of it is hurtful, because it takes off thy thoughts and hinders thy endeavours from what is alone of any importance—the great business of thy eternal salvation. All thy thoughts and actions ought to centre towards this great matter, the attainment of which is all the more important because it is so doubtful. But when thou art absorbed in the pursuit of some object that it is difficult to attain, thou, alas! overlookest the fact that, by directing thy energies to obtain what in itself may possibly prove a hindrance to thy salvation, thou in reality neglectest the true interests of thy soul. Do bear in mind that thou art a pilgrim, and that thy fatherland is heaven, and give thy time and attention to what alone is of real importance, namely, to acquaint thyself with the sure path that leads to it.

III. Consider that the time accorded thee to obtain possession of the one important end and object of thy existence, is both short and fleeting; how, then, canst thou reconcile thyself to lose it in searching after aught else than what alone is worth searching after? Thy time is short, because it is for a few days only—*numero dierum;* it is fleeting, because it *passeth like a shadow—velut umbra præterit.* Do not, therefore, waste it going in pursuit of objects which themselves pass away with time, but use it only in making way along the safe road to thy true country, and in acquiring a right to an everlasting inheritance. With what anxiety and diligence would not that pilgrim wend his weary way, who was bound to reach his country within a very short period of time, under penalty of forfeiting his father's inheritance ? His one fear would be lest time should fail, and to gain more time he would deprive himself of sleep, of conversation, and certainly of all idle amusements. This is just what thou hast to do ; thou art a pilgrim, and if thou dost not reach thy journey's end by the time Our Lord has appointed, it is all over with thee, thou wilt never enter into possession of thy inheritance for all eternity !

THURSDAY IN THE TWENTY-THIRD WEEK AFTER PENTECOST.

Cum accepero tempus, ego justitias judicabo.—Ps. lxxiv. 2.
When I shall take a time, I will judge justices.

I. CONSIDER how Our Lord allows thee ample time and opportunity now to do good, if only thou on thy part art willing to make use of it to gain a happy eternity : *Dedit illi tempus, ut pœnitentiam ageret*—Apoc. ii. 21—*I gave her a time that she might do penance.* And what then ? After a while He will summon thee unexpectedly to judgment, and then thou wilt no longer have any time for thy affairs—no, not even one second : *Tempus non erit amplius*—Apoc. x. 6—*Time shall be no longer.* Oh, what a strict account thou wilt have to render of the precious time which He has given thee : *Vocavit adversum me tempus*—Thren. i. 15—*He hath called against me the time.* Ponder now awhile how thou employest thy time, if usefully, or uselessly. Our Lord's object in giving thee time is that thou mayest turn it to good account for the purchase of Paradise; and wouldst thou think little of it? Oh, what a sad waste thou makest of such precious time! and how thou wilt learn to value it—but, unfortunately, too late for thy own interests—when thy lease of life is over, and the day of the Lord is come!

II. Consider that, as soon as time is ended for thee, it will be thy Lord's time to judge thee. But what, pray, is the meaning of *justitias judicabo—I will judge justices?* It means, as the Hebrew phrase indicates, that He will judge with uprightness, with severity, and according to the rules of strict justice, so that on that dread day mercy will have to withdraw and leave justice sole possession. How comes it, then, that thou heedest not, and scarcely deignest to give a thought to the appalling severity of this awful day? The holiest even of God's saints have trembled and shuddered at the thought of the extreme rigour with which their Lord was to pass sentence on their every deed at the end of their lives; hence they never gave over bewailing their sins and cancelling their debts by penance, and continually sifting their consciences with the greatest nicety, in order to settle their accounts at a tribunal of mercy during their lifetime, and not be constrained to do so at a tribunal of severe justice by continual delay. Unfortunately, thy line of conduct is just the reverse; thou entertainest but little fear of the cross-questioning to which the justice of Almighty God will subject thee on that last day, and allowest that precious time to run by in which thou art free to avail thyself of His all-forgiving mercy.

III. Consider that the words *justitias judicabo—I will judge justices*, mean also, that on that awful day Our Lord will judge not only thy wickedness, but thy justices also—that is to say, thy good works. He will examine if thou hast performed them in due season, with an upright intention, in the proper manner, and with all the requisite circumstances. Good God! if this be the case, what will become of thee and thy good works? How will it fare with so many works, excellent, indeed, in themselves and which thou performest in the daily routine of a religious life, such as prayer, choir, sacraments, and the like? In what manner dost thou discharge these duties? What an amount of distraction, and listlessness, and shortcomings of all sorts thou interminglest with them! Yet thou hast to be judged with the utmost severity with regard to each one of those good works so ill performed by thee! Remember, it is not the mere material action that will avail thee, it is the way in which it is performed. Why, then, dost thou not dread this judgment? Pray Almighty God to give thee light to know and appreciate it more thoroughly.

FRIDAY IN THE TWENTY-THIRD WEEK AFTER PENTECOST.

Hæc mihi sit consolatio, ut affligens me dolore non parcat, nec contradicam sermonibus sancti.—Job vi. 10.
May this be my comfort, that afflicting me with sorrow, He spare not, nor I contradict the words of the Holy One.

I. CONSIDER the strange consolation which holy Job begs of Almighty God in the midst of his afflictions: he asks for a fresh trial, and together with the trial he asks also for patience: *ut affligens me non parcat, nec contradicam sermonibus ancti*—that afflicting me He *spare not, nor I contradict the words of the Holy One.* It is easy enough—though but little matter for real spiritual consolation—to be resigned to the Will of God, when He prospers thee and does not try thee. But to be fully resigned to the Will of Almighty God and to derive consolation from trials when His fatherly hand lies heavy on us—ah yes! this affords solid consolation to the heavenward-bound sighs of a perfect soul. Thrice happy wilt thou be when thou reachest this lofty stage of perfection that will enable thee to look for thy consolation in enduring lovingly and patiently fresh and still heavier trials! And yet to this thou must aspire, because we are not here in order to enjoy ourselves but to suffer, and hence it is that thou wilt never find true joy or contentment until thou succeedest in deriving all thy consolation from sufferings and trials.

II. Consider the great longing that holy Job had for suffering. There he sat on his dunghill, one mass of wounds from head to foot; and yet in this state of terrible affliction he puts forth an especial prayer for desolation of soul, which of all trials is the most heart-rending and distressing. He was afraid lest Our Lord, on beholding him in such great suffering, should in His tender-heartedness be moved to pity him, and he therefore, as it were, encouraged Him to continue to show severity in his regard until he should be reduced to dust and ashes. See here an example of the perfection at which frail flesh and blood—as thou art thyself—is capable of arriving by energy and determination of soul. At any rate, be ashamed of thy own weakness, and beg Our Lord to give thee light to understand how great are the benefits to be derived from suffering in this life for God's sake, and to strengthen the frailty of thy flesh by His holy grace.

III. Consider that when holy Job asked for sorrows, he asked with the same breath for the grace of not seeking to shirk them when they were at hand, but to receive them with full resignation: and thus he gave proof of the distrust in which he held his own desires, as is the wont of all humble souls. Thou also at times, perhaps, conceivest a desire to undergo some toil or suffering for the love of God; but because thou art self-confident and trustest to thy own resources, and, therefore, failest to beg Almighty God from thy inmost heart to assist thee, no sooner does the occasion present itself than all thy good desires disappear, and thou art wanting in that perfect conformity to the Will of Almighty God which is requisite under every trial. So perfect ought this conformity of will to be, that no circumstance of time, of disposition, or of health ought to make any suffering irksome, or cause thee to fail in receiving it from the hands of God with full resignation. Now this is precisely what Job prayed for when he asked for fresh sufferings; and it is this for which thou also must ask, but with far greater reason, because thou art so much weaker in spirit than he, and oughtest therefore to place the less reliance on thy own desires. However earnest and holy thy dispositions may seem to be, they will never prove firm and stable without the assistance and especial help of Almighty God.

SATURDAY IN THE TWENTY-THIRD WEEK AFTER PENTECOST.

Beatus homo quem tu erudieris Domine, et de lege tua docueris eum.—Ps. xciii. 12.

Blessed is the man whom Thou shalt instruct, O Lord, and shalt teach him out of Thy law.

I. CONSIDER that nothing so effectually spurs on a scholar in the pursuit of learning as the devotedness and natural good-heartedness of his master. Now, where, pray, can a better master be found, all the world over, than Jesus Christ; where, one that is able to teach those that frequent his school so well as He? And yet, how few there are that make any effort at all to study the profound lessons of so great a master, inasmuch as by far the greater number of mankind betake themselves in thronging crowds to the treacherous school of the world. Reflect, therefore, under what a great obligation thou liest of thanking Almighty God, Who has not only caused thee to be born at a time when the school of this great Master is open to all, but has actually called thee to the religious state—His own especial school, where thou hast so many opportunities for deriving the fullest benefit from His heavenly teaching—especially during time of prayer. If thou hearkenest not, and failest to take in His doctrines, the fault lies entirely with thyself!

II. Consider that no master is ever wont to lead on his scholars to deeper learning if he finds that they are not well grounded in the first rudiments of the science he is teaching, and in the previous elementary lessons he has so earnestly laboured to explain to them. So also reflect in thy own case what great pains thy Saviour has taken with thee individually to form and guide thy spiritual life—that is to say, how He has laboured to detach thee from the world and from thy own evil tendencies to haughtiness, ambition and excessive self-love. Yet after so many years during which thou hast frequented His school, in thy character of religious, thinkest thou, thou art sufficiently grounded in, and formed on, the teaching of thy Master? What reason, therefore, hast thou to be surprised that He should refuse to impart to thee those more advanced and elevated lessons in the shape of especial interior lights, which He usually gives in time of prayer to such as have made greater progress? Thou canst never hope to be taught the highest and sublimest doctrines of so profound a Master if thou art not first of all thoroughly grounded in first principles. Abandon thyself, therefore, to His guidance, give Him full liberty to strip thee of thy excessive love of comfort and of thy own will, and then He will take thee on to another and higher standard.

III. Consider that the chief result of a method of teaching which is peculiar to and worthy of so great a Master, is the practical fulfilment of His holy law. Thou mayest well be saved and be most holy without possessing a profound speculative knowledge of the mysteries of God: but without the practical knowledge of His holy law thou canst never be saved: hence it is all-important that thou shouldst aim at making progress in its practical fulfilment, and it is this alone that will make thee truly happy. What in the world will all thy knowledge of philosophy and theology, of rhetoric and mathematics, avail thee, after all the toil they have cost thee, if in the end thou art lost? Yet it is quite possible, notwithstanding the possession of all these sciences, to lose thy soul unless thou learn from this greatest of Masters the real practical knowledge of the law of God. He teaches thee this science as being of all others the most important in itself, and the most necessary to make thee truly happy : *Beatus homo quem tu erudieris Domine, et de lege tua docueris eum—Blessed is the man whom Thou shalt instruct, O Lord, and shalt teach him out of Thy law.**

TWENTY-FOURTH OR LAST SUNDAY AFTER PENTECOST.

Erit tunc tribulatio magna, qualis non fuit ab initio mundi usque modo.—Matth. xxiv. 21.
There shall then be great tribulation, such as hath not been from the beginning of the world until now.

I. CONSIDER that as every individual man has to undergo a particular judgment at the end of his life before God's tribunal, so also at the end of the world a general judgment will be held for the whole of mankind. This general judgment will tend to enhance the glory and the reward of the elect, as also will it increase the shame and punishment of the reprobate. It will serve as a public vindication of the plan that divine Providence follows up now in the actual government of the world, and which is so grossly misrepresented and misunderstood, simply because it is a well-known fact that the good are so often unfortunate, whilst the wicked prosper—that the most virtuous are often deprived of this world's goods, whilst evil-doers become rich. It will then be shown how these arrangements and dispositions of Providence, which seem to us now

---

* The Meditations for any supernumerary weeks between this day and the last Sunday after Pentecost may be supplied from the corresponding intercalary weeks from the Third to the Sixth Sundays after the Epiphany.—*See* Vol. I.

a medley of inextricable confusion, are all prearranged with consummate wisdom for the attainment of an end, namely, the glory of God and our own good; therefore, if at any time thou shouldst happen to observe anything, which to the short ken of thy understanding may appear badly arranged either in the government of the world, or it may be of thy own community, bethink thee of the warning of the apostle : *Nolite ante tempus judicare, quodusque veniat Dominus*—1 Cor. iv. 5—*Judge not before the time, until the Lord come,* because it will be only on the judgment-day that the exquisite beauty and order of Providence will discover itself in all that at present seems to us disorder. Providence is like an elaborate piece of needlework which, when looked at from the wrong side, looks like a confused mass of uneven and disorderly stitches, but when looked at on the right side proves to be a lovely masterpiece of elaborate design.

II. Consider that just as when a man is in the act of dying, the humours of the body cease from their functions, his eyes become glazed and dim, his countenance grows livid, and all his strength and senses fail him, so also at the end of the world all the elements will become as it were out of gear, and in confusion; the sun, moon and stars will be eclipsed, the earth will rumble and heave with dreadful quakes, and an awful fire will burn up forests, dwellings, cities, and their inhabitants, and whatever else exists on the face of the earth. Ah, then indeed it will be clearly understood what is the real worth of the goods of this world which are now so fondly cherished and sought after by mankind : then worldlings will learn how to set a just value on the mansions, the pleasure-grounds, the country-seats, and all their lavish luxury and wealth, which they will behold swallowed up in an instant by the devouring flames. How thankful thou oughtest to be to Almighty God for having enabled thee to give up and forsake, to thy own great merit, all these temporal advantages and possessions, which will so shortly be reduced to ashes!

III. Consider that as soon as the world shall have been destroyed by the devouring flames, the blast of that dread trumpet will resound in all the four quarters of the globe, which will summon the dead from their tombs to judgment: *Surgite mortui, et venite ad judicium*—S. Hieron, Reg. Monach. c. 30—*Arise ye dead, and come to judgment.* On a sudden all the bodies of the dead will be reunited to the souls that formerly quickened them, and be conducted by the ministry of angels to the valley of Josaphat. There will be no distinction on that day between rich and poor, between persons of high degree and low degree, between liege and vassal, but simply and solely between good and bad. Oh how this great truth will flash across the minds of all, namely, that real riches, real worth, are to be found only in virtue, as, on the other hand, that real evil is exclusively confined within the boundaries of those vices and passions which in lifetime are so sadly overlooked and unheeded! Consider, moreover, what a great difference will be seen between the elect and the reprobate. The souls of the elect will be united to their bodies, become new, more lightsome than the sun, endowed with the four properties of glorified bodies,* and will be borne aloft amongst angels and placed nigh to the throne of their Judge. The souls of the reprobate,

---

* These four properties, as enumerated by divines, are: 1. Impassibility or immunity from all suffering; 2. Subtility, by virtue of which a glorified body can penetrate any other body, or co-exist with it in the same space; 3. Agility, or the faculty of exercising motion with freedom and speed; 4. Brightness, by which a glorified body will become, both externally and internally, resplendent and transparent.— *Translator.*

also, will be rejoined to their bodies, destined now to become the hideous and darksome firebrands of hell, and they will be left to take up their stand in the gloom of the valley in the company of the demons. Oh awful truth! one of these two lots must fall to thy share! Choose now which thou listest. If thou art so anxious to enjoy health of body now during thy short lease of life, and to work thy way to an honourable position in this world; and if, on the other hand, it is so distasteful to thee to see others preferred before thee and thyself left behind, and if thou regrettest so bitterly having perhaps a poor constitution or some chronic ailment—how much more earnestly oughtest thou not to strive after an honourable position and a glorified body on that all-important day of judgment? that day which will decide thy eternal lot for weal or woe!

MONDAY IN THE LAST WEEK AFTER PENTECOST.

Videbunt Filium hominis venientem in nubibus cœli—
Matth. xxiv. 30.

They shall see the Son of man coming in the clouds of heaven.

I. CONSIDER how different will be the dispositions of mind with which the elect and the reprobate will stand in readiness for the coming of the Son of God. He will come down from heaven in great majesty, accompanied by all His legions of angels in visible form, carrying aloft the standard of His cross with the utmost display of honour and respect. The Gospel says that on the appearance of the cross both the elect and the reprobate will weep; the tears of the elect will be tears of consolation at having embraced it during their lifetime, to their own great advantage; the tears of the reprobate will be tears of regret at having, to their own irreparable loss, shunned and scorned it. If thy present frame of mind regarding the cross of Christ were to form the basis of what thy feelings will be when, on the great stage of Josaphat, thou wilt gaze on that great emblem of Christ's judiciary power, what, pray, would thy tears betoken?—joy and consolation, or regret and fear? Yet the day will come when thou thyself wilt have to take part in that great spectacle. Strive, therefore, to be now at this present time of the number of the lovers of the cross, and not of the number of its enemies, *quorum finis interitus*—Philip. iii. 19—*whose end is destruction*.

II. Consider how immediately behind the cross, Jesus the Supreme Judge will be seated on a throne amidst the clouds of heaven. So great will be the majesty of His divine Nature, and so great the glory of His deified Humanity, that the sun, moon and stars will pale away in His sight. Oh, how unutterable will not the fear and dread of the reprobate be on the appearance of their Judge! What a matter of consolation it would be for them on that awful day to be buried under the ruins of the mountains, rather than behold the angry countenance of that Jesus Whose meekness and forbearance they have so shamefully abused! On the right of the Judge will be the Blessed Virgin, but no longer, alas, the refuge and advocate of sinners! on the left the apostles as chief jurors, and together with them a throng of apostolic souls, who, like them, have abandoned all they had in the world for God's sake, and embraced the Gospel counsels. How honoured will virtue and the imitation of Christ be on that day! what disgrace and confusion will overwhelm vice and the foolish slavery of worldlings!

III. Consider how at this point of the proceedings the books will be opened, that is to say, the consciences of each individual. Every one will see with the greatest distinctness not only all and each of his own actions, good and bad, performed during life, but those also of every one else; so that all and each of thy thoughts, words, and deeds, all the good and evil thou hast wrought in thy lifetime, will be displayed to the searching ken of angels and men; the good for their approval, the evil for their disapproval. Remark, too, that the estimation formed there of good and evil will not be like that which exists at present in the world at large, but will be modelled in the estimation formed of both in the mind of God; that is to say, good will appear. infinitely more precious, and evil infinitely more guilty than they either do now. How unspeakable, therefore, will not the shame of the wicked be on seeing all their most hidden sins brought to light and displayed before the eyes of all! How overwhelming the honour heaped on the good, at the laying open of their unknown and unappreciated virtues! Their very sins will no longer be matter of shame to them, but rather of consolation, on account of the tears with which they have washed them out in the sacrament of penance. How then comes it that thou, who now layest so much store by what men think of thee, that their opinion influences thy whole manner of acting and tenor of life—how comes it that thou heedest so little this searching judgment which will be passed on thee in the valley of Josaphat? Ponder seriously on this, and thou wilt soon learn to overcome all human respect, to be anxious to perform works which will stand thee in good stead at that last day, and to avoid all that might prove matter of shame and confusion.

TUESDAY IN THE LAST WEEK AFTER PENTECOST.

Venite, benedicti Patris mei, possidete regnum . . . . . Discedite a me, maledicti, in ignem æternum.—Matth. xxv. 34, 41.
   Come, ye blessed of My Father; possess you the kingdom . . . . Depart from Me, ye cursed, into everlasting fire.

I. CONSIDER the sentence which the Judge will pass in favour of the elect, to whom He will address with a loving and smiling countenance those thrilling words—*Venite, benedicti Patris mei*—Come, ye blessed of My Father—come from toil to rest, from sorrow to gladness, from combat to the reward; *possidete regnum*—possess you the kingdom—by which words is denoted the continuous and peaceful security with which they will enjoy the possession of the glory of heaven for never-ending ages. *Qui vicerit, possidebit hæc*—Apoc. xxi. 7— *He that shall overcome, shall possess these things.* The bliss of heaven is styled *regnum— the kingdom*, to signify the stateliness and magnificence which will belong to the elect by their possessing all the good that belongs to God Himself. Ponder awhile on the thrill of joy that will gladden the hearts of the blessed on hearing themselves called to take possession of so great a kingdom, and that too for ever, a kingdom which is adjudged to them as their due in recompense for the short-lived and insignificant trials they had endured during life in the faithful service of their Lord and Master. Oh, how thankfully they will exclaim in their rapturous astonishment : *Lætati sumus pro diebus quibus nos humiliasti ; annis quibus vidimus mala*—Ps. lxxxix. 15—*We have rejoiced for the days in which Thou hast humbled us ; for the years in which we have seen evil.* Thou also wilt one day partake of this their joy, if now thou sharest their trials.

II. Consider how no sooner will the Judge have pronounced sentence in favour of the elect, than He will turn towards the reprobate with every token of dreadful wrath, and will hurl against them the sentence of everlasting damnation—*Discedite a me, maledicti, in ignem æternum*—*Depart from Me, ye cursed, into everlasting fire.* Oh, what unutterable woe! to be banished for ever from before the lovely face of God! What a frightful addition to their woe, to be banished to the dark depths of hell, to become the fuel of its everlasting flames! *Discedite a me* . . . . *in ignem æternum*—*Depart from Me* . . . . *into everlasting fire.* Yet all this will be nothing but what is strictly just, because in the act of sinning the sinner perpetrates two evils : the first is that he contemptuously turns his back upon Almighty God ; and the second is that he gives his affections to creatures, despite the claims of his Creator. Hence, in the sentence of damnation, the pain of loss is the penalty of his turning away from God—*Non videbit gloriam Dei*—Isa. xxvi. 10—*He shall not see the glory of the Lord*—and the pain of sense is the penalty of his turning towards creatures—*Cruciabuntur die ac nocte in sæcula sæculorum*—Apoc. xx. 10—*They shall be tormented day and night for ever and ever.* The agony which these damned souls will have to undergo for all eternity in the flames of hell, will be equivalent to every conceivable kind of pain ;

it will equal the racking throes of the most barbarous instruments of torture, it will exceed anything the mind of man can possibly imagine. Make up thy mind, therefore, to avoid, at all costs, the falling under so dreadful and disastrous a sentence.

III. Consider that Christ will first of all call His elect to the enjoyment of His kingdom, and then drive away the reprobate to the flames of hell, for a twofold reason. Firstly, that the elect may be all the more highly honoured by receiving their reward in the presence of their sworn enemies, who ill-treated them in life and turned them to scorn; and secondly, that the reprobate may be all the more cruelly disappointed on beholding the glory of the elect and the depths of their own woe, as they wistfully gaze on the saints winging their flight with Christ and the angels to the realms of bliss, whilst they are being swallowed up in gaping chasms and buried in the innermost depths of the earth: *Ibunt hi in supplicium æternum: justi autem in vitam æternam*—Matth. xxv. 46—*And these shall go into everlasting punishment: but the just into life everlasting.* Think seriously on these two so widely-differing lots, and on what thy fate will be on the day of judgment: there will then be no middle course—thou wilt have to take thy stand either on the right side or on the left, thou wilt either reign for ever in paradise or rave for ever in hell.

WEDNESDAY IN THE LAST WEEK AFTER PENTECOST.

Videte, vigilate et orate ; nescitis enim quando tempus sit.—Marc. xiii. 33.

Take ye heed, watch and pray ; for ye know not when the time is.

I. CONSIDER how in the fulfilment of these three duties is comprised all that is required of thee—to be ready for death and to save thy soul. The first is that thou take heed—*videte:* not indeed with the eyes of thy head, but with the eyes of the soul, reflecting in good earnest on the shortness of this fleeting life, on the uncertainty of the moment when death will overtake thee in its rapid course, and on the eternity of the future life that awaits thee. See how quickly these twenty, thirty, or forty years of life thou hast already spent have glided by, and remember that the few that still remain for thee to live will pass away more quickly still. Besides, what guarantee hast thou that death will not rob thee of even these few years on which thou reckonest, at a moment when thou least expectest it ? Look around thee, and see how many there are who from day to day are snatched away in the very flower of life ! how many, blessed with the soundest health, die suddenly, contrary to all expectation ! one from apoplexy, another from paralysis or some unforeseen accident. *Videte . . . nescitis enim quando tempus sit*—*Take ye heed . . . for ye know not when the time is.* Remark, too, that the Evangelist does not say, *quand tempus* "*erit*"—*when the time " shall be,"* but *sit*—*when the time " is ;"* because there is no circumstance, no moment, which may not be thy last. Yet thou livest just as though there were no such thing as death for thee, and as though thou wert not on the brink of an eternity. If thou lovest thyself, think on death, think on eternity, and think well on them. Be not so foolish as to cherish the hope that Jesus Christ will prove Himself to be a liar; and He warns thee: *nescitis quando—ye know not when.*

II. Consider the second condition that is needful, which is that thou watch—*vigilate.* Now, this has two meanings. The first is, that thou be not guilty of carelessly losing that precious time which is granted to thee on purpose to lay by treasures for eternity: time is too valuable to be killed as those do who give too much to sleep: *Noli diligere somnum, ne te egestas opprimat*—Prov. xx. 13—*Love not sleep, lest poverty oppress thee.* The other meaning is, that thou must not, by the sleep of an idle and sluggish life, be put off thy guard, and thus lay thyself open to the jibes and insults of thy hellish foes and disorderly appetites. Arouse thyself, therefore, and be on the alert against thy enemies, both internal and external, because they will stab thee if they get the chance when thou least expectest it. Arouse thyself by giving ear to the voice of thy Saviour, Who calls thee to a perfect life, and beware of again falling asleep; He may not, haply, call thee again, but let thee sleep on in thy negligence and tepidity.

III. Consider the third thing that is needed, which is prayer—*orate.* The meaning of this is, that thou must never give over recommending thyself to thy good Lord and Master. Thou canst not always be engaged in actual prayer: but in the first place, thou must not omit to fulfil this duty at its own proper times; then thou oughtest from time to time during the day to raise thy heart to God, and lay open to Him, as it were, thy eager craving for His divine aid. *Desiderium pauperum exaudivit Dominus*—Ps. ix. 17—*The*

Lord hath heard the desire of the poor. Let these affections and desires be all the more frequent by reason of the short time they take to make. Then, again, betake thyself as often as thou canst into the presence of the Blessed Sacrament Who is so near to thee. Above all, think about death, because the dread of death will cause thee to recommend thyself with all thy heart to thy Jesus, and to entreat Him earnestly and frequently.

THURSDAY IN THE LAST WEEK AFTER PENTECOST.

Cum metu et tremore vestram salutem operamini ; Deus enim est qui operatur in nobis, et velle et perficere pro bona voluntate.—Philip. ii. 12.

With fear and trembling work out your salvation ; for it is God Who worketh in you, both to will and to accomplish according to His good Will.

I. CONSIDER that thy salvation is an undertaking which depends altogether on God, and at the same time depends altogether on thyself; and hence it behoves thee to work unceasingly with the deepest concern, because up to the last thou must remain in uncertainty as to whether thou wilt succeed, owing to the many dangers that hem thee round. Thou must toil *cum metu et tremore—with fear and trembling*, for below thee are the yawning depths of hell, whence the spirits of darkness sally forth to assault thee; around thee thou beholdest a cheating world, with snares laid for thee on all sides ; whilst within thee is the lair of thy disorderly appetites. How, then, canst thou but be affrighted and tremble in the midst of so many and great perils, when thou recollectest that the object at stake is one which if thou failest to attain, thou wilt be lost for never-ending ages!

II. Consider in what this fear must chiefly consist. It has to consist in keeping thyself humble: for however great be the amount of good thou performest, it is always true that the efficacious helps of Almighty God's grace are absolutely needful to enable thee to act; whilst, on the other hand, it is equally true that He doles out His grace from sheer generosity, and not from any indebtedness in thy regard, and therefore He can cease making His largesses whenever He pleases. See, therefore, how great reason thou hast to fear and tremble in His divine sight, and freely own that whatever good thou performest, it comes from Almighty God. Moreover, *operatur in vobis velle et perficere*—*He worketh in you both to will and to accomplish;* because His preparatory grace—*gratia præveniens*—is the means by which He engenders in thy heart the first design of doing good, by enlightening thy understanding and strengthening thy will: and in this manner *operatur velle*—*He worketh in thee to will.* Then His accompanying grace—*gratia concomitans*—follows thee up, step by step, in its performance right up to the end: and thus, *operatur perficere*—*He worketh in thee to accomplish.* Now, if such be the case, how canst thou fail to recognise the continual need thou hast of that efficacious grace of His, which He is in nowise bound to bestow on thee?

III. Consider that although Almighty God can if He likes, at any moment, cease giving thee this especial grace to do good—*gratia efficax*—still, as a matter of fact, He never will give over lavishing it on thee, provided thou art not thy own enemy by failing to have recourse to Him and to commit thyself to His keeping. This, therefore, has to be the practical result of thy fear: thou must be constantly betaking thyself to Him for protection, calling on Him and beseeching Him to save thee from the dangers that surround thee. The moment thou givest over recommending thyself to Him, it is all over with thee. The first link in the chain of grace is bestowed independently of any petition made for it; but after the first grace—if we may believe S. Augustine—no other grace will be accorded but that which is asked for. Our Lord gave thee the grace of vocation without thy asking for it; but He will not give the grace of faithfully persevering in the religious state till the end, if thou failest to recommend thyself to Him, and to entreat Him both earnestly and perseveringly. Our Lord says: *Effundam super habitatores Jerusalem spiritum gratiæte precum*—Zach. xii. 10—*I will pour out upon the inhabitants of Jerusalem the spirit of grace and of prayers;* thus giving thee to understand that just as thou wilt never have the spirit of prayer without His preparatory grace—*sine gratia præveniente*—so also thou wilt never be aided by His accompanying grace unto the end—*gratia concomitante*—without the same spirit of prayer.

FRIDAY IN THE LAST WEEK AFTER PENTECOST.

Expecta Dominum et custodi viam ejus, et exaltabit te, ut hæreditate capias terram: cum perierint peccatores, videbis.—Ps. xxxvi. 34.

Expect the Lord and keep His way, and He will exalt thee to inherit the land: when the sinners shall perish thou shalt see.

I. CONSIDER that as the life of man is made up of days and nights, so also is it chequered with alternate prosperity and adversity. Sometimes all is bright and prosperous, at other times all looks dark and goes wrong; much in the same way as with light and darkness, each has its own turn—though both come from God: *Tuus est dies, et tua est nox*—Ps. lxxiii. 16—*Thine is the day, and Thine is the night.* If only thou art steadfast at both times, thou wilt receive a fitting reward from Almighty God in due season. If thou wouldst be steadfast during the night-time of adversity, be content with patiently awaiting thy Lord; keep alive thy trust in Him, and fail not in the performance of thy accustomed exercises of regular observance and private devotion. *Expecta Dominum—Expect the Lord* because thy trials will come to an end, and very shortly He will visit thee again with increased love, and amply console thee. So be faithful to Him in prosperity, endeavour to practise discretion; be not like a river which, when it abounds with water, overflows its bed and abandons its proper course: *Custodi viam ejus—Keep His way.* Thrice happy art thou if thou only succeedest in being faithful to Almighty God under all circumstances, whether prosperous or adverse, because *exaltabit te—He will exalt thee* from earth to heaven.

II. Consider that when this exaltation, this rousing up, comes about, thou wilt take possession of paradise —that true land of promise—by right of inheritance. Do not, however, imagine that thou wilt obtain this inheritance without deserving it, as is sometimes the case when a son comes in for property he would never have enjoyed if his father had not happened to die intestate. If thou wouldst earn thy claim to thy inheritance in thy father's lifetime thou must obey him, respect him, and conduct thyself like a dutiful son in his regard. Thus, in the same way, paradise is an inheritance to be gained from a Father who will never die, and thou must, therefore, needs earn it for thyself by thy dutifulness, and by proving thyself steadfast both in adversity and prosperity; otherwise He will deprive thee of this inheritance, as He deprived those amongst the Hebrews of their inheritance of the promised land, who did not stand firm under the proof to which He subjected them in the desert.

III. Consider that, until the day of judgment, thou wilt never grasp the full meaning of this wonderful exaltation—*exaltabit te*—with which Almighty God will honour thee if only thou prove thyself worthy of it; *cum perierint peccatores videbis—when the sinners shall perish thou shalt see;* because it will be only from comparing the rigorous justice Almighty God will display in His condemnation of the wicked, that thou wilt appreciate the loving mercy He has shown thee in saving thee. When thou beholdest on that dreadful day the misery and the dismay of the reprobate on being condemned to be buried body and soul, in the awful cesspool of hell, and when on the other hand thou beholdest the happiness and the honour accorded to the elect on being raised to heaven to reign there with Christ—oh, then indeed thou wilt fully understand the enormous difference there is between these two extremes! Oh, how heartily thou wilt then thank thy good Lord for having, by thy vocation to the religious state, enabled thee to be faithful to Him, and so to be of the number of those *qui servient ei die ac nocte*—Apoc. vii. 15; that is, who serve Him both in the daytime of prosperity, and in the night-time of adversity!

SATURDAY IN THE LAST WEEK AFTER PENTECOST.

Deus meus es tu, ne discesseris a me: quoniam tribulatio proxima est: quoniam non est qui adjuvet.—Ps. xxi. 12.

Thou art my God, depart not from me. For tribulation is very near: for there is none to help me.

I. CONSIDER that these words ought to be constantly on thy lips, imagining thyself to be near death—that hour of trial when thou most of all requirest help. Death will be a great trial to thee, both for body and soul. Thou wilt suffer in thy body, by reason of accompanying pain and distressing ailments, from sleeplessness and restlessness, which will allow thee no repose or ease. Thou wilt suffer even more in thy soul, from its natural dread of going away from this world and of quitting that body which is so dear to it: then again, and which is still worse, thou wilt suffer from pangs of conscience arising from the knowledge that thou art about to render a strict account of thy whole life, and of all thy sins, which at that dread moment will appear to thee far more numerous and heinous than thou art wont to consider them now. Oh, what a trial will not this be to thee in these last moments, on which hangs an eternity of reward or of punishment! Beg Our Lord earnestly every day of thy life not to withdraw Himself from thee at that hour.

II. Consider that this great trial—death—is nearer to thee than thou art apt to imagine. What a variety of accidents may not befall thee at any moment! Dost thou not see how speedily the ten, twenty or thirty years of life that thou promisest thyself are gliding by? Look back on the years already gone, and it will come home to thee how quickly they pass! Lose no time, therefore, in putting matters straight, and in being in readiness for that great journey: *Vasa transmigrationis fac tibi*—Jer. xlvi. 19—*Furnish thyself to go.*

III. Consider that not only is this tribulation—death—close at hand, but there is no help for it; and if Our Lord comes not to thy aid, woe betide thee! no one else can. Who else is there, pray, in that awful moment that can ward off the attacks and temptation of thy hellish foes and preserve thee from falling a prey to their fiendish malice? Who else is there that can bestow on thee especial help to enable thee to overcome the difficulties that will come in thy way, and may hinder thee from making that passage from time to eternity as it ought to be made? Oh, how important then it is that thou shouldst secure the goodwill of thy Lord now, since it is He only that can come to thy assistance then! Often take into thy hands that crucifix which thou wilt probably clasp on thy deathbed, and kiss it over and over again; and swear fealty to Him, and at the same time entreat Him with burning tears *ut non te deserat et non te derelinquat*—Heb. xiii. 5—*not to leave thee nor forsake thee.* If only thou canst be sure of having Jesus at thy side at that hour, thou wilt not require assistance from any one else, and thou mayest courageously exclaim: *Dominus mihi adjutor: non timebo quid faciat mihi homo* —Ps. cxvii. 6—*The Lord is my helper: I will not fear what man can do unto me.*

IN OMNIBUS GLORIFICETUR DEUS.

INDEX.

TRINITY WEEK.

	PAGE
TRINITY SUNDAY. On the Holy Trinity	1
MONDAY. On preparation for Holy Communion	3
TUESDAY. The paschal lamb the type of the Holy Eucharist	5
WEDNESDAY. On preparation for Holy Communion	7
CORPUS CHRISTI. On the excessive love of Jesus in the institution of the Blessed Sacrament	9
FRIDAY. On the circumstances of the institution of the Blessed Sacrament ...	11
SATURDAY. Why Jesus remains on our altars ...	14

WEEK WITHIN THE OCTAVE OF CORPUS CHRISTI.

SUNDAY. On the Sacrifice of the Mass	16
MONDAY. On the intimate union of Jesus with our souls in the Blessed Sacrament...	19
TUESDAY. The Blessed Sacrament our Medicine, our Armour, and our Comfort ...	21
WEDNESDAY. Jesus in the Blessed Sacrament the food of our souls	23
THURSDAY (OCTAVE). The Blessed Sacrament a pledge of life eternal...	25

FRIDAY. The Feast of the Sacred Heart—the
          fountain of all grace 28
SATURDAY. The efficacy of Christ's maxims ... 30

THIRD WEEK AFTER PENTECOST.

SUNDAY. Jesus the Good Shepherd 33
MONDAY. On performing our actions with a right
          intention 35
TUESDAY. On the foolish presumption of sinners 36
WEDNESDAY. On the remembrance of the four last
          things 38
THURSDAY. On the hatred God bears to sin and the
          sinner 41
FRIDAY. On mortification 43
SATURDAY. On the sentence of eternal damnation 45

FOURTH WEEK AFTER PENTECOST.

SUNDAY. On the miraculous draught of fishes ... 47
MONDAY. On the reward promised to those who
          persevere 49
TUESDAY. On the particular judgment 51
WEDNESDAY. On confidence in God in time of
          spiritual dryness 53
THURSDAY. On the evil of overlooking small faults 55
FRIDAY. On the eternal reward of the short
          sufferings of this life 58
SATURDAY. On sudden death 60

FIFTH WEEK AFTER PENTECOST.

SUNDAY. On the perfection required by Jesus
          Christ 62
MONDAY. On the last judgment 64
TUESDAY. On lasting sorrow for sin 66
WEDNESDAY. On thwarting self-will 68
THURSDAY. That this life is a time of warfare
          which passes quickly 71
FRIDAY. On the "exaltation" of Our Lord ... 73
SATURDAY. On preparation for temptation ... 75

SIXTH WEEK AFTER PENTECOST.

	PAGE
SUNDAY. On the miraculous multiplication of the loaves	77
MONDAY. On death and judgment	80
TUESDAY. On suffering and humiliation	82
WEDNESDAY. On peace and union with our neighbour	84
THURSDAY. On hearkening to the voice of conscience	86
FRIDAY. On confidence in God in time of adversity	88
SATURDAY. On cleanness of heart	90

SEVENTH WEEK AFTER PENTECOST.

SUNDAY. On the words: "Beware of false prophets!"	92
MONDAY. On the reward to come	94
TUESDAY. On our duty to ourselves, to our neighbour, and to God	97
WEDNESDAY. "The kingdom of heaven suffereth violence"	99
THURSDAY. On the value and merit of temptation	101
FRIDAY. On the contempt of all things for Christ	103
SATURDAY. The duties of Christians as soldiers of Christ	105

EIGHTH WEEK AFTER PENTECOST.

SUNDAY. On the parable of the dishonest steward	107
MONDAY. On true mercy towards our neighbour	109
TUESDAY. As a man lives, so shall he die	111
WEDNESDAY. On the entrance of Jesus into Egypt	113
THURSDAY. That we must fight if we wish to be crowned	115
FRIDAY. On the death of the fervent and the tepid follower of Christ	117
SATURDAY. On hope and confidence in God	119

NINTH WEEK AFTER PENTECOST.

	PAGE
SUNDAY. Jesus weeps over Jerusalem	122
MONDAY. On the last judgment	124
TUESDAY. On the invitation of Jesus: "Come to Me, all you that labour"	126
WEDNESDAY. On the folly of worldlings	128
THURSDAY. On the workings of the Holy Ghost in the soul	131
FRIDAY. On the threefold warfare of the Christian	133
SATURDAY. Almighty God our Teacher	135

TENTH WEEK AFTER PENTECOST.

SUNDAY. On the parable of the Pharisee and the publican	137
MONDAY. On the necessity of circumspection	140
TUESDAY. On taking up the yoke of Christ	142
WEDNESDAY. Our life is a pilgrimage	144
THURSDAY. The results of good and evil works	145
FRIDAY. The passion of Christ our armour	147
SATURDAY. On the advantages we should derive from our frailties	149

ELEVENTH WEEK AFTER PENTECOST.

SUNDAY. On the healing of the deaf and dumb man	152
MONDAY. On the goodness and the severity of God	154
TUESDAY. On pride and its consequences	156
WEDNESDAY. On the duty of helping our neighbour	158
THURSDAY. On the final separation of the good from the bad	160
FRIDAY. On the remembrance of the passion of Jesus Christ	163
SATURDAY. On the importance of prompt resistance to the suggestions of the Evil One	165

TWELFTH WEEK AFTER PENTECOST.

		PAGE
SUNDAY.	On the love of God	167
MONDAY.	On the love of our neighbour	169
TUESDAY.	On the love of God for the sons of His adoption	171
WEDNESDAY.	On the three great "days of the Lord"	173
THURSDAY.	On the words: "If thou wilt separate the precious from the vile," etc.	175
FRIDAY.	On being crucified to the world	177
SATURDAY.	How Almighty God deals with the proud and the humble	179

THIRTEENTH WEEK AFTER PENTECOST.

SUNDAY.	The parable of the ten lepers	181
MONDAY.	On attachment to the goods of this world	183
TUESDAY.	On love for one's enemies	185
WEDNESDAY.	On the patience of Almighty God	187
THURSDAY.	On the eternal fire of hell	189
FRIDAY.	The claims that Christ's love has on man	191
SATURDAY.	Motives for self-humiliation	193

FOURTEENTH WEEK AFTER PENTECOST.

SUNDAY.	On the impossibility of serving two masters	194
MONDAY.	On the house of eternity	196
TUESDAY.	The evils of riches	198
WEDNESDAY.	On God's dealings with the proud	201
THURSDAY.	On the holy fear of God	203
FRIDAY.	Jesus our Model	205
SATURDAY.	On the mastery over our passions	207

FIFTEENTH WEEK AFTER PENTECOST.

PAGE

SUNDAY. The raising to life of the widow's son 209
MONDAY. On the consequences of yielding to passion ... 211
TUESDAY. The obligation of the law of the Gospel ... 212
WEDNESDAY. On self-denial ... 214
THURSDAY. On Eccl. xvii. 6: "Cum consummaverit homo," etc. ... 216
FRIDAY. On the consequences of Christ's redemption ... 218
SATURDAY. On worldly wisdom ... 220

SIXTEENTH WEEK AFTER PENTECOST.

SUNDAY. On the necessity of humility ... 222
MONDAY. On criticising the faults of our neighbour ... 224
TUESDAY. On the honour we should pay to our own soul ... 226
WEDNESDAY. On fidelity to grace ... 228
THURSDAY. On godly wisdom ... 230
FRIDAY. On living for God ... 232
SATURDAY. On the difference between the wise and the foolish man ... 234

SEVENTEENTH WEEK AFTER PENTECOST.

SUNDAY. On the love of God ... 236
MONDAY. On persevering unto death in the service of God ... 238
TUESDAY. On confessing Christ before men ... 240
WEDNESDAY. On the efficacy of grace ... 242
THURSDAY. On conformity to the Will of God ... 244
FRIDAY. On predestination ... 246
SATURDAY. On fidelity in small things ... 248

EIGHTEENTH WEEK AFTER PENTECOST.

PAGE

SUNDAY. On the healing of the man sick of the palsy ... 250
MONDAY. On confidence in God ... 252
TUESDAY. On the conversion of the sinner ... 255
WEDNESDAY. On pusillanimity ... 257
THURSDAY. On the path of perfection ... 259
FRIDAY. On the test of true love ... 261
SATURDAY. On our ignorance of our state before God ... 264

NINETEENTH WEEK AFTER PENTECOST.

SUNDAY. The parable of the wedding feast ... 266
MONDAY. "Blessed are the dead who die in the Lord" ... 268
TUESDAY. On fidelity to the inspirations of grace ... 270
WEDNESDAY. The folly of human greatness... ... 272
THURSDAY. On tepidity in the service of God ... 274
FRIDAY. How we are freed from the slavery of Satan ... 277
SATURDAY. On three qualities of true love ... 279

TWENTIETH WEEK AFTER PENTECOST.

SUNDAY. On the healing of the ruler's son ... 281
MONDAY. On entire obedience ... 283
TUESDAY. On fidelity in little things ... 285
WEDNESDAY. On the disproportion between guilt and its penalties ... 287
THURSDAY. That we should keep our eyes fixed on Our Lord ... 289
FRIDAY. On trusting ourselves to the providence of God ... 291
SATURDAY. On the fear of God ... 293

TWENTY-FIRST WEEK AFTER PENTECOST.

SUNDAY. On the parable of the two debtors ... 295
MONDAY. On brotherly love ... 298

	PAGE
TUESDAY. How we can, and should, pray always	300
WEDNESDAY. On living a life of faith	302
THURSDAY. How to prepare for a good death	304
FRIDAY. Jesus, the Way, the Truth, and the Life	306
SATURDAY. On true riches	308

TWENTY-SECOND WEEK AFTER PENTECOST.

SUNDAY. On the double tribute	310
MONDAY. On the fear of God's judgment	313
TUESDAY. On the reward of fidelity	315
WEDNESDAY. On patience under trials	317
THURSDAY. On the presence of God	319
FRIDAY. Man's life a pilgrimage	321
SATURDAY. Man's life a warfare	323

TWENTY-THIRD WEEK AFTER PENTECOST.

SUNDAY. On the raising of Jairus's daughter	325
MONDAY. On persevering watchfulness	327
TUESDAY. On the evils of impatience	329
WEDNESDAY. On leaving well alone	331
THURSDAY. On the good use of time	333
FRIDAY. On the value of suffering	335
SATURDAY. Jesus our Teacher	338

THE LAST WEEK AFTER PENTECOST.

SUNDAY. On the end of the world	340
MONDAY. On the second coming of the Son of Man	343
TUESDAY. On the sentence of the just and the reprobate	346
WEDNESDAY. On preparation for death	349
THURSDAY. On working out our salvation	351
FRIDAY. On the reward of patience and fidelity	354
SATURDAY. On the tribulation of death	356

IN OMNIBUS GLORIFICETUR DEUS.

THE END.

www.ingramcontent.com/pod-product-compliance
Lightning Source LLC
Chambersburg PA
CBHW020311240426
43673CB00039B/771